HOSTILE HUMOR IN RENAISSANCE FRANCE

HOSTILE HUMOR IN RENAISSANCE FRANCE

Bruce Hayes

UNIVERSITY OF DELAWARE PRESS
Newark

DISTRIBUTED BY THE UNIVERSITY OF VIRGINIA PRESS

University of Delaware Press
© 2020 by Bruce Hayes
All rights reserved
Printed in the United States of America on acid-free paper

First published 2020

1 3 5 7 9 8 6 4 2

978-1-64453-177-8 (cloth)
978-1-64453-178-5 (paper)
978-1-64453-179-2 (e-book)

Library of Congress Cataloging-in-Publication Data is available for this title.

Cover art: Mado Hayes

To Tony Corbeill, my mentor and friend

CONTENTS

Acknowledgments   ix

Introduction   1

1 · The Affaire des Placards and the Early Stages of Pamphlet Warfare   15

2 · Early Evangelical and Reformist Comic Theater   30

3 · Artus Désiré, Renaissance France's Most Successful, Forgotten Catholic Polemicist   55

4 · Geneva's Polemical Machine   92

5 · Abbeys of Misrule on the Stage   120

6 · Ronsard the Pamphleteer   133

Conclusion   163

Notes   167

Bibliography   199

Index   211

ACKNOWLEDGMENTS

I have many people to thank for helping me complete this book. Before getting to people, let me begin with my home institution, the University of Kansas. I have received tremendous support from my university, starting in the fall of 2011 when I was granted a sabbatical that allowed me to begin this new project in earnest. In the spring of 2011 I was awarded a Keeler Intra-university Professorship, thanks to the co-sponsorship of my department and the Classics Department. During that semester, it was a real treat to be able to sit in on Tony Corbeill's Latin grammar class and Tara Welch's graduate seminar on Roman satire, not to mention the helpful conversations I had with both of them about my project. Next came a Hall Center for the Humanities residential faculty fellowship in the spring of 2014 that gave me a semester to do some serious research and writing. (As a side note, it was my good fortune to have Jorge Perez and Laura Mielke as "fellow fellows" that semester.) My department has been incredibly supportive, and I would like to acknowledge in particular the course release that my chair Caroline Jewers secured for me in the spring of 2015. Further support for my research included a KU General Research Fund grant in 2014 and travel grants from the Hall Center and the Office of International Programs in 2015.

Since becoming department chair in 2016, two deans, Carl Lejuez and Clarence Lang, provided critical support and cheered me on as I completed the manuscript under less than optimal circumstances. Also, I have loved having my colleague and dear friend Kim Swanson as my "study buddy"; we make a good team, encouraging each other and keeping each other accountable. Let me conclude my thanks to people at KU by acknowledging all the terrific people from KU Libraries that have helped me, from Fran Devlin, who is always willing to do whatever she can to provide support, to Lars Leon, who makes sure that the service provided by KU's interlibrary loan is always exceptional; from Karen Cook and Elspeth Healey at the Spencer

Research Library to Pam LeRow, who can format, collate, and bring order to a chaotic manuscript with efficiency and ease. I feel fortunate to work where I do.

Next, I want to acknowledge the important external support I have received that allowed this project to move forward. The short-term fellowship I received from the Newberry Library in the fall of 2011 enabled me to begin seriously reading polemical pamphlets, including the one I refer to in the introduction. At the Newberry, Carla Zecher and Karen Christianson at the Center for Renaissance Studies were particularly supportive. The following summer, thanks to a Summer Stipend from the National Endowment for the Humanities and a Franklin Grant from the American Philosophical Society, I was able to travel to Lyon, Geneva, and Paris to read dozens and dozens of pamphlets. I appreciated the help I received at the Bibliothèque municipale de Lyon and the Bibliothèque de Genève. In Paris, the Bibliothèque nationale de France provided me with a wealth of materials and the occasional helpful librarian. Without a doubt, my favorite place to work in Paris has been the Bibliothèque du protestantisme français, a charming and intimate space I have returned to each summer since 2012, overseen by the inscrutable Mme. Poinsot, who scared me at first but who is in fact kind and generous.

I would like to thank colleagues and friends at Brigham Young University, the Virginia Military Institute, Wichita State University, the University of Pennsylvania, and the University of Vermont who invited me to their campuses to give talks related to this book. There are too many wonderful people in my field to mention who have been incredibly supportive and who inspire me. Let me try a partial list: Kitty Maynard, Bob Hudson, Scott Francis, Charles Morand-Metivier, Mary McKinley, Cathy Yandell, Gary Ferguson, Jeff Persels, Dora Polachek, Jessica DeVos, and I could go on. Special thanks to Jeff Persels and Mary McKinley, who generously read early chapter drafts and provided invaluable feedback. Julia Oestreich at the University of Delaware Press is a consummate professional and I have very much enjoyed working with her. I was fortunate to have three readers who provided extremely useful feedback; one in particular, and he knows who he is, went above and beyond to help make this a better book. All three readers caught mistakes and provided helpful suggestions. All remaining faults and shortcomings are mine.

Finally, I am grateful for family and friends. Despite the fact that my wife often jokes that she has no idea what I do for a living, she is a real sport, not to mention an incredibly generous and giving person whose tireless ability to help others puts me to shame. In that way that only parents can do, my parents think that their son is a genius who can do no wrong. However untrue that is, it is still nice to have such unconditional support and love. As for friends, I cannot believe my good fortune to have people in my life who lift me up, who motivate me by their example, and who keep me smiling (and laughing). This book is dedicated to one of those friends who has played a special role in my life that started shortly after this book project began. He has since left the University of Kansas for greener fields, and I continue to feel the loss.

Part of chapter 2 was published as "'De rire ne me puys tenir': Marguerite de Navarre's Satirical Theater," in *La Satire dans tous ses états*, edited by Bernd Renner (Geneva: Droz, 2009), 183–200.

Part of the introduction and chapter 1 were published as "The *Affaire des placards*, Polemical Humour, and the Sardonic Laugh," *French Studies* 70, no. 3 (2016): 332–47.

HOSTILE HUMOR IN RENAISSANCE FRANCE

Introduction

Of course it's a joke, just not a very funny one.
—Tyrion Lannister, *Game of Thrones*, "Mockingbird" (S4 E7)

To begin, a word about the title of this book. "Hostile humor," a phrase meant to highlight my focus on the increasing use of aggressive satire by religious polemicists in Reformation-era France, tells only part of the story. The other side to this, also important in understanding this phenomenon, is the accompanying emergence of hostility toward certain types of humor previously considered acceptable. At the start of this project, the alliterative phrase I used was "castigating comedy."[1] I remember sharing with a colleague in classics this provisional title. She asked me what part of speech "castigating" was. Her question was as simple as it was astute: Was it the comedy that was doing the castigating, or was it comedy that was being castigated? This question proved the impetus for one of the more surprising discoveries in my research. My initial intent was to focus on humor that castigates—attacks, satirizes, and reproaches—within the context of growing religious conflict in sixteenth-century France. The further I went in my research, however, the more I realized that there were just as many examples in the material where satire itself was castigated, rebuked, and censured as a form of irreligion and blasphemy. This makes sense, of course, since so often the targets of polemical humor were people or practices considered sacred by the other side.

In the early years of the religious conflict in sixteenth-century France, there emerged a particular form of satire that was deliberately harmful and destructive and that, in its most extreme manifestations, could even be characterized as not funny. The purpose of this book is to understand this phenomenon in the context of the Catholic and Protestant conflict and to see what it reveals about the society that both exploited and vilified this kind of satire.[2] I am interested in aggressively hostile jokes and satire, as well as the accompanying backlash against certain types of humor in sixteenth-century France. I am looking at plays and pamphlets, two of the most popular vehicles of propaganda during these sectarian fights. Pamphlets, frequently referred to as *libelles*, represented an entirely new medium, which allowed for the quick dissemination of polemics. The sectarian clashes in Europe saw the first such use of the relatively new technology of the printing press.

While many types of laughter are explosive and unrestrained, and can therefore be described as liberal or generous, the particular form of laughter that is the focus here, sardonic laughter, is a forced laugh that is acrimonious and resentful, as well as aggressive. In considering the role of humor during the turmoil leading up to the Wars of Religion, I am trying to answer this question: At what point are laughter and satire so dominated by invective and diatribe that the destructive subtext smothers all forms of laughter except the sardonic laugh? While humor and laughter can interrupt and even defuse anger, they can also be used detrimentally to incite acts of violence. Drawing upon some of the same pamphlets and plays examined in this study, Antónia Szabari has proposed the concept, connected to but distinct from traditional modes of satire, of a literature of vituperation.[3] Building on this, I focus on a particular form of humor that is so negative and aggressive, so vituperative, that it highly circumscribes the type of laughter it can elicit. It often serves as a prelude to or justification for violence. As George Hoffmann has observed regarding the emphasis on shock in reformist satire, "Such shock could at times shoot past laughter entirely and end in revulsion."[4]

Two episodes from Rabelais's *Quart livre*, his most mordantly satirical and even bitter work, provide instructive examples of the phenomenon that is the object of this study. In the episode of Lord Basché and the Chicanous (chapters 12–15), a story Panurge tells to justify his own excessive violence against Dindenault, Basché sets up a theatrical scene with a fake wedding in order to beat up the pestering Chicanous.[5] As he provides stage directions to his troupe, he reminds them, "Telz coups seront donnez en riant" (566) (Such blows must be given with a laugh [463]).[6] Such disingenuousness is a key quality of the type of humor and laughter I am examining. In the works and performances I investigate, laughter often serves as a pretext for aggressive and even violent polemics. The second example from Rabelais's *Quart livre* also features fake, violent laughter. In describing the impossible actions of Quaresmeprenant, the text indicates that he "Rioit en mordant, mordoit en riant" (32:614) (He laughed as he bit, bit as he laughed [506]). This is an even more pertinent example, as this section of the *Quart livre* introduces two opposing groups, with Quaresmeprenant and his followers representing a group of fanatical Catholics, and their enemies the Andouilles, a band of zealous Calvinists. The laughter I examine in this book is primarily militant, partisan laughter.

In an anonymous pamphlet published in 1564, a year after the conclusion of the first War of Religion and during a period known as the "Armed Peace,"[7] a nobleman asks the king for help. The extended title of the pamphlet, typical of its time, tells us much of what we need to know: *Remonstrance envoyée au roy par la noblesse de la religion reformée du païs et comté du Maine, sur les assassinats, pilleries, saccagements de maisons, seditions, violements de femmes et autres exces horribles commis depuis la publication de l'Edit de pacification dedans ledit comté; et presentée à Sa Majesté à Rossillon le 10 jour d'aoust, 1564* (Admonition sent to the king by the nobility of the reformed religion in the country of Maine, on the assassinations, pillaging, plundering of houses, seditions, raping of women, and other horrible abuses committed since the publication of the Edict of pacification of said county, and presented to his majesty in Roussillon the tenth day of August 1564). While the pamphlet is ostensibly intended for the king, Charles IX, it was aimed at a wider audience, both to garner sympathy for the Huguenot cause and to put extra pressure on the Crown and even includes at the end an "Advertissement aux Lecteurs" (Warning to Readers).[8]

This unnamed nobleman describes an extended scene of carnage in Le Mans, the capital of Maine, following the formal end of hostilities and the royal publication of the Edict of Amboise. (This edict granted certain liberties to Huguenots and, like most if not all of the royal edicts during this extended conflict, left both sides deeply dissatisfied.) The author describes a series of assassinations, notable for their savagery. One nobleman is torn to pieces and his mutilated body delivered to his wife; the mob then kills three servants and burns down the residence. The naked body of another murdered nobleman is paraded in front of the magistrates. In describing the cruelty of yet another assassination, our writer blurs the line between human and animal, asserting that these monsters' furor is worse than that of a tiger.[9]

After these accounts of the carnage, our author, in his litany of crimes, refers to exactly the kind of laughter that is the focus of this book: "les pillories et brisemens de maisons, les seditions, excez, meurtres, les violemens de femmes, et *les risées publiques* qu'ils font de vos Edits dedans la ville" (the pillaging and destruction of homes, the seditions, abuses, murders, raping of women, and *the public mockery [or laughter]* they make of your Edicts in the city).[10] Here he suggests to the king (and to his larger audience) that Catholics are laughing at the king by making a mockery of his edict. This laughter is seriously criminal—it directly follows rape in the list of atrocities. The suggestion is that these people are violating the Crown symbolically by publicly laughing at its law and literally by murdering royal representatives, which they do while laughing. Laughter and violence are inseparably bound together here.

The *Remonstrance envoyée au roy* continues with a description that combines festivities and violence. In the middle of the city, two dogs are hanged; strung about their necks are signs bearing the names of two of the king's local officers. A carnival-like parade takes place, with masked men and children dressed as nuns, "avec des gestes si ords et impudiques, qu'ils eussent fait rougir une [*sic*] Heliogabale,[11] *que se rire à bouche ouverte*, et avec un mépris desordonné de vos Edits" (with gestures so dirty and indecent that they would have made Heliogabalus blush, *laughing with their mouths open*, and with an immoral contempt for your Edicts).[12] This horrifying scene encapsulates much of what this book seeks to uncover. Reading it, we are shocked by the violence, and yet all of this takes place in a festive, carnivalesque setting, with people in drag parading past the murdered dogs, the king's servants hanged in effigy, all while laughing "à bouche ouverte." Increasingly prevalent in the period I am examining, this particular form of laughter is vicious and menacing, described by contemporaries as the sardonic laugh. The *Remonstrance envoyée au roy* presents this laughter as worthy of contempt. It is condemnable because it is abusive, and there is little that is humorous about the scene described. In this pamphlet, laughter is both castigating and castigated, as it will continue to be amid the increasing religious conflict that dominated this era in France.

To provide a theoretical framework for what I am examining, I have turned to both modern and sixteenth-century theorists for help. First, there is Freud's concept of "tendentious humor," which aims to do harm.[13] In his study of jokes, he draws a distinction between innocent jokes and tendentious ones. He observes, "Where a joke is not an aim in itself—that is, where it is not an innocent one—there are only two purposes that it may serve.... It is either a *hostile* joke (serving the purpose of aggressiveness, satire, or defence) or an *obscene* joke (serving the purpose of exposure)."[14] Hostile humor is the primary subject of this study, as is an increasing hostility toward this type of humor. I am looking for instances where, as Freud notes, tendentious humor seeks "to turn the hearer, who was indifferent to begin with, into a co-hater or co-despiser, and creates for the enemy a host of opponents where at first there was only one."[15]

Next to consider are two sixteenth-century writers, one well known, the other less so, both of whom addressed the concept of cruel humor. The first is Erasmus and the second is Laurent Joubert, a chancellor of the medical school in Montpellier and one of Henri III's physicians. One of Erasmus's most impressive and prodigious works is his *Adages*,[16] in which he includes a proverb concerning the *risus sardonicus*, the sardonic laugh.[17] He notes that it has been called a false laugh, a bitter laugh, or a crazy laugh ("De risu ficto aut amarulento aut insano denque").[18] He then traces the etymology to the island of Sardinia, where Carthaginian colonists enforced a draconian retirement system, murdering all men over seventy years old. While committing these murders, they supposedly laughed and embraced each other. Another possible connection with Sardinia is a wild parsley that grows there and is poisonous. Those who eat it die in agony, their mouths twisted as though smiling.

As one finds throughout the *Adages*, in his discussion of the *risus sardonicus*, Erasmus displays his immense knowledge of antiquity, citing among others Cicero, Lucian, and Plato. He notes many appearances of the *risus sardonicus* in literature but situates the origin of the expression in Homer's *Iliad*, when the warrior Ajax has been chosen to engage in combat with Hector. In the Latin version that Erasmus cites, the passage says: "Sic ingens Aiax surgebat, murus Achivum, / *Terribili ridens vultu*" (Thus mighty Ajax rose up, wall of the Greeks, / *With a laugh on his grim face*).[19] The juxtaposition is striking in the second verse, where the warrior, about to fight, laughs with a terrible grimace. In fact, Erasmus cites sources that explain how this laugh is a deadly one, and he gives examples of dogs and horses that show their teeth as if smiling before biting. He also refers to the baring of teeth as a sign of insincerity, since sardonic laughter is essentially counterfeit. Thus Erasmus brings together two key notions about the sardonic laugh: disingenuousness and violence. The sardonic laugh is forced, vicious, and menacing.

Laurent Joubert was an erudite physician who published several treatises and scholarly works. His *Traité du ris*, published in 1579, three years before his death, is particularly important for the present study.[20] In it, Joubert addresses a variety of issues pertaining to laughter, including physiological descriptions of the various body parts and bodily functions involved. This relatively unexamined work is both amusing and insightful. Several of the chapter titles alone are attention grabbing. One that would have pleased Rabelais is, "D'où vient qu'on pisse, fiante, et sue, à force de rire" (Whence It Comes That One Pisses, Shits, and Sweats by Dint of Laughing),[21] which recalls several episodes in the tales of Gargantua and Pantagruel. Another intriguing physiological observation Joubert makes is, "Quelques uns font des pets sans puanteur, autant qu'ils veulent, et de divers sons: tellement qu'ils samblent chanter du cu" (Some let farts that do not smell, as many as they want and of diverse sounds, so much so that they seem to sing from their arse).[22] Another memorable chapter title suggests a possible new diet plan that requires the elimination of laughter: "Pourquoy est-ce, que les grans rieurs deviennent aisemant gras" (Why It Is That Great Laughers Easily Become Fat).[23]

In the second section, Joubert attempts to categorize different types of laughter. Early on, he defines a particular type of laughter as "batard, ou non legitime: qui est, un Ris seulemant equivoque: d'autant qu'il n'exprime que le geste et maintien externe des rireurs, sans avoir les accions qui precedent le vray Ris" (bastard or illegitimate, which is a laughter that is only equivocal since it expresses only the gestures and external manner of laughers without having the internal actions which precede true laughter).[24] Most compelling for the present study is Joubert's elaboration on the sardonic or Sardinian laugh in a chapter titled "Des autres differences du Ris, et ses epithetes" (On the Other Differences in Laughter and on Its Epithets). After mentioning Erasmus, he refers to Alessandro Alessandri's observation in his *Dies geniales* (Genial Days), "On use de ce mot, *Ris Sardonien*, à l'androit de ceus qui contrefont les joyeus, ayans martel an taite, outrés de facherie: et qui d'une caresse voilent et couvrent leur mal-veulhance" (The expression *sardonian laughter* is used to designate those who act joyous while machinating evil and who, filled with anger, gently hide and cover their malevolence).[25] Joubert adds that this laughter is

> manteur, simulé et traitre, plein d'amertume et mal-talant, ou (pour le moins) de feintise ... comme le Ris qu'on dit vulgairement *d'Hotelier*.

> Aussi bien anciennemant celuy qu'on nomme aujourdhuy *Hospes* an Latin, s'appelloit *Hostis* (sinifiant annemy) d'où les Français ont retenu ces mots de *hote* et *hotelier*. Le Ris Sardonien est dit aussi de quelques uns, pour un ris de folie, ou d'arrogance, ou d'injure, ou de moquerie.
>
> (lying, simulated, and traitorous, full of bitterness and ill will, or (at least) falseness... as with the laughter commonly called *hostile* laughter. The one that long ago was called *hospes* in Latin used to be called *hostis* (signifying enemy), from which the French have retained the words *hote* and *hotelier*. Sardinian laughter is also used by some people for a laughter of folly, arrogance, injury, or mockery.)[26]

The differing Latin roots contribute to the ambiguity and suspicion surrounding this term—from host and hospital to hostile and hostility.

If Erasmus's and Joubert's work can be seen as a secular description of a particular type of humor, what about biblical or religious rationales for this biting humor? Many of the authors and playwrights discussed in this book were well read in the humanist tradition; all were well versed in Scripture. Within this highly charged conflict, explaining or justifying harsh satire (or condemning it) in scriptural terms was extremely important. Especially in the later years of the Catholic-Protestant conflict in France, support from classical sources could easily be dismissed as atheistic and ungodly.[27]

To address the issue of biblical justification for or disapproval of harsh humor and invective, it is helpful to look at M. A. Screech's *Laughter at the Foot of the Cross*.[28] At the beginning of his study, Screech makes the somewhat overgeneralized observation that "laughter flourished in the soil of Renaissance Christian controversy."[29] However, by the end of his study he concludes, "Christian laughter will never have it easy. Hovering in the background there remains a curious alliance of disapproving forces."[30] It is precisely this "curious alliance of disapproving forces" that is notable. Screech begins with the New Testament references to the mocking of Christ:

> In both Matthew and Luke the Latin Vulgate word for "to mock" is *illudo*. It is a compound word, containing within it the verb *ludo*, to sport, to play, to amuse oneself. It means that the scoffers made sport of Jesus, mocked him, made a laughing-stock of him. It is a harsh and emotive term. In context, the laughter implied by it is cruel.[31]

These references buttress arguments used against mordant satire that attacked religious institutions and practices. Through a metonymic association, it is not uncommon to find those attacked in this war of words equating these attacks with the vicious mocking endured by Christ. A key difference, however, is that in these pamphlets and performances, no one ever turns the other cheek, and outrage over the mockery endured is immediately followed by the use of comparable tactics. Whereas humor can often serve to diffuse a conflict, in these instances, it serves the opposite purpose and escalates mutual hatred and contempt.

Screech discusses two key Old Testament stories, one condemning and the other supporting harsh satire.[32] The first concerns a crowd of children who mock the prophet Elisha for his baldness. When Elisha curses them, two bears come out of the woods and tear apart forty-two of the children (2 Kings 2:23–25). Screech emphasizes that this scriptural event preoccupied sixteenth-century theologians and was cited repeatedly as a warning against harsh satire and mocking laughter. But there is also the better-known story of Elijah and the priests of Baal (1 Kings 18:22–40). Elijah challenges the priests to prove their God real by slaughtering a bull and calling down fire from heaven for the sacrificial blaze. When this fails, Elijah roundly mocks the priests of Baal before ordering all 450 of them seized and slaughtered. At least for some of the religious polemicists considered in this study, this story confirmed that violence was a completely justified response to religious insults and blasphemous satirical writings and performances. George Hoffmann has pointed out another divine endorsement of hostile mirth: "French reformed satirists found further license for laughter in citing a biblical warrant: 'He that sits in the heavens shall laugh at them: the Lord shall mock them' (Ps. 2:4)."[33]

Within the context of early sixteenth-century religious conflict in France and through an examination of some key polemical pamphlets and plays, I am seeking to draw connections between humor and violence, between laughter and cruelty. Although I draw on examples that antedate the following timeline, my symbolic starting point is 1534, with the most notorious Protestant *libelle*, the *Articles veritables sur les horribles, grandz et importables abuz de la Messe papale*. I end in 1562, when the first War of Religion broke out, with a discussion of the best-known Catholic *libelle*, Ronsard's *Discours des miseres de ce temps*. For specialists in this field, 1534 has a particular resonance—it is the date of the notorious Affaire des placards in France. With his sister Marguerite de Navarre's encouragement, François I had been fairly open to religious reform and often opposed the Sorbonne's extremely conservative theological faculty, going so far as to banish its firebrand leader, Noël Béda, in 1533. That tolerant attitude changed dramatically on the night of 17 October 1534, when placards were hung up in Paris, Amboise, Orléans, Blois, Tours, and Rouen, denouncing and attacking the Catholic Mass. It was rumored that one was even hung on the door of the king's bedchamber in the royal château at Amboise.[34] The likely author of this daring propaganda stunt was Antoine Marcourt, a Frenchman who had moved to Switzerland and become pastor of the Protestant congregation in Neuchâtel. The royal reaction was severe: masses and processions were held, suspected sympathizers were rounded up, and soon heretics were being burned at the stake. Many reform-minded humanists fled Paris, including two of France's most important satirists, the poet Clément Marot and the eventual leader of the Geneva-based Protestant faith, Jean Calvin, both of whom fled south to Nérac, where the king's sister resided. Another similar propaganda stunt the following January led to further royal crackdowns, including a brief ban on printing.

My project ends with the outbreak of war. It was also the moment when France's most celebrated poet, Pierre de Ronsard, rather unexpectedly published a pamphlet titled *Discours des miseres de ce temps*. This would lead to others over a period of approximately eighteen months, including a rebuttal of a Calvinist *libelle* attacking the poet. Later Ronsard would combine these *plaquettes* in a definitive edition also titled *Discours des miseres de ce temps*. Coming at a key historical moment and serving as a counterbalance to the Affaire des placards, Ronsard's pamphlets represent an emblematic endpoint for this study.

This book is organized into six chapters. In the first, I look at some of the earliest pamphlets from the 1530s. While the symbolic starting point is Antoine Marcourt's placards, I begin with Marcourt's first anti-Catholic satirical work from the previous year, the *Livre des marchans*.[35] The comparison of Marcourt's two pamphlets illustrates a larger phenomenon I am exploring: as new forms of satire are developed,[36] humor becomes paradoxically both more constrained and more violent,[37] and unrestrained, bawdy laughter becomes marginalized, viewed increasingly as a form of blasphemy. This is certainly true of Jérôme de Hangest, who, at the request of the Sorbonne, produced two responses to Marcourt's placard in Latin and the other in French, the latter intended for a more general audience.[38] It should be noted that at this early stage in the propaganda battle between Protestants and Catholics, the Catholic side was slow to figure out how to engage effectively in this war of words. One of the limitations was an initial hesitancy to produce treatises in French instead of Latin.[39] Hangest's work, along with publications by his fellow Sorbonne theologians, tended to be very dry and with a strong emphasis on theological considerations, not the sort of material that would have found a wide readership.[40] In the last part of the chapter, I draw attention to one of the only female voices of the nascent Calvinist movement, Marie Dentière, who reached out to Marguerite de Navarre for help in a pamphlet. Like the other pamphlets, there is much that is serious in her writing, but there is humor as well, humor that can be aggressive and mocking.[41]

The most powerful woman in France at this time, and Marie Dentière's putative protector, was Marguerite de Navarre. The focus of my second chapter shifts to theater from the 1520s and 1530s, ending with three farces that Marguerite de Navarre wrote.[42] These plays provide insights into the queen's reformist views and reveal the different ways she gently used humor and satire to communicate these views. Before getting to Marguerite's plays, I first look at some of the earliest examples of reformist plays that may have informed hers.

In chapter 3, I examine several pamphlets by the Catholic polemicist Artus Désiré.[43] Désiré was one of the first Catholic polemicists who understood how to reach a wider, more popular audience. Most of his tracts are written in French rhymed verse and are relatively short. The language is simple and populist sentiment dominates. Denis Crouzet speculates that between 1545 and 1562 there were likely 60,000 to 70,000 copies of Désiré's *libelles* circulating, making him a remarkably successful author, though all but forgotten today.[44] Throughout Désiré's polemical tracts, laughter is almost always sardonic, and humor is simultaneously castigated (when it is a question of Protestant satire) and castigating (when it is Catholics or Christ himself laughing at the punishment of apostates). The chapter ends with Conrad Badius's play, the *Comedie du pape malade et tirant à la fin*, an intriguing work in which characters representing Désiré and other Catholic polemicists play supporting roles to a corrupt and dying pope. Badius's work both illustrates the fluid relationship between pamphlets and plays and is a pertinent example of radically altered attitudes toward humor and its function in society.

Chapter 4 centers on some of the most important satirical output from Geneva from the 1540s to the start of the first War of Religion. The main polemicists discussed are Pierre Viret and Théodore de Bèze. Viret was a prodigious writer and defender of the Geneva-based faith and produced more than fifty works over the course of his career, yet he is little known outside of theological studies. This points to a challenging aspect of many of the works discussed in this study; as Hoffmann points out, many of these *libelles* are "too theological for literary critics, too literary for historians, and too historical for theologians." He adds, "The period's vast vernacular religious literature constitutes an awkward corpus."[45] Though this awkwardness helps explain, at least in part, the relative neglect of these works, they are nevertheless essential to understanding the religious conflicts that, more than anything else, would define the century.

The fifth chapter centers on plays produced by two of the best-known *sociétés joyeuses* in France, the Conards de Rouen and the Parisian Basoche. Between 1535 and 1545 a series of polemical morality plays were performed in Rouen by the Conards.[46] These plays are remarkable for their heterogeneity, reflecting conflicting currents in a city that was both a hotbed for reformist ideas and notorious for burning heretics. These plays show various ways derisive humor could be used in a populist context to generate anger. The last work examined in this chapter is a curious morality play performed in Paris after the first War of Religion ended with the Peace of Ambroise in 1563. In 1564 the Basoche, the most famous *société joyeuse* in France, with a long tradition of putting on farces and other theatrical productions since the Middle Ages, staged a play titled *Mars et Justice*.[47] The views expressed are stridently Catholic, blaming the unrest and conflict in France on Protestants and their nefarious foreign allies. After the various characters have completed their critique of Protestants, the play ends by referring to several scabrous stories, primarily on the topic of marital infidelity. This surprising ending seems a melancholy reminder of the former spirit of the Basoche, now lost under the rubble of war. At the end of the play, there is laughter, but it is rueful and removed, recalling rather than acting out the mirthful misbehavior of farce.

The last chapter focuses on the most famous poet of France and the leader of the Pléiade, Pierre de Ronsard, who published a series of anti-Protestant pamphlets, beginning in 1562, eventually published together as the *Discours des miseres de ce temps*. These elicited a strong response from Geneva and generated remarkable enthusiasm among Catholics.[48] The last part of the chapter discusses one of the many responses to Ronsard from Geneva, a three-part *libelle* by Antoine de la Roche-Chandieu and Bernard de Montméja that inspired Ronsard's final pamphlet, the *Response aux injures et calomnies, de je ne sçay quells predicans et ministres de Genève* (1563). The humor used by both sides in this skirmish is bitter and sardonic, meant to convince readers of the sheer awfulness of their opponents. It is perhaps more than a coincidence that open warfare would break out in France in the middle of this much-publicized polemical dispute between Ronsard and Geneva.

Before the Protestant Reformation in Europe, late medieval humorous genres such as *fabliaux* and farce had already poked fun at the clergy, the legal system, and schoolmen. The disruptive forms of humor in medieval comedy were ideal for the more targeted theological satire and polemical critiques brought about by the Reformation and Counter-Reformation.[49] Humor in medieval comic forms such as farce is often derived from representations of lascivious monks, dissolute priests, and con men hawking relics and indulgences. Clerics in these works behave abominably, but one also finds a resigned acceptance of their conduct, since no one was calling for abolishing the monastic tradition or radically reforming the priesthood. All of this changed dramatically with the advent of the Reformation. Anticlerical representations became a key feature of later comedic forms, as popular entertainment and performance began to be used for specific ideological and religious reasons. In short, they became weaponized.[50] The initial satirical scope of late medieval comedy was expanded and its playfulness eventually supplanted by bitter partisan satire and polemics.[51]

This study is interested in a particular form of humor and laughter, the *risus sardonicus*. In examining plays and pamphlets of this period, one encounters many different types of humor; sardonic humor does not exist in isolation. For example, Marguerite de Navarre's plays contain several types of humor, including the "rire mystique" first described by Daniel Ménager,[52] and this despite Edwin Duval's recent assertion that Marguerite is never funny.[53] Even though Conrad Badius's *Comedie du pape malade* is dominated by a tense blend of sardonic humor and pious pronouncements, Hoffmann rightly observes that there are parts of the play that "quickly slid[e] into ejaculatory, excessive laughter."[54] Ronsard's increasingly sardonic tone in his *libelles* contains an unmistakable element of schadenfreude toward his Huguenot adversaries, which motivates his satiric attacks. These are just a few examples of the complexity and heterogeneity of the humor in these plays and pamphlets, even if the focus here is primarily on sardonic humor and laughter.

Perhaps surprisingly, while satire is an important element of my study, it contains only minor references to possibly the three greatest satirists of sixteenth-century France: François Rabelais, Clément Marot, and Jean Calvin. Why is this so? There are two primary reasons. First, this study focuses on a particular form of humor that is extremely strident and aggressive, angry and even violent. For the most part, the satirical tone of writings by these three canonical authors is much more playful, ironic, and even generous.[55] The second reason for partially excluding these authors (though each is discussed) is that this book aims to bring to light writers and works lesser known to modern readers but important to our understanding of the mentalities on either side of the growing religious divide during this time. While I have included works by established authors Marguerite de Navarre and Pierre de Ronsard, even for them the focus is on less-studied works, and the bulk of examples I use are from little-known or even anonymous polemicists.

The year 1534 marks a turning point in the history of religious satire in France. Much has been written about the change in the political climate in France following the Affaire des placards. An important part of that change was that jokes and satirical attacks that were previously off-limits, such as mockery of the Eucharist, were to become commonplace. With this growth in religiously inspired acerbic satire came an increasingly distrustful and even violent reaction to it, which resulted in an inevitable crackdown on humor now considered unacceptable. It has been argued that during the sixteenth century attitudes to humor changed profoundly, leading to new restrictions on what was deemed appropriate. Daniel Ménager characterizes this shift as a move from the "rire" to the "sourire."[56] This elegant phrasing, however, in some respects masks the violence of the religiously inspired vitriolic satire that played a central role in this evolution. During this turbulent period, sardonic laughter became progressively more prominent. Far from being harmless, this type of humor was aggressive and menacing and could in fact be dangerous and even deadly. Debates over acceptable forms of humor and satire mirrored similar arguments over what types of violence (torture, massacres, regicide) were to be condoned. In a period of growing sectarian violence, culminating in nearly forty years of civil wars, France saw a comparable increase in verbal violence, including aggressive and dehumanizing jokes, a phenomenon on which this study seeks to shed further light.

1

The Affaire des Placards and the Early Stages of Pamphlet Warfare

Celuy qui veult plusmer... est plusmé.
—[Marie Dentière], *La Guerre et deslivrance de la ville de Genesve*

The use of the printing press to disseminate religious polemics widely and rapidly certainly did not begin in 1534, but that year's Affaire des placards marked a turning point. The sheer audacity of this aggressive publicity stunt was without precedent in France. Taking aim at the most sacred ritual of the Catholic Church and hanging these militantly anti-Catholic broadsides throughout the kingdom, possibly even on the door of the king's bedchamber, predictably resulted in a strong backlash against nascent French Protestantism. Less than three decades after this polemical attack, France would be thrown into civil war, and less than four decades later the St. Bartholomew's Day Massacre would prove to be the century's deadliest in France. It may not be possible to establish a direct or causal relationship between vitriolic language and violence, but the polemical pamphlets and plays that are the focus of this study certainly heightened tensions and provoked angry responses. They could also provoke laughter, frequently the type described in the introduction as sardonic. I am interested in particular in the use of humor and satire with purely destructive aims. I will start with the likely author of the placard broadside, Antoine Marcourt, a zealot whose belligerent style is noteworthy in the history of religious polemics. I will also highlight *libelles* by Jérôme de Hangest, one of the first Catholics in France to engage in the propaganda battle with Protestants. Hangest's

Contre les tenebrions Lumiere evangelicque (1534) represents the first Catholic response to Marcourt's broadside. Finally, I will look at a curious *libelle* by Marcourt's coreligionist Marie Dentière, an enigmatic figure of the Reformation movement in Geneva. At this early stage, there was not an enormous number of polemical pamphlets in France, and most of the Catholic ones, as well as some of the Protestant ones, were in Latin.

Before getting to Marcourt's notorious placard, the *Articles veritables sur les horribles, grandz et importables abuz de la Messe papale*, it is helpful to back up a year to examine his first anti-Catholic satirical work, the *Livre des marchans, fort utile à toutes gens pour cognoistre de quelles marchandises on se doit donner garde d'estre deceu* (1533), translated into English in 1534 as *The Boke of Marchauntes*.[1] In this brief tract (under one hundred pages), Marcourt sets a sarcastic tone with the title itself, followed by a prologue that mocks the "difficulté Sorbonnique" (Sorbonnic difficulty). The premise is simple and populist, typical of reformist diatribes: beware of the shenanigans, masked in an impenetrable veil of scholastic balderdash, propagated by the Sorbonne.[2] The economic metaphor satirizes the motivations of Marcourt's Catholic adversaries, framing his argument as a caveat emptor. Instead of being a high-minded religious institution, the Sorbonne is like a petty merchant, seeking to dupe naïve clients (believers) through the obfuscation of their "difficulté Sorbonnique." The *Livre des marchans*, in contrast, is written in accessible French, with a small number of Latin citations glossed in French. The second edition of the tract (1534) ends with a whimsical poem, in later editions moved to the front, titled, "Dizain pour les marchans":[3]

> Il ne fut jamais telz Marchans,
> Que ceulx qui vendent au marc Chantz:
> Plus dru que sort ne marche en dé,
> Marchans marchantz ont Marchandé:
> Et quoy que meschant Marchant dise,
> Il n'y a que Marchandise:
> Mais garde soy tout Marchandeur,
> Que son mal ne luy Marchande heur:
> Et que après avoir bien marché,
> Il ne trouve mauvais Marché.
>
> (There have never been such merchants,
> As those who sell songs for money.

More common than chance in a game of dice,
Itinerant merchants have peddled their wares.
And whatever the traitorous merchant says,
It's nothing more than merchandise.
But let every buyer beware
Lest fortune sell him his downfall;
And lest after having been taken,
He end up having made a bad deal.)[4]

The poem is reminiscent of the *grands rhetoriqueurs'* playful, pun-filled poetry, bursting with equivocal rhymes based on the root words "marchand/marché." Early editions end with the populist dichotomy, "Riche marchant/ou paouvre poullaillier" (Rich merchant/or poor little chicken coop).[5] In later editions, the end is changed to the associative pun, "Marchant ou larron" (Merchant or thief), to highlight the deceptive practices of the Sorbonne. Catholicism is presented as a sort of shell game, with the word/Word constantly moved around ("marcher") in a marketplace ("marché") full of tricksters, ultimately revealing its true identity through a homonymic association. For the converted, the poem evokes spiteful laughter at both duper and duped. This brings up an important question, and one that I will return to throughout this book: Who is the intended audience? The *Livre des marchans* pokes fun not only at the Sorbonne but at Catholic believers as well. Was the strategy to create more Protestant converts, or rather to fortify the Protestant faithful by making fun of their religious adversaries? It is hard to imagine this tract as a conversion tool; its appeal might extend to those less sure of the Catholic faith, but the text also provided Swiss Protestants with a chance to laugh at and mock their French Catholic enemies.[6]

There is a notable difference between the first and subsequent editions of the *Livre des marchans*, namely references to Rabelais's *Pantagruel*, the first such allusions found in print.[7] These were taken out the following year, but in this satire aimed at the Sorbonne, and more generally at the Catholic Church, it is intriguing that the title page of the first edition lists as its author "le sire Pantapole[8] . . . prochain voysin du seigneur Pantagruel" (Sir Pantapole . . . next-door neighbor of Lord Pantagruel). The prologue refers to the "preux et venerable seigneur Pantagruel, lequel droictement en scaura juger: car autresfois il a sententié merveilleusement au profit des parties" (the valiant and noble Lord Pantagruel, who will know how to judge correctly, since in the past he gave a marvelous ruling that satisfied both parties), a reference to the Baisecul and Humevesne episode, and the main body of the text mentions the gifted trickster Panurge. While later in the religious conflict Rabelais would become associated with atheism and hedonism by both sides, here he is referenced likely in the hopes of attracting an audience familiar with *Pantagruel*.⁹ This tells us something about reader reception and about the popularity of Rabelais's work, which had reached deep into Switzerland in its first year. Marcourt, like others after him, was hoping to gain readership by associating his pamphlet with a scandalous best seller.¹⁰ It has been suggested that the deletion of the references to *Pantagruel* the following year suggests Marcourt's aversion to the controversy that soon surrounded Rabelais's work, but this argument is not entirely convincing, as Marcourt could hardly be accused of being cautious in the face of controversy.¹¹ A more plausible explanation is that as Marcourt's militant ideological position hardened (the spirited tone of the *Livre des marchans* would be replaced the following year by the compressed stridency of his notorious placard), Rabelais's work became too liberal minded and too heterodox for him.¹² The removal of the reference can thus be seen as presaging Calvin's eventual condemnation of Rabelais, as Calvinists became increasingly intolerant of irreverent ideas.¹³

Before attacking Catholic "marchans," the pamphlet begins by praising "loyaulx marchans" (faithful merchants) whose work is "louable et fort utile, pourveu qu'il soit fidelement entretenu" (praiseworthy and quite useful, as long as it is conducted honestly). Catholic priests and monks, on the other hand, are "furieux larrons, et insatiables loupz ravissans" (raging thieves and insatiable, ravenous wolves). As Marcourt berates these deceptive merchants, he derives humor principally from the putative dominant desires of the Catholic clergy: food and sex. These are the same crude clerical motivators one finds in medieval *fabliaux*, farces, and *contes* going back hundreds of years, but, barely a decade after Luther's excommunication and with the growth of reformist sects in Europe, Marcourt's use of these satirical tropes takes on new meanings and is more aggressive.

Gluttony and lust motivate the prelates portrayed in the *Livre des marchans*, connecting gastronomic overindulgence with theological extravagance, a common theme in Protestant polemics. It is hard not to see Rabelais's influence in many of the vivid descriptions. Marcourt refers to the kingpin of the merchants as the "grand galiffre"; Cotgrave defines "galiffre" as "A greedie feeder, a ravenous eater." (This expression will return in Marie Dentière's writing and in the *Satyres chrestiennes de la cuisine papale*.)¹⁴ Monks and clergy fight for "leur grasse soupe, leur ribauldise . . . leur gourmandise et trop friande cuisine" (their fatty soup, their debauchery, their gluttony, and their rich cuisine).

This polemical tract brings performativity and theatricality to the forefront. Priests and monks in their various costumes, wigs, and tonsures are "semblables à basteleurs, mommeurs, ou joueurs de passe-passe" (similar to jugglers, buffoons, or tricksters). They are "un tas de deguisez et contrefaits galans" (a troop of disguised and crafty scoundrels). Heteronormative attacks also play a role in this: Catholic clergy members are "gens effeminez" (effeminate people). Different forms of "farder," to apply powder or makeup, describe their deceiving ways. Gender-bending representations are meant to antagonize and dehumanize the Catholic clergy, provoking the *risus sardonicus* by means of what Freud described as tendentious jokes, which call into question the heteronormativity and virility of priests and monks. Male virility is connected to religious authority and patriarchy. With each suggestion that the powerful male Catholic clergy is in fact impotent, both undermining the virility and mocking the celibacy of Catholic prelates, the text seeks to symbolically castrate them. In the one mention of women, the text describes female victims who are taken captive into convents and abandoned; unsurprisingly, femininity is equated with weakness. The author asserts that effeminate priests are violating heteronormative roles and suggests that male leaders of the Catholic Church are either sexless or feminine. These crude gender portrayals are the stuff from which so much tendentious, misogynistic humor is derived.

Humor cedes repeatedly to piety in the *Livre des marchans*, especially in subsequent editions of the tract.[15] There are recurrent instances where pious pronouncements about the "parole de verité" eclipse mockery of Catholic clergy. Priests in drag hawking indulgences, meant to provoke laughter, disappear and are replaced by biblical passages and references to Christ's parables. This shift becomes more pronounced in subsequent versions, when references to Rabelais and other scabrous allusions are replaced by more devout sentiment, which I would argue supports the notion that as Marcourt became more zealous, there was less room for irony and playfulness in his writing.[16]

While his *Livre des marchans* would see a dozen editions and be translated into English, Dutch, and German, Marcourt's notoriety comes from his placard, a much shorter treatise in small gothic letters printed on a sheet measuring just 37 by 25 centimeters, titled the *Articles veritables sur les hor-*

ribles, grandz et importables abuz de la Messe papale.[17] The sarcastic portrayals and satirical barbs of Marcourt's *Livre des marchans* are almost entirely absent here, replaced by earnest fanaticism. Fanaticism leaves little room for irony, the lifeblood of humor, and the *Articles veritables* is the work of a fanatic. Of the four sections or articles in the broadside, the first three focus almost exclusively on the Eucharist and transubstantiation, the very topic that will dominate the vast majority of *libelles* and treatises during this period. The fourth and final section contains the only slight deviation from strictly doctrinal declarations, ending with a sardonic representation of the so-called false faith:

> Mais le fruict de la messe est bien aultre, mesme comme experience nous demonstre, car par icelle, toute congnoissance de Jesus Christ est effacé, predication de l'evangile rejectée et empeschée, le temps occupé en sonneries, urlemens, chanteries, ceremonies, luminaires, encensemens, desguisemens et telles manieres de singeries, par lesquelles le paovre monde est comme brebis ou moutons miserablement entretenu et pourmené, et par ces loups ravissans, mangé, rongé et devoré. Et qui pourroit dire ne penser les larrecin de ces paillardz? Par ceste messe ilz ont tout empoigné, tout destruict, tout englouty, ils ont desherité princes et rois, marchans, seigneurs, et tout ce que on peult dire, soit mort ou vif. Par icelle ilz vivent sans soucy, ilz n'ont besoing de rien faire, d'estudier encore moins, que voulez vous plus? Il ne se fault donc esmerveiller se bien fort ilz la maintiennent, ilz tuent, ilz bruslent, ilz detruisent, ilz meurtrissent comme brigans tous ceulx qui a eulx contredisent, car aultre chose ilz n'ont plus que la force. Verité leur fault. Verité les menasse. Verité les suyt et pourchasse. Verité les espouvante. Par laquelle briefvement seront destruictz.

> (But the fruit of the mass is rather different, even as experience shows us, for by it, all knowledge of Jesus Christ is removed, preaching of the gospel is rejected and impeded, time is spent with ringing bells, hollering, chanting, candlelit ceremonies, incense, disguises and all sorts of monkeying around, the result of which is that the poor people are like sheep miserably held captive and led along, and by these ravenous wolves they are eaten, gnawed on, and devoured. And who could assert the contrary of this larceny committed by these depraved people? Through this mass they have seized everything, destroyed everything,

swallowed up everything, they have dispossessed princes and kings, merchants, lords, and all that one can say, dead or alive. Through this mass they live without a care, they do not have to do anything, and study even less; what more do you want? It should come as no surprise that in order to maintain it, they kill, they burn, they destroy, they murder like outlaws all those who contradict them, because they can only act by force. They need the truth. Truth harasses them. Truth follows and pursues them. Truth scares them, by which truth soon they will be destroyed.)

The satirical description of the Catholic clergy, spending their time "en sonneries, urlemens, chanteries, ceremonies, luminaires, encensemens, desguisemens et telles manieres de singeries" (ringing bells, hollering, chanting, candlelit ceremonies, incense, disguises and all sorts of monkeying around), harks back to the *Livre des marchans*, but the chance for a sardonic laugh is lost by the conclusion of the phrase, as the poor are like sheep before the slaughter, "mangé, rongé et devoré" (eaten, gnawed on, devoured) by the rapacious wolves of the Catholic Church.

The comparison of the *Articles veritables* with the *Livre des marchans* elucidates a larger phenomenon during this period—as new forms of satire evolve, humor becomes both more acerbic and more violent,[18] while unrestrained, bawdy laughter increasingly becomes marginalized. This phenomenon recalls a key moment, rarely discussed by scholars, in the Papimanes episode of Rabelais's *Quart livre*. In chapter 50, after Homenaz has shown them the portrait of the pope and described him as God on earth, Frère Jean tells a rather innocent joke from his time in the Seuilly monastery about a group of beggars bragging about their earnings, the most successful being teased for having a "jambe de Dieu" (God's game leg),[19] in other words, as Mireille Huchon explains, a phony disability devised to elicit pity.[20]

What is shocking is Pantagruel's extreme reaction to Frère Jean's light humor: "Quand (dist Pantagruel) telz contes vous nous ferez, soyez records d'apporter un basin. Peu s'en fault que ne rende ma guorge. User ainsi du sacré nom de Dieu en choses tant hordes et abhominables? Fy, j'en diz fy. Si dedans vostre moynerie est tel abus de paroles en usaige, laissez le là: ne le transportez hors les cloistres." ("When you tell us such stories," said Pantagruel, "remember to bring a basin: I'm almost ready to throw up. To use the holy name of God in such filthy and abominable things! Fie! I say Fie! If such an abuse of words is customary in your monkery, leave it there, don't bring it outside the cloisters.")[21] Michael J. Heath offers the following explanation for Pantagruel's rebuke: "Perhaps excusable at such times of crisis as the storm and the battle with the Spouter, Frere Jan's blasphemy cannot be forgiven when it merely provides the punchline of a joke; Rabelais knew the excesses of monkish humor. *Noblesse oblige*: polite towards his hosts, Pantagruel can be ruthless towards his own team."[22] This seems like a defining moment, in which Rabelais realizes that the type of humor he had built his reputation on is no longer acceptable to the radicals on either side of the divide, here represented by the Papimanes.

Both Catholics and Protestants use humor and satire as weapons to further their causes, but the viciousness of the debates and the intensity of belief progressively drained the ironic possibilities of the form. In an increasingly divided society, the ambiguities of wordplay, puns, and jokes, as well as the occasional blasphemy, become less innocent and less tolerated. Derogatory and sarcastic quips become increasingly bitter, as the *risus sardonicus* becomes the dominant form of laughter for both Catholic and Protestant zealots. There remain, however, many examples where equivocation and play remain possible, despite strong religious and political forces pushing against them.

Jérôme de Hangest, one of the first Catholic polemicists, was chosen by the Faculty of Theology (at the Sorbonne) to respond to Marcourt's *Articles veritables*. It has been suggested that Rabelais's character Janotus de Bragmardo, the hapless Sorbonniste who delivers a farcical harangue in an attempt to convince Gargantua to return the bells of Notre Dame Cathedral, represented Noël Béda. It is equally plausible, given the timing of Hangest's response, that Rabelais had the latter in mind when creating his inept Sorbonniste.[23] Hangest's nickname was "le Marteau des Hérétiques" (The Hammer of the Heretics).[24] He produced two treatises immediately following the dissemination of Marcourt's broadside, one in Latin and one in French. The Latin treatise, *De Christifera Eucharistia adversus nugiferos symbolistas* (1534), is almost entirely theological, limiting its audience to other theologians and those humanists engaged in these rather arcane debates. It would not have found a wide readership outside of university and perhaps humanist circles and illustrates a central weakness of the initial Catholic response: early Catholic polemicists were primarily Sorbonne theologians. The idea of producing a theological treatise not in Latin was almost unheard of, if not unthinkable. By refuting with inaccessible Latin texts on questions of doctrine the Protestant arguments that were being distributed widely in France, the initial efficacy of the Catholic response, measured by breadth of readership, was greatly curtailed.

Hangest did follow up this Latin treatise with a second attack, written in French, *Contre les tenebrions Lumiere evangelicque* (1534), which he addressed to Anne de Montmorency, the king's most trusted military advisor. As Claude Postel observes about this second treatise,

> Quoiqu'on décèle encore une forte latinisation dans la forme du discours, le style combattant est là, avec son cortège de vigoureuses apostrophes contre ces "abominables ténèbrions . . . insidiatifs pirates . . . pervers calomniateurs", que sont les disciples de Luther. À ce "maistre asnier à la langue pestilente", il adresse un "Tu crains ta peau" préludant à l'exhortation finale: face à la sédition ou à la trahison de ces hérétiques, "Fault doncq en les extirpant obvier" et le plus tôt sera le mieux.
>
> (Although one still finds the writing strongly Latinate, the combative style is there, with its string of vigorous attacks against these "abominable tiny clouds of darkness . . . insidious pirates . . . perverse calumniators" that are Luther's disciples. To this "master donkey-driver with a pestilent tongue," he launches a "You're afraid of your own skin," a prelude to the final exhortation: faced with the sedition or the treachery of these heretics, "it is necessary to take precautions while eliminating them" and the sooner the better.)[25]

Postel's summary of Hangest's diatribe brings out the liveliest part of what is otherwise a long-winded, tedious, and dry theological treatise. For well over a hundred pages, the reader is subjected to arcane considerations surrounding the Eucharist. While *Contre les tenebrions* represents one of the first examples of the Catholic side in France participating in the propaganda war with Protestants, it is a rather feeble start. As Luc Racaut reminds us, however,

> It can be argued that the French Wars of Religion were lost and won by the ability of Catholics and Huguenots to create and to block competing narratives and representations of each other. The Protestant representation of Catholicism is more familiar to the modern reader because it achieved greater notoriety with time. . . . Catholic representations were nonetheless more successful in the short term in fostering distrust and hatred of the Protestants.[26]

Racaut seeks to correct the modern view of this propaganda war, arguing that the Catholic side was in fact much more effective than previously acknowledged.[27] Despite the tedium of *Contre les tenebrions* for the modern reader, Hangest was certainly effective in creating distrust and hatred of Protestants in this and other tracts.

Hangest produced a much more succinct and satirical work two years later, *En controversie voye seure* (1536). While the title page is filled with Latin, and there is Latin throughout, this work is shorter and more engaging and appeals to a wider audience. It contains several satirical attacks against Protestant practices, attacks that use gender and class in ways that reinforce the conservatism of the Catholic position. Describing Protestant worship in a way that would become characteristic of Catholic diatribes, he writes, "le tabourin de liberté sensuelle a faict tres haultement sonner, de volupté la baniere apertement a deployée, et a faict doulcement resoner la trompette de deceptive palliation ... que concede ladicte secte, plus que epicurienne" (the tambourine of sensual liberty has been loudly played, the banner of voluptuousness plainly unfurled, and the trumpet of deceptive pleasure has enticingly been sounded ... which proves that this sect is utterly epicurean). This lascivious representation of Protestant practices recalls Natalie Zemon Davis's observation that

> the new Calvinist liturgy, with its stress on the concerted fellowship of the congregation, used the vernacular—the language of women and the unlearned—and included Psalms sung jointly by men and women. Nothing shocked Catholic observers more than this. When they heard the music of male and female voices filtering from a house where a conventicle was assembled, all they could imagine were lewd activities with the candles extinguished.[28]

In addition to Hangest's lewd portrayal of this "epicurean" sect, in *En controversie voye seure* he mocks them for something else that introduces gender and class into the debate: "Voyla entre les hommes dangereux debatz, entre les femmes pernicieuse disputation, entre varletz et chambrieres temeraires contrariete, entre jeunes enfans folle vociferation, de chamberiere ou varletz contre leur maistre" (Look at these dangerous debates among men, pernicious disputation among women, contradictions between servants and impudent chambermaids, pandemonium among young children, female and male servants against their master). For this Catholic polemicist, the excesses of Protestantism are twofold: their conduct is vulgar and they disrupt the social order by allowing women and servants to participate actively in theological debates, thus turning servant against master, emblematic of the larger religious conflict in France. Hangest's sardonicism is very Juvenalesque in tone, decrying the chaos brought about by this upstart heretical sect. The aim of *En controversie voye seure* is not only to shock the Catholic populace but also to get them to laugh at Protestants, who are so absurd that they allow women, children, and servants to debate matters of faith. This is a good example of Freud's concept of tendentious humor, evoking laughter by denigrating the lower levels of society occupied by women and servants. And in fact, as we will see, early reformists did emphasize the involvement of women and children in their cause, drawing upon the New Testament paradox of the powerful laid low by the powerless.

One woman to take up the Protestant cause was Marie Dentière. As one of the few female voices from Geneva, Dentière has received a fair amount of scholarly attention.[29] A former nun from Tournai, she was the first reformist woman in France to be excommunicated.[30] She left her Augustinian convent and married Simon Robert, a former priest in that city, in the 1520s. They fled to Strasbourg, where they were introduced to one of the future leaders of the Protestant movement in Geneva, Guillaume Farel. Dentière's husband was named a reform pastor in Bex. The couple had two daughters. After Robert died in 1533, Dentière married Antoine Froment, with whom she had three more children, and the family ended up in Geneva.[31] Both she and Froment became defenders of Farel and Calvin, especially when these future leaders of the Geneva-based Protestant movement were banished from that city by the Council of Two Hundred in 1538. After much conflict, Geneva had officially become a Protestant city in 1536. That same year, a *libelle* was published, *La Guerre et deslivrance de la ville de Genesve* by "un Marchand demourant en icelle." It was not until the nineteenth century that this anonymous pamphlet was attributed to Marie Dentière. More recently scholars, among them Mary McKinley, have doubted this attribution.[32] McKinley states that "the author of *The War and Deliverance* shows little concern about gender. Women are portrayed as passive victims and are generally absent from the heroic account."[33] There is, however, one exception to this, and it occurs in the only humorous part of the tract. The main adversary of Protestants in Geneva was the Duke of Savoy. In a particularly trenchant satirical passage, the author asserts:

> Mais, ce Duc, voyant bien qu'il perdroit ses plusmes, comme il a faict par ses [ces] derniers jours, a tant faict et machiné deçà et delà qu'il a eu

grandes alliances avec plusieurs princes et seigneurs. Mais tout n'a rien servy.... La crainte ne luy a pas esté sans dommaige, car ung chescun luy a tiré une plume, et est plusmé tout nud et est sans plusmes. Aussy est bien rayson que celuy qui veult plusmer et est plusmé, qui [qu'il] soit sans elles. Femmes boutés hardiment poussins couver, car les ducs ne les mangeront plus. (42)

(But this Duke/Owl, seeing that he would lose his feathers, as he had done these last days, did so much and plotted hither and thither to establish great alliances with several princes and lords. But it did him no good.... His fear was not without loss, for everyone plucked one of his feathers, and he was plucked until he was naked and without feathers. Thus it is true that he who wants to pluck is plucked, so that he is without feathers/wings. Women fearlessly cover their chicks, so that the dukes/owls will not eat them anymore.)

In French, *duc* can mean both duke and horned owl. This lays the foundation for an extended joke about how the duke has lost his feathers, and the people of Geneva are now safe. There is even a modified proverb from the world of farce, "celui qui veut tromper est trompé" (the one who wants to trick is tricked), which here becomes "celuy qui veult plusmer ... est plusmé" (he who wants to pluck is plucked). Now the women of Geneva can sit on their eggs to hatch their chicks, since the duke will no longer eat them—he is left without *elles*, a homonymic pun referring to both feathers (*elles*) and wings (*ailes*).[34] In this description, the plucked duke has been symbolically castrated by the women of Geneva, rendered impotent by the life-giving force of Geneva's female inhabitants. This portrayal, both humorous and acrimonious, calls attention to gender and highlights the strength of Geneva's women.

Three years later, Marie Dentière published a much more radical *libelle*, the *Epistre tres utile faicte et composée par une femme chrestienne de Tornay, envoyée à la Royne de Navarre seur du Roy de France: Contre les Turcz, Juifz, Infideles, Faulx chrestiens, Anabaptistes, et Lutheriens* (1539). In this case there is no debate over authorship, and the work has a decidedly female perspective. McKinley remarks that "the epistle brings together, if only in print, two women who played very different roles in [the Protestant Reformation] movement."[35] This extraordinary document contains the "first explicit statement of reformed theology by a woman to appear in French."[36]

The back story of this pamphlet is that when Marguerite de Navarre found out that Farel and Calvin had been banished from Geneva, she supposedly wrote to Marie Dentière (Marguerite was the godmother of one of Dentière's daughters) to find out what had happened. Marie's response became the tract.[37] As McKinley notes,

> While Marguerite is the designated recipient of the *Epistle*, Dentière clearly intended a wider audience for her work. Those targeted readers would include people she criticizes and attacks: the authorities in Geneva who had made Calvin and Farel leave, the powerful hierarchy of the Catholic Church, believers in reform who stayed in the Catholic Church, and members of the French court who tolerated or supported them.[38]

The work created quite a stir in Geneva. Officials raided Jean Girard's printing shop (no one was fooled by the publisher falsely listing Antwerp as the place of publication, as Girard was close to Farel and Calvin) and burned the copies they found there. Some refused to believe the pamphlet could be the work of a woman and referred to it as "Froment's epistle."[39]

The most explicitly feminist section of the *Epistre tres utile* is titled "Defense pour les femmes."[40] In it, Dentière makes the argument that women should be allowed to write about matters pertaining to Scripture. Countering the traditional misogynistic biblical example of Eve corrupting Adam, she gives multiple biblical examples of righteous women, including the Samaritan woman who preached to Jesus. The resurrected Christ first showed himself to women, but as Dentière observes, it was a man, Judas, who betrayed Christ, and none of the false prophets in the Bible were women. This radical treatise would be silenced, and Dentière would eventually be attacked by the very person she was trying to help, Jean Calvin. As Natalie Zemon Davis has ruefully noted, "no book by a woman was printed in Geneva for the rest of the century."[41] The initial exuberance of reform-minded women like Dentière was soon crushed, as Calvin and other Protestant leaders insisted on women's total submission. Still, one finds in this section an audacious, if short-lived, insistence on the importance of women in this nascent religious movement.

Ironically, Dentière employs a common gender trope for comic effect elsewhere in the *Epistre tres utile*, saying to those who blindly follow Catholicism: "Lesquelz comme paovres bestes attachées vous mennent à l'abbreuoir. Avezvous le nez de cire, qu'on le vous tourne à tous ventz? *il semble que soyez du tout effeminez*, hors du sens, sans crainte de Dieu [emphasis mine]." (They are leading you to the watering-place like poor, tied-up beasts. Are you so pliable that they can turn you about every which way? *You seem to be completely emasculated*, out of your senses, without fear of God.)[42] Whereas Dentière focused on women's strength in her "Defense," here she ridicules Catholics for being weak and emasculated—essentially for being too feminine. This is typical misogynistic humor, a tendentious joke that equates femininity with weakness and one that was used repeatedly by both Catholics and Protestants. It is a curious inclusion for a woman as fearless as Dentière; it also problematizes gender divisions, as men are portrayed as acting womanly while a woman, the author of the pamphlet, is acting in manly fashion.

Among her satirical digs at Catholics, one of the funnier ones is her description of Catholic superstitions; in their search for cures, the ignorant faithful turn to a litany of saints: "S. Roct du vomissement. S. Loup des dens. S. Renard du manger. S. Cosme des chastrés, et Damien des rompus de tous costez." (Saint Rock for vomiting, Saint Wolf for the teeth, Saint Fox for eating, Saint Cosmos for the castrated, and Damien for the crippled on all sides.)[43] This piling on of funny-sounding saints' names, both real and fictitious, and connecting them to such corporeal and scatological activities as vomiting and castration makes for a lighter, entertaining moment in an otherwise heavily sententious and even violent epistle. As George Hoffmann has argued, this is not the sort of satire that would likely make converts of moderate Catholics; while funny, it is also quite aggressive.[44] Dentière pulls no punches in this pamphlet and refers to Catholics repeatedly as "fous." As for the Geneva council that had Calvin and Farel banished, she mocks them and calls them "cafards" (religious hypocrites). Overall, it is a bold and bellicose work. Because of the way it attempts to address gender inequalities, the section on the defense of women was omitted in Herminjard's nineteenth-century edition.[45] Dentière's *Epistre tres utile* is a remarkable document produced during a time of transition, when possibilities seemed to be opening up for women, fueled by the enthusiasm of new converts like herself.

Before leaving Dentière, there is one final satirical performance by her to examine, one that we know about only from a 1546 letter from Calvin to Farel, the very people Dentière had previously sought to defend.[46] As Calvin describes a recent run-in with her, his tone is sarcastic and mocking. He prefaces his account, "Now I'm going to tell you a funny story" (Narrabo hic iocosam historiam).[47] Apparently it had got back to Calvin that Dentière had been going around town attacking the Geneva church's male authorities for their ostentatious dress, particularly their long garments, which she compared to those worn by the scribes whom Jesus warned his followers against in Luke 20:45–47. In Calvin's description of their confrontation, her response is telling: "Since she knew that it had got back to me, she excused herself, *laughing*" (Quum id mihi fuisse indicatum sciret, excusavit se *ridendo* [emphasis mine]). She did not back down and chastised Calvin and the male leadership. Calvin concludes, "Feeling that she was closely pressed, she complained of our tyranny, because no one was allowed to chatter about anything he or she wants. I treated the woman as I should have." (Quum sentiret se urgeri, conquesta est de nostra tyrannide, quod non cuivis liceret quidvis garrire. Tractavi mulierem ut debui.)

Here we have two registers of laughter, both of them forms of the *risus sardonicus*. The first laugh is Dentière's. It suggests that her apology to Calvin is insincere, and her laughter is lightly subversive and sardonic. Forced to apologize, she grits her teeth, yet laughter escapes. Dentière's impudence is countered, rather defensively, by Calvin's final sarcastic quip in his letter to Farel, intended to ridicule and humiliate the absent Dentière, who cannot defend herself.[48] Calvin tells the story in this way because he wants Farel to laugh at the end, mocking the supposed airs of this obstreperous woman. The punchline is left unspoken, if indeed it was ever delivered. By insisting, "I treated the woman as I should have," Calvin implies that he made a witty retort that put her in her place. That Calvin leaves unsaid his supposed rejoinder suggests that this is an *esprit de l'escalier* moment for the Genevan leader. It is hard not to feel, in reading his letter, that it was Dentière, in fact, who had the last laugh and that Calvin reimagined the encounter to save face.

In this first chapter, the focus has been on the types of humor and satire found in pamphlets from the 1530s, a period when confessional boundaries were still fluid and ambiguous, when the definition of heresy was debated, and when reformists and their conservative counterparts were beginning to work out how to use the relatively new medium of print to widely disseminate polemical ideas and responses. It is also the period that produced the most (in)famous of all the French religious polemical *libelles*, Marcourt's *Articles veritables*, and the only example we have of a female pamphleteer, Marie Dentière. As we move further into this pamphlet battle, the disappearance of female voices is regrettable. The Catholic side fared no better, and in these pamphlet exchanges it is nearly impossible to find any female voices.

2

Early Evangelical and Reformist Comic Theater

De rire ne me puys tenir.
—Marguerite de Navarre, *Trop Prou Peu et Moins*

Attention now shifts from pamphlets to theater, while recognizing the fluid boundaries between the two, as theater pieces could be circulated in print, pamphleteers could appear onstage as characters, and pamphlets contain many performative qualities. In this chapter, I want to examine some important theatrical performances that unite comedy and religious polemic. Before focusing on three plays composed by Marguerite de Navarre, which she styled farces, I would like to consider some key earlier plays that provide important context for them. A common trope in reformist polemics, especially in theater, is to represent Christianity as a sick patient in need of a cure.[1] Early examples include a pair of *sotties* performed in Geneva in the 1520s, as well as Matthieu Malingre's *Moralité de la maladie de chrestienté* in 1533, and Louis de Berquin's *La Farce des theologastres*, performed in the late 1520s.

While Calvin's church produced and disseminated a large number of pamphlets, as we will see in chapter 4, plays were another matter. Calvin has been called "the least theater-friendly reformer of all."[2] In his discussion of differences between German and French pamphlets, Francis Higman suggests that the Geneva-based church aimed at a more intellectual public and that "le théâtre, genre également populaire, est peu exploité" (theater, a genre that is also low-brow, is hardly taken advantage of).[3] Before Calvin's arrival, an interesting pair of *sotties* were performed in Geneva in 1523 and 1524, the *Sottie des béguins* and the *Sottie du monde*.[4] One could view these as two acts of the same play, as the *Sottie du monde* takes up where the *Sottie des béguins* leaves off and contains many of the same characters. Unusually, we actually know a lot about when and where these plays were performed and even the names of the actors. The *Sottie des béguins* was performed on 22 February 1523, the first Sunday of Lent, in the Place Molard. At this early stage in the turbulent events that would eventually lead to Geneva becoming a Protestant city, tensions were high between those who followed the Duke of Savoy, aligned with the Hapsburg Empire, and the Swiss confederates, the Eidgenosse (a name that may be the origin of the term *Huguenot* in French).[5]

The plot is rather straightforward: Mère Folie and her fools are in mourning, thinking that Bon Temps is dead; a messenger, Printemps, arrives with a letter from Bon Temps revealing that he is still alive. They write a letter in reply and Printemps leaves with it, at which point there is a musical interlude. After this pause, everyone springs into action, wanting to perform a farce for Bon Temps when he returns. The fools need hats (in a farce fools would wear hats resembling donkey ears and cover their faces with flour), but they lack fabric to make them. Mère Folie suggests they take it from her shirt, near her rear end, but the shirt is too short. She then says that she will lengthen the shirt and give birth to another fool, which she does onstage. When they make their hats, they only have enough fabric for the left ears, implying inadequacy or ineptitude. The right ear, which would enable them to understand things correctly, is lacking. The fools despair, decide that it is impossible to put on the play, and bid farewell to the audience, announcing that they are heading out to drink.

Much of the humor in the play is gestural, but there are jokes as well. The satire is rather oblique and general. However, there is a reference in Bon Temps' letter to "ces predicants" who have caused a ruckus in Geneva since he left four years earlier. "Predicants" (preachers) by 1529 referred to Protestant ministers, and here the term is used pejoratively.[6] In the letter replying to Bon Temps, one of the fools, Antoine, complains that they have not been allowed to perform, a common lament in plays of this period (vv. 154–55). Further on in the letter, there is a mocking complaint that while these poor actors lack fabric for hats, the ladies and lawyers of Geneva are certainly well dressed (vv. 212–15). The satire here is lighthearted; nonetheless the play announces general themes that with time will become much more mordant.

The *Sottie du monde* was performed a year later, in 1524, on the first Sunday of Lent like its predecessor.[7] Although the play was originally scheduled to be performed in the Place Molard, because of rain it was performed indoors in the Palace of Justice. In prefatory remarks in the printed version of the play, it is noted that the Duke of Savoy and his wife were supposed to attend, but "pour ce qu'on ne leur avoit pas dressé de place . . . ils n'y voulurent pas venir. Aussi pour ce qu'on disoit que c'estoient Huguenots qui jouoyent." (because they had not set up a place for them . . . they did not want to come. Also because it was rumored that Huguenots were performing the play.)[8] This comment alone alerts us to a change in tone in what could be considered Act II of this play about a world that is sick. The first lines grimly recall the previous year's *sottie*—Bon Temps has still not arrived, and Mère Folie has died. As in the previous play, next comes an interlude, with the fools following after and attempting to serve the allegorical figure Monde. The second part becomes more serious and more overtly partisan. As it begins, Monde makes the fools work, but as they transform themselves into different artisans (a tailor, a cobbler, a milliner, etc.), he is unsatisfied with their labor. New characters appear—Conseiller, Prestre, and Medecin—and then we learn that Monde is sick. As Medecin notes, "Il est blessé / Du cerveau" (He is wounded / in the brain") (vv. 226–27).

Monde is resistant to Medecin's advice, and at the rather ambiguous end of the play,[9] Medecin launches into a tirade:

> Tu ne te troubles pas
> De voyr ces larrons attrapards
> Vendre et achepter benefices,
> Les enfants ez bras des nourrices
> Estre abbez, evesques, prieurs.
>
> (Are you not bothered
> To see these robbing thieves
> Selling and buying benefices,
> Children in the arms of their wet nurses
> Who are made abbots, bishops, priors.) (vv. 246–50)

Medecin's outburst grows more intense and ends with the accusation that the Catholic Church for no reason declares war on fellow Christians (vv. 255–56). Monde, reacting indignantly to this diatribe, responds, "Ce sont des propos du pays / De Luther, reprouvez si faulx" (These are ideas from the country / Of Luther, and must be condemned) (vv. 260–61). Medecin responds defensively, bemoaning that any such diagnosis is immediately met with an accusation of Lutheran heresy. The earlier humor, as the bumbling fools try to appease Monde, has only been a pretext for this biting polemic. This is the nature of the *risus sardonicus*, in which joking serves as a prelude to something much more aggressive, in this case a piercing satire of corruption and hypocrisy in the Catholic Church.

In 1533, the same year that Pierre de Vingle published Marcourt's *Livre des marchans*, he also published a play by Matthieu Malingre, a Dominican monk from Normandy who had joined the cause of the Reformation and fled to Switzerland. This work, the *Moralité de la maladie de chrestienté*, was performed in Beaulmes in 1549, possibly in Geneva in 1546, and in La Rochelle in 1558 in the presence of Marguerite de Navarre's daughter, Jeanne d'Albret, who had joined the Protestant cause.[10] The primary purpose of this morality play, like the majority of Reformation-era morality plays, is polemical. As Jean-Pierre Bordier has noted, two aspects that unite *sotties* and *moralités* are revealing the meaning of allegorical figures and the recourse to laughter.[11] This play contains many of the themes already encountered in the previous two *sotties*. A notable addition is the comic presence of the Aveugle and his Varlet. This is a device dating back hundreds of years, meant to provide comic relief. Another addition is a doubling of doctors; in this play, the Medecin providing the ultimate cure is Christ himself (*Christus medicus*, made explicit at the end of the play), and there is the Docteur, who consults with the former, his superior. This allows the Docteur to express satirical sentiments inappropriate for the Medecin, in much the same way Rabelais has Panurge say and do things that Pantagruel, the Christian humanist prince, cannot.

The protagonist of the *Moralité de la maladie* is Chrestienté, though an "honneste dame" suffering from illness and harassed by Hypocrisie, dressed as a nun, and Péché. On the other side are Inspiration and Bon Œuvre, who attempt to lead Chrestienté in the right direction. The play is filled with Lutheran doctrine, insisting on the centrality of grace and the need to remove all forms of mediation for salvation. Both sides try earnestly to get Chrestienté to partake of their respective remedies, with Péché's efforts mirroring those of Satan and Eve in the Garden of Eden.

In the first half, the part of the play with the most movement and interaction among characters, Chrestienté is besieged on all sides. When Chrestienté says that only Jesus Christ can save her, Hypocrisie, who reveals herself to be an execrable character, responds, "Il nous fault bien des advocatz / Comme l'on voit chez les prelatz" (We really need lawyers / Just as one finds among the prelates of the Church) ([A8]r). When Chrestienté insists that salvation is a simple matter, Hypocrisie stresses the need for mediation, using the verb "gloser" (to gloss), a satirical barb easily understood by both humanists and reformists.[12] Chrestienté is seduced and changes course, and tells the Docteur she is going to Rome to receive absolution and give gold to the pope. When poor Aveugle asks for help, she tells him to go away because her money is reserved for saints, masses, and the "confrairie."[13]

In an interlude with the Aveugle and his Varlet, the former launches a satirical attack on the Catholic Church, which will be amplified by the Docteur in the last part of the play. As the Aveugle offers critiques, Varlet says he agrees but does not want any trouble. This back-and-forth continues until the Aveugle declares,

> Prebstres ont tout nostre vaillant
> En chandelles et en offrandes
> Por nourrir leurs putains friandes:
> Helas n'est il nul Jérémie
> Pour les prescher?
>
> (The priests have taken what we have
> In candles and offerings
> In order to feed their lecherous whores:
> Alas, is there no prophet Jeremiah
> To preach to them?)[14]

The Aveugle offers a now-familiar critique of Catholicism and laments the absence of a new Jeremiah to condemn the abuses of the Church. This biblical intertext prepares the way for the Docteur's more virulent satire.

Once diseased Chrestienté's urine has been taken for examination,[15] the Docteur delivers an extended tirade, regularly punctuated by the Medecin's refrain, "C'est par péché et la poison" (It is through sin and poison), in response to a series of "if" hypotheticals. First the Docteur asks,

> Si les moynes et religieux...
> Par charnelle corruption
> Sont lubriques et scandaleux
> Pervers et avaricieux
> Pleins de toute confusion.
>
> (If monks and clerics...

Through carnal corruption
Are lecherous and scandalous,
Perverse and miserly,
Full of all sorts of confusion.)¹⁶

Here the aggressive language continues.¹⁷ At the end of the diatribe, he claims that the law is complicit with the corruption and that there is no place to seek justice. He continues:

Si bigottes et papelars
En secret font leurs raliars
Puis après fornications
Vont quester doubles et liars.

(If these bigots and papists
In secret make their money
Then after fornications
Go looking for more coin.)¹⁸

As always, the emphasis is on the clergy's rapacious greed and gluttony, insults that are aggressively sardonic. Finally, the Docteur reaches a crescendo of invective condemning the Catholic clergy:

C'est donc le caterre immunde
Qui les a faictz simoniacles . . .
Qu'on doibt dire plus priapistes
Bacchanaliens et papistes
Veneriens gentz de Sodomes
Que l'on ne doibt saincts et preudhommes.

(It is thus the squalid disease
Which has made them practitioners of simony . . .
Such that it is more correct to call them priapists
Bacchanalians and papists
Venereal-disease-ridden sodomites
Than to call them saints or honest men.)¹⁹

Even the comic aspects of this diatribe (such as the pun in rhyming papist with priapist) are harshly sarcastic, as Malingre uses invective and comic tropes to provoke the sardonic laugh, a laugh reserved for those who share his religious views.

Louis de Berquin, one of the earliest French reformists defended by Marguerite de Navarre, is the likely author of *La Farce des theologastres*, a play with many of the same themes as the *Moralité de la maladie de chrestienté*. ("Theologastres" is a pun conflating "theologians" with "gastric," based on the cliché that prelates were gluttonous; Cotgrave defines "theologastre" as "a smatterer in Divinitie.") The play was performed in Paris sometime between 1526 and 1528.[20] Three times Marguerite intervened on Berquin's behalf, but despite her efforts, he was eventually burned at the stake in 1529, becoming an early martyr to the Protestant cause in France.[21] *La Farce des theologastres*[22] both draws upon the medieval anticlerical comic tradition and anticipates more partisan and mordantly satirical works such as the *Comedie du pape malade* (1561), as playful mockery is replaced by acerbic attacks paired with sententious moralizing. Dramatically, the play is fairly stilted, and the characters, although ostensibly engaging in dialogue, seem at times to be doing nothing more than taking turns offering various dogmatic observations. Given this format, and the presence of a number of allegorical figures, the play in certain respects fits more comfortably in the tradition of the *moralité*. The dialogue is laden with erudite references, which suggests that the play was intended for an educated audience. The play scornfully mocks the two irascible and witless companions, Fratrez and Theologastres, who represent the Sorbonne and, to a lesser degree, the Catholic Church.

The performance begins with the clerics Fratrez and Theologastres discussing the horrors of the new Protestant heresy. As they are decrying the current state of affairs, the character Faith enters, explaining that she is ill and seeking a cure. They attempt to control Faith and make her follow their regime, hoping to exploit and abuse her. In rapid succession, the play then presents two additional characters, Text and his daughter Reason (underscoring Luther's insistence on *sola scriptura*); Text is battered and bloody but hopeful that someday he will be treated with respect, after the violence done to him by the Sorbonne's "sotz argumentz" (v. 145). Text and Reason help guide Faith away from the trap of the clerics and lead her eventually to Mercury, a figure representing Berquin.[23] The humor of *La Farce des theologastres*, which is sardonic and heavily didactic, even pedantic at times, centers on the two bumbling characters representing the Catholic hierarchy and, more specifically, the authority of the Sorbonne. When the two clerics ask Faith to identify her malady, for example, she replies that it is "Sorbonnique," wordplay suggesting a sort of theological colic.

Fratrez and Theologastres assume the traditional role of tricksters in farce, attempting to deceive Faith and seeking to gain from her demise. Here the tricksters are tricked, however, and the audience is aware from the start that this reversal is inevitable. Again drawing upon a well-established comic convention, Theologastres illustrates his ignorance from the start, speaking in garbled kitchen Latin,[24] ranting about how everyone speaks Greek now ("Omnes nunc leguntur grecum" [v. 7]), and admitting that while he does not understand Greek, he suspects it must be heretical ("est suspectus de heresi" [v. 13]). The Latin is both bad and heavily inflected with French, producing a comic effect at the Sorbonne's expense.[25] Appreciating the puns and quips generally requires a knowledge of the scholastic method employed by these self-designated "apostres de Sorbonne" (v. 125). Their attempts at deception are blocked by a stream of Protestant dogma from the other characters and mockery of the excesses and abuses of Sorbonne theologians. As Text remarks, "Leur fait est plain de desraison / Par un tas de sotz argumentz" (Their opinions are utter folly / Supported with a pile of stupid arguments) (vv. 144–45).

Toward the end of the play Reason dismisses Fratrez and Theologastres's logic (and by extension the Sorbonne's disputes with Luther) as sheer gibberish. In the middle of Reason's diatribe, there is an intentional slip, as she confuses "lunatique" with "sorbonnique" (vv. 409–10), meant to evoke reformist laughter at the Sorbonne and its excesses. The carnal excesses that are punished in medieval comic plays are here replaced with theological excess, which is critiqued and silenced. The would-be tricksters are utterly inept and ineffectual, unable to play any tricks, and verbally cordoned off by a constant stream of pious pronouncements.

This verbal castration of the clerics is all the more remarkable because of the place women occupy in this play. Gender takes on a surprising role that counters previous representations of women in traditional comic texts. In such a highly misogynistic society, women were very commonly objects of derision; farces such as *Les Femmes qui se font passer maîtresses* and *Les Femmes qui apprennent à parler latin* roundly ridicule female pretensions to learning. Although the Protestant movement would end up being as patriarchal and misogynistic as the Catholic Church (if not more so, at least in Calvin's Geneva), in these early years Catholic polemicists such as Pierre Gringore and Jean Bouchet ridiculed reformists and "Lutherans" because of the elevated status they granted women. As Claude Longeon points out in his edition of *La Farce des theologastres*,[26] a key passage in the text takes on some of these misogynistic satires, with Fratrez clumsily complaining,

> Ha! Les femmes l'ont emporté [la Bible]
> Hors la Sorbonne et translaté
> Tellement que, sy n'eussïons
> Trouvé des gloses à foisons,
> Chascun fust aussy clerc que nous.
>
> (Ha! Women took the Bible
> Away from the Sorbonne and translated
> So much of it that if we hadn't
> Found plenty of glosses,
> Everyone would be clerics just like us.) (vv. 292–96)

Instead of women being mocked for their temerity, as one finds in the comic literature of the period,[27] in this play they carry more authority than the theologians, and at the end Mercury tells Theologastres that he has been "banny de madame Rayson" (banished by Lady Reason) (v. 564).

In the end, *La Farce des theologastres* undermines the role of the trickster, and this undermining provides the ultimate comic effect. The would-be tricksters are tricked, in a deviation from traditional farce. However, instead of using a ruse to trick the tricksters, which would produce the comic effect of a typical farce, the theologians' adversaries are utterly earnest in their arguments, which does serve to deflate to a certain degree the comic impact of the play. A traditional farce would be funny to anyone who appreciates that sort of physical and scatological comedy. Here, appreciation of the jokes requires adhesion to a particular belief system. If one compares this play to Rabelais's satires of the Sorbonne, such as the "propos torcheculatifs" episode (*Gargantua*, ch. 13) and the Janotus de Bragmardo episode (chs. 17–20), one finds both similarities and differences. Both authors poke fun at the Sorbonne for its perceived excesses and obfuscation. Both entertain the reader or spectator with caricatures. But Gargantua and his entourage, while having a good laugh at Janotus's expense, in the end are generous and forgiving, making the laughter generous as well. In *La Farce des theologastres*, on the other hand, laughter is limited to smirks derived from tendentious jokes, the type of sardonic laughter one finds with increasing frequency in the escalating polemics of religious controversy.

In 1533, a play was performed at one of the colleges of the University of Paris. The play is now lost, and we do not even know the title of it, if one ever existed. This play was a result of a larger controversy that year, involving Marguerite de Navarre and Gérard Roussel, Marguerite's personal preacher and a member of the Circle of Meaux. (This group of reform-minded Catholics, led by Guillaume Briçonnet, attempted many religious reforms until broken up in 1525.) While her brother François I was away in Picardy, Marguerite had Roussel preach a series of Lenten sermons at the Louvre, which attracted as many as five thousand people.[28] The sermons were heavily inflected with evangelical ideas; the Faculty of Theology of the Sorbonne were furious and pushed the Paris Parlement to put Roussel on trial. As the year wore on, tempers flared on both sides of the dispute, leading François I to banish the head of the Sorbonne, Noël Béda, in May. In this context of heightened tensions, in October of the same year, students at the Collège de Navarre at the University of Paris staged an aggressive farce that featured two characters that clearly represented the queen and Gérard Roussel. The character representing Marguerite is spinning yarn when she is overcome by some sort of fury (female hysteria), takes up the Bible and denies the faith, spurred on by the character Mégère, whose name unmistakably refers to M[aître] Gér[ard] Roussel.

Marguerite was frequently attacked and was almost always exceptionally restrained in her responses. This time, however, according to Patricia Cholakian and Rouben Cholakian, she reacted strongly and insisted to her brother that the perpetrators be arrested.[29] The Provost of Paris, accompanied by royal archers, went to the college to arrest the author of the play and the participants. They were met by a barrage of stones thrown by faculty and students. The king's representatives managed to arrest some of the actors, but the author was never discovered, nor was the text. According to limited reports,[30] the performance had evoked tremendous laughter among the crowd. The story of this play illustrates the ephemeral nature of the media I am examining—both pamphlets and performances were motivated by current events and created for the moment, and many of them disappeared into obscurity or were altogether lost. Here we are fortunate to have recorded accounts that provide enough information to understand the basic structure of the play and identify the targets of its biting satire.

All of the plays thus far discussed serve as a useful backdrop as we now turn our attention to three plays written by Marguerite de Navarre. Her plays, a previously little-known area of her literary and creative output, have been the subject of increased interest in the twenty-first century.[31] The celebrated author of the *Heptaméron* and numerous works of poetry also composed almost a dozen theatrical pieces, a corpus including both biblical and non-biblical plays. Among Marguerite de Navarre's non-biblical plays, the most centered on evangelical and reformist ideas are three she identified as "farces"—*Le Mallade*, *L'Inquisiteur*, and *Trop Prou Peu Moins*. All three contain varying levels of satire, primarily aimed at those unsympathetic to religious reform. The first two contain structural elements of the genre of farce, while the third fits more comfortably within the genre of the *sottie*. That said, generic classifications were extremely fluid during this time, and designating a play a "farce" simply meant that it contained comedic material.[32] In the 1530s, at the same time Rabelais was composing his tales of Gargantua and Pantagruel, Marguerite and others were reconfiguring established comedic forms for overtly polemical purposes, heightening the satiric element as a tool of reformist propaganda.[33] While Marguerite's use of this material is not an isolated phenomenon, there are many distinctive elements of her plays that merit particular attention.

Her plays have often puzzled critics; even their classification has evoked mild controversy. In his edition of the comedic plays, V.-L. Saulnier labeled them "théâtre profane," a categorization convincingly dismantled in Geneviève Hasenohr and Olivier Millet's later edition of Marguerite's plays. Hasenohr and Millet rightly point out that making a distinction between religious and non-religious or secular ("profane") plays produces an ill-suited taxonomy, as all the plays are laden with religious topics and concerns.[34] They propose instead a division between biblical and non-biblical plays, with the farces belonging to the latter category.[35] Whatever the purported subject, religious questions dominate all of Marguerite's dramas, including the farces.

The connection between Marguerite's plays and the late medieval tradition of farce and comic theater is not immediately obvious. Charles Mazouer has asserted, "Encore un théâtre qui se préoccupe seulement de la leçon religieuse et mystique! Décidément, avec ses préoccupations spirituelles, Marguerite de Navarre aura parcouru une voie singulière qui rend en réalité son théâtre inclassable et sans postérité." (Again her theater only focuses on religious and mystical lessons! Clearly, with her spiritual preoccupations, Marguerite de Navarre followed a singular path which makes her plays unclassifiable and without posterity.)[36] Mazouer makes two assertions that while in some ways are correct are ultimately overreaching. First, it is true that the plays in question are highly didactic, with a heavy moralizing tenor that hardly calls to mind the playfulness of comic theater. Second, Marguerite's pronounced evangelism and the examples of negative theology[37] in the plays set them apart from their more popular counterparts, such as farces, *sotties*, and morality plays. However, as Jelle Koopmans has demonstrated, the critical distinction between form ("old" medieval genres) and content ("new" reformist, polemical ideas) that leads to the assertion Mazouer makes is inadequate. When one considers that medieval genres such as farce were still very popular during the Renaissance, as well as the fact that allegory continued to have an important presence in the sixteenth century, one understands Koopmans's assertion that Marguerite's theater "fait le pont entre les moralités dites médiévales et le moralités polémiques qui . . . sont bien postérieures aux œuvres de la princesse" (bridges the gap between so-called medieval morality plays and the polemical morality plays which . . . come much later than the works of the princess).[38] By examining Marguerite's comic plays, I will show how they are connected to their medieval counterparts while also containing a level of didactic satire much more pronounced than in late medieval farce, an element that could be considered dangerous for the period in which they were produced, likely between 1534 and 1536.

In farces, every action and all dialogue have one goal: the humiliating reversal, often corporeal and obscene, that comes at the end of the play. In these typically brief plays, the character being tricked is guilty of some form of excess or exaggerated appetite. The volte-face central to the genre represents a restoration of the status quo, as someone who has stepped beyond certain prescribed social limits is put back in his or her place. Women are seldom the object of these punishments, which is attributable to an underlying misogynistic assumption that they are simply too skilled at deception to fall prey to such trickery and because, as Natalie Zemon Davis has rightly noted, the topos of "women on top" (women dominating men) is always comical because of its perceived absurdity.[39] This points to the essentially conservative ethos of pre-Reformation farce: despite certain subversive elements (for example, it is almost always someone in a higher social position who is punished by a social inferior), the dramatic movement of farce is toward a reestablishing of norms that have been transgressed.[40] This comic restorative gesture certainly contains a level of satire, as forms of conduct deemed unacceptable are condemned and the offenders humiliated. In Marguerite's recasting of farce, the latent satire is exploited, heightened, and made more subversive, and rather than reestablishing societal norms, it attacks and destabilizes established Catholic orthodoxies.

Of Marguerite's so-called farces, *Le Mallade* most closely resembles a traditional farce, with a cast of generic stock characters: "Le Mallade," "La

Femme," "Le Medecin," and "La Chambriere." It has also been suggested that the play draws inspiration from Berquin's *Farce des theologastres*.[41] To give a brief overview: a sick husband sends his wife to fetch the doctor, which she agrees to do, while insisting he would be better served by her folk remedies. In her absence, the female servant explains to the husband that, through faith in God's word, he can be healed. He accepts this and is restored to good health. The wife returns with the doctor, who is berating her mercilessly for her superstitious beliefs. The physician suggests a course of treatment and is extremely irked to discover his patient already cured. Like her husband, the wife realizes the source of the cure, but the doctor refuses to accept this and storms out, furious.

It is unsurprising that many critics have interpreted *Le Mallade* as an allegory, as the evangelical message is readily discernible. Building on the belief that sickness is an exterior manifestation of inward transgression, the husband, a sinner, is presented with three options to be healed: first, the doctor/priest/theologian, who poses as an authoritative intermediary; second, the wife's folk remedies/superstitious beliefs; or third, the solution offered by the maidservant, the evangelical belief that only faith in the Word of God can heal. Both husband and wife come to understand the efficacy of the third option, while the doctor/theologian remains ignorant and leaves in a state of unbelief, exasperated that his authority is being undermined.

Because of the prominent figurative nature of this farce, with allegory serving as a thin mask for an underlying critique of those opposed to evangelical thought, the doctor's humiliation represents a more subversive, dangerous form of satire. Marguerite replaces a familiar and fairly anodyne character—the blundering, incompetent physician more interested in getting paid than in healing—with an equally hapless doctor who most likely represents the doctors of divinity at the Sorbonne. Like a traditional farce, this play portrays the doctor as woefully ignorant and easily confused; though the husband is already cured, he hands him a prescription and a request for payment anyway:

> Voylà par escript vostre cas.
> Je m'en voys jusques à demain.
> Or sus, baillez moy les ducatz.
>
> (Here are my written directions,
> I shan't return till tomorrow,
> But give me my ducats now.)[42] (vv. 287–89)

The physician's repeated emphasis on the need to follow his "directions" (vv. 287, 409), "protocols" (v. 355), and "remedies" (v. 391) contributes to the satire, as a representative of the Sorbonne tries in vain to insist that others obey instructions portrayed as superfluous, if not detrimental.

The possibilities for satire in traditional farce are limited because the characters punished are chiefly anonymous and interchangeable; farce's mocking portrayal of type characters such as the bumbling doctor is a crude satire of a particular group, similar to today's ubiquitous lawyer jokes. In Marguerite's play, the choice of the doctor as a target reflects an explicit ideological concern, and thus the satire is much more pointed—he embodies the reactionary mentality of those opposed to reformist ideas and must be deflated and ridiculed in order to cure society's ailing spirituality. Base appetites and greed motivate the combatants in traditional farce; Marguerite's characters, especially the doctor and the maid, are motivated by competing systems of belief. This ideological antagonism, which leads to the physician being humiliated by the maid, gives rise to a degree of satire and polemical discourse that is much more pronounced.

There is another key alteration in *Le Mallade*, as well as in the next play we will examine, *L'Inquisiteur*. While the doctor is indeed humiliated, there is also the matter of the husband's evangelical conversion. Clearly the concept of conversion, from the Latin verbs *conversare*, "to turn around," and *convertere*, "to turn back, to reverse," fits nicely within the parameters of reversal that characterize farce. In *Le Mallade*, the husband's spiritual change eclipses the doctor's humiliating volte-face, and in his concluding soliloquy there is a clear demarcation, including a paragraph break, between mockery of the doctor's pretension and a final emphasis on evangelical conversion. Moving from satire to piety, the husband concludes,

> Mais je croy qu'il [le médecin] vouldroit encores
> Que l'on creust en luy comme en Dieu.
> Mais puisque, sans ung seul moyen,
> Dieu m'a mis hors de tout danger,
> A luy seul, où gist tout mon bien,
> Doresnavant me veulx renger
> Sans jamais ce propoz changer,
> En priant à tous chrestiens
> En Celluy, d'où ne veult bouger,
> Tenir telle foy que je tiens.

(Yet he [the doctor] would want us, I believe,
To believe in him as in God.
Out of danger I feel safe,
By God's work, with no mediator;
To Him alone, my only good,
To Him forever, I belong.
My determination will not fail,
And thus I pray that all Christians
May keep in Him, with whom I stay,
A faith, like mine, everlasting.) (vv. 429–38)

This drastic change in register recalls an observation in the *Heptaméron*, following the humiliating and amusing outcome of the lighthearted tale of the monks who erroneously believed they were going to be slaughtered (Nouvelle 34). After a sententious discussion by the participants, Simontault proclaims, "Mais regardons . . . de là où nous sommes venus: en partant d'une très grande folie, nous sommes tombés en la philosophie et la théologie" (But look where we have come from: starting from great foolishness, we have landed on philosophy and theology).[43] *Le Mallade*, like the *nouvelle*, ends on a high moralizing register, in contrast to traditional farce and comic plays, which are designed to end with laughter. Reform-minded idealism and spiritual transformation have here replaced carnal appetites and scatological punishments. Satire takes on a new form, much more insistent on proposing change and rejecting the status quo. The farces of Marguerite de Navarre reveal the vast range of the possibilities of satire and demonstrate the profound changes the genre was undergoing in early sixteenth-century France.

Marguerite's modification of farce in *Le Mallade* shows some radical reformulations of the genre. One of these is the juxtaposition of the doctor and the maidservant. Like other evangelicals, Marguerite drew inspiration from scriptures such as, "So the last will be first, and the first will be last" (Matt. 20:16) and "All who exalt themselves will be humbled, and all who humble themselves will be exalted" (Matt. 23:12), verses that exemplify reversed expectations in the same way satire does and that lend themselves well to performance possibilities. Farce in particular functions as a performative representation of such sentiments, as often a character of inferior social status tricks someone of a higher social position. In *Le Mallade*, the humble maid finishes in a position of dominance, while the erudite doctor is made to look like a bumbling fool who is roundly humiliated. What is in many respects the key moment of the play actually contains a rare stage direction.[44] Right after the patient informs the doctor that the servant is not making this up and really has cured him appears the stage direction, "La chambriere rit" (after v. 326). The doctor angrily responds, "Voyez vous ce visaige fainct, / Qui en derriere faict la moue?" (Look at her, acting innocent, / While she mocks me behind my back!) (vv. 327–28). The doctor is indeed the object of satire in this play because of his lack of understanding and his insistence on the infallibility of his own knowledge and authority. There is an important connection to the *risus sardonicus* here, as the play subtly presents the servant's actions as potentially duplicitous and mocking. The issue of laughter in Marguerite's plays is of foremost importance, as it often takes the form of what Daniel Ménager refers to as Marguerite's "rire mystique," laughter that denotes that "La joie est à son comble, mais le rire qui jaillit est finalement un rire qui se détache du monde et le méprise" (Joyfulness is at its height, but the laughter that is provoked is, in the end, a laugh that is detached from and contemptuous of the world). Here, however, the servant's laughter appears to be sarcastic and even satirical, mocking the doctor's lack of comprehension.[45]

The conflict between the physician and the servant is a metonymic representation of a larger struggle concerning language and hermeneutics, over what words (and more particularly, the Word) mean and who controls their interpretation. The exasperated doctor, furious that his authority is being ignored and even derided by a simple servant (and a woman at that), exclaims,

> Qui vous a apprins ces haultesses
> Et ce gentil jargonnement?
> Ce sont paroles d'enchanteurs,
> Parler ainsi par parabolles.
> Nous avons de saiges docteurs
> Qui ont frequenté les escolles.
> Ilz nous servent de prothocolles;
> Ceulx là nous debvons escoutter.

> (But who has taught you such lofty thoughts
> And this elegant gibberish?
> It is the art of sorcerers
> To confuse us with parables.

> We have wise and learned doctors
> Who have frequented colleges:
> They are our only proctors;
> To them alone we must listen.) (vv. 349–56)

The female servant's "gentil jargonnement" trumps the arrogant and elevated register of her learned male adversary. The maid's response to this assertion is instructive: "Mais, s'ilz disent folles parolles, / Font mal les femmes de doubter?" (But if what they [the "learned doctors"] say is nonsense, / Are women wrong to doubt their words?) (vv. 357–58).

It is hard not to see in this a subtle form of revenge for the violent farce mocking Marguerite performed at the Collège de Navarre in 1533, and for a lifetime of insults, big and small, almost all of which she had endured in silence. It is helpful to recall that the most notable mockery of Marguerite in the 1533 performance occurred precisely at the moment when the character representing her, apparently a victim of possession or sorcery, spoke as if hysterical or insane, provoking a *risus sardonicus* from the crowd. In *Le Mallade* the doctor echoes that scene, decrying the "paroles d'enchanteurs" that lead the servant to speak "gentil jargonnement."

In all of this, it is also impossible to ignore the issues of gender and performance. In the satirical performance at the Sorbonne in 1533, all participants and audience members would have been men, including the actor playing Marguerite. In *Le Mallade*, gender roles are reversed (and if Brantôme was correct, the performers were all women). Before the central debate between the servant girl and the doctor, when the wife gently suggests to him a possible remedy, the physician condescendingly and aggressively replies, "Vous me troublez l'entendement. / Taisez vous, folle que vous estes" (Still your tongue, you silly woman! / All your chatter muddles my mind) (vv. 195–96). And when the female servant audaciously suggests that the lofty discourse of the learned doctors may be nothing better than "folles parolles," the physician once again lashes out,

> Regardez comme elle respond!
> Va, va mener tes oysons paistre
> Et veoir si la geline pont:
> C'est le lieu où il te fault estre.
>
> (Listen to the way she answers!
> Go fatten your geese in the field,

46 · Hostile Humor in Renaissance France

And see whether the hens have laid:
That is the place where you belong.) (vv. 359–62)

The underlying message of the 1533 satirical farce was that women should not speak—when they do, they are portrayed as delusional, possessed, or deranged. This same sentiment is taken up again in this play, with the same misogynistic characterizations. This time, however, women gain the upper hand and roundly rebuke and reject male authority. It is easy to imagine this play as a sort of revenge fantasy for the queen, who created this farce within a couple of years after the attack. *Le Mallade* functions in part as a response to the Sorbonne's satire against her, provoking its own form of the *risus sardonicus*.

In her own quiet way, Marguerite de Navarre in this play is making the radical assertion that language and interpretation cannot be controlled by the theologians of the Sorbonne or anyone else, but rather true understanding is an intensely personal affair, unmediated and unobstructed by the "protocols" of scholastic theology. Traditional male authority as exemplified by the physician is undermined, satirized, and portrayed as inept and inconsequential; its claims of superiority based on the medieval tradition of *auctoritas* are simply ignored and supplanted by the counsels of a lowly, uneducated female servant. The play portrays the educated character's supercilious prescriptions as being as inefficacious as the wife's superstitious folk remedies, which the doctor so scorns. This debasement and humiliation of the haughty learned man moves beyond mere moralizing, producing a level of mordant satire that evokes the *risus sardonicus* at the expense of those who previously ridiculed the Queen of Navarre.

L'Inquisiteur is likely the second of Marguerite's farces.[46] As the main character, the Inquisitor has given rise to various theories as to which historical person he represents. In his edition of the plays, Saulnier suggested Noël Béda as a likely candidate, while Hasenohr and Millet suggest Mattieu Ory, who was in fact the royal inquisitor in France, appointed in 1536.[47] The important issue to bear in mind here is that the very fact that this character has been so consistently assumed to represent a historical figure highlights an important difference between Marguerite's play and traditional farce. As mentioned before, traditional farce is typically anonymous, with characters who are simply stock figures. While type characters such as the lascivious monk and the scheming merchant might suggest a general social malaise, traditional farce proposes no alternative vision, and the satire usually remains diffuse and unfocused. The negative portrayal of *L'Inquisiteur* contains an ideological dimension that extends the satire beyond the generic setting of farce and into the realm of theologically motivated polemics. Such satire is more subversive and potentially more dangerous, and in fact, when Marguerite published her *Marguerites de la Marguerite des princesses tres illustres royne de Nauarre* in 1547, she included several plays but notably omitted this play and *Le Mallade*.[48] However, despite the risky content, both of these plays keep destructive polemics to a minimum, and both remain primarily positive and optimistic, a quality that will become harder to find as religious conflict in France increases.

The Inquisitor is portrayed in such a way that the audience cannot help but draw connections between him and the reactionary theologians of the Sorbonne. In fact, in his opening monologue, he casts aspersions on "Ce savoir neuf, qui le nostre surmonte" (this new knowledge eclipsing ours) (v. 5), a clear reference to evangelical, humanist thought. He is also explicitly linked to the Sorbonne when he continues, "Grant temps y a que suis passé docteur / Dedans Paris par ceulx de la Sorbonne" (Learned theologians of the Sorbonne / Many years ago made me a doctor) (vv. 17–18). His confessions in the opening monologue include acknowledging that evangelicals know Holy Scripture better than he does (vv. 9–13); that his solution is to burn all potential heretics, even those who are in fact innocent (vv. 33–36); and that he is a hypocrite (v. 56).

As in *Le Mallade*, in *L'Inquisiteur* the adversaries of authority are of an inferior social position (the Inquisitor's servant and a group of children), a deliberate dynamic created both to generate sympathy for those persecuted by inquisitorial zeal and to heighten the sense of triumph when the Inquisitor's power is overthrown. The choice of children, in particular, carries with it a specific, evangelical connotation, recalling biblical passages such as Matthew 19:14, "but Jesus said, 'Let the little children come to me, . . . for it is to such as these that the kingdom of heaven belongs.'" Additionally, Marguerite links the children to the world of farce with a notable reference. When the Inquisitor asks his valet who these children are, the servant replies, "Ce sont enfans . . . sans soulcy" (They are children without worry) (v. 291). This is a play on words, as the children are in fact "sans soulcy" because of their evangelical conversion, yet it is also a clear reference to the Enfants sans souci confraternity, a group that, along with the Conards and the Basoche (discussed in chapter 5), produced *sotties* and farces, and to whom Clément Marot dedicated his first ballad, "Des enfans sans soucy."[49]

The Enfants sans souci were one of the biggest *sociétés joyeuses* in Paris. Their best-known performance was Pierre Gringore's *Jeu du prince des sotz et de mère sotte*, a satirical work that took aim at Pope Julius II.[50]

The hybrid nature of Marguerite's *L'Inquisiteur* is reinforced through the use of singing. As Marot says of the Enfants sans souci, "Saulter, dancer, *chanter* à l'advantage, / Faulx Envieulx, est ce chose qui blesse?" (jump, dance, sing exceedingly well, / To those who are envious hypocrites, does this do any harm?) (vv. 7–8, emphasis mine). The children here have just begun to sing when the Inquisitor asks about them. The disparate worlds of farce and evangelism are brought together through Marot, as what the children have just commenced singing is his translation of Psalm 3, a translation that would send him into exile again when it was published in 1539. (Copies of the manuscript of Marot's translations circulated well before their publication, and Marguerite likely had access to these.)[51]

When the Inquisitor's valet explains to his master why, despite the frigid weather, the children playing outside are not cold, the Inquisitor responds by hitting him. This act, common in traditional farce, takes on an entirely different significance in this play. In a typical farce, a master hitting his servant is a simple comic device. But because the Inquisitor is not a stock character but instead represents a particular ideological position and is a known public figure, his action, however innocuous or lighthearted it would be considered within the realm of traditional farce, is portrayed here in a purely negative way, an act of unwarranted violence further reinforcing his persona as a cruel persecutor.

The central conflict of *L'Inquisiteur*, as in *Le Mallade*, is based on language and meaning. Before talking to the children, the Inquisitor has already admitted that the evangelicals have a better understanding of sacred language and that as a result, he and his colleagues must resort to violence to block the dissemination of new knowledge. When he strikes his servant, he does so to silence him, exclaiming, "Te tairas tu?" (Will you shut up?) (v. 105). Already his servant has identified the Sorbonnist's limitation—he cannot move beyond strictly literal meanings and is locked in a mind-set that prevents him from reaching higher understanding. For example, when the servant tries to explain to his master that the children playing in the snow are not cold because they transcend physical conditions through the heat of spiritual conversion, this figurative explanation is lost on him. Exasperated, the Inquisitor derides the proposed paradox:

Voylà la raison d'un follet:

> Quant l'enfant joue par nature
> A la neige ou au chastellet,
> Dire qu'il n'a poinct de froidure.
>
> ('Tis the reasoning of a dolt
> When children play games in the snow,
> Build castles, or run to and fro,
> To conclude that it is not cold.) (vv. 93–96)

Unsurprisingly, this is his last contribution to their discussion before resorting to violence. His inability to comprehend the symbolic dimension of evangelical discourse recalls Lefèvre d'Étaples's concept of *duplex sensus literalis*, where two literal meanings exist, one governed by human reason and the other by divine inspiration.[52] The Inquisitor's understanding is limited to the former, and he is incapable of comprehending the latter. When he encounters divergent interpretations, he is reduced to reacting brutally.

After listening to the children, who use figurative language to express the source of their strength and convictions, the cleric is evidently perturbed and interjects,

> Il vauldroit myeulx qu'à noz leçons
> Feussent par leurs parens induictz,
> Qu'ainsi en jeux et en chansons
> Passer leur temps; ilz sont seduictz.
> —Enfans, enfans, vous perdez temps:
> Vous feriez mieulx d'estudier.
>
> (I would prefer that their parents
> Brought them to hear our lessons.
> Wasting their time in games and songs,
> Away from us they are misled!
> —Children, children, time is wanting!
> You would do better studying.) (vv. 159–64)

While he claims that the children are engaged in trivial pursuits, in fact he is attempting to rein them in with "noz leçons." The purpose of the proposed study is to curtail the children's enthusiasm, to bring them back to a more circumscribed comprehension similar to that promulgated by the Sorbonne. He asserts that the children have been "seduictz" by this new form of understanding, which threatens the status quo he has been charged to maintain.

The remainder of *L'Inquisiteur* consists of the children speaking metaphorically about their faith, with the prelate unable to comprehend their coded language. For example, when the Inquisitor demands to know who the father of one of the children is, one of the children replies, "Le vostre," a play on the double meaning of *father*, as all are children of the Heavenly Father; the prelate misses this linguistic play and replies, "Non est. Par sainct Pere, / Nous ne sommes en rien parens" (Not so! By God the Father, / You and I are not related) (vv. 213–14). The Inquisitor's mounting frustration is registered throughout: "Qui leur a apprins à respondre / Et dire chose si haultaine?" (Who taught these children to argue / And to speak with such arrogance?) (vv. 187–88); "Pardieu, ce ne sont poinct paroles / Qui puissent procedder d'enfans" (These dangerous and foolish words / Are not from the minds of children) (vv. 267–68), followed by the vain threat, "Comme dangereuses et folles / Plus en parler je vous deffendz" (They are, by God, much too brazen. / I forbid you to speak further!) (vv. 269–70). At almost the exact middle of the play, the servant is converted, telling his master, "Mais avecques eulx je riray" (And I will share in their laughter) (v. 330). The issue of laughter is important, both for its connection to satire and as a sign of conversion, representing what Daniel Ménager calls "le rire mystique."[53] It also relates to the Renaissance requirement that satire contain moralizing, subjective criticism, and a noble form.[54] The priest himself is finally converted, and the play ends with the whole group singing a hymn. They discuss preparations for a feast, with a small child saying, "Allons, allons, allons meignan" (Let's go eat) (v. 670). This ending is very similar to that of many farces, with one character announcing that all should eat and drink to celebrate. Yet despite this clear parallel, Marguerite's conclusion takes on an entirely different significance, as the meal proposed alludes to a Eucharistic celebration.

Rhetorically, *L'Inquisiteur* presents three distinct types of laughter. First, when the servant says he will laugh with the children, this is the innocent laughter of the converted, symbolic of an insouciant attitude and joyfulness. One can envision many moments in the play when the children onstage sing, dance, and also laugh, encouraging the audience to laugh with them. Second and on the opposite end of the spectrum is the Inquisitor's cruel laughter, a sign of his hypocrisy. In his opening monologue, he highlights both his cruelty and his deceptive tactics, saying dismissively, "Assez de gens se sont mal contantez / De ma rigueur, mais je n'en faiz que rire!" (Many a man is somehow displeased / With my rigor. I only scoff at them!)

(vv. 45–46). His scornful laughter underscores his counterfeit attitude; he cloaks his wrath in piety—"Car ma fueur en zelle je desguyse" (Because I cloak my wrath in piety) (v. 56)—and his laugh is another cruel disguise, an extreme version of the *risus sardonicus*. The third type of laughter is found once again with the children and, more importantly, in the Inquisitor's reaction to them. On the one hand, their laughter proclaims their innocence; on the other hand, the Inquisitor rightly detects in it a mocking tone. When he hears them singing a psalm, he exclaims, "Je les oy chanter. Qu'est cecy? / De moy se mocquent, ce me semble" (I hear them singing. What is this? / It seems that they are mocking me) (vv. 289–90). Despite the ostensible innocence of their laughter, the children are also gently chiding and mocking the Inquisitor. It is not difficult to imagine a reform-minded audience laughing as well, as the children move around him, dancing, singing, and making fun of his comments and questions, while also ignoring him. This sort of laughter is slightly tendentious and polemical but in a context that is positive and hopeful.

Such satire entailed serious risks, and of the three plays Marguerite deemed farces, it is unsurprising that *Trop Prou Peu et Moins*, the most esoteric, was the only one published in the queen's lifetime.[55] What little has been written about this unusual play has emphasized the impenetrable language the characters use.[56] However, one of the main themes of their exchanges is unquestionably laughter; there are dozens of uses of the word, and it is a word that is debated among the characters. There are clear indications that the play is intended to be comic; two pairs of characters—Trop and Prou, who start the play, followed by Peu and Moins—are wearing traditional comic costumes, with Trop and Prou sporting donkey ears and Peu and Moins wearing horns. The play is generically hybrid, combining elements of farce, *sottie*, and morality play. The humor is based in populist sentiment—the rich against the poor, with the former being bested by the latter. After examining plays like *Le Mallade* and *L'Inquisiteur*, it is impossible to ignore the polemical framing of *Trop Prou Peu et Moins*, despite the generic quality of the characters. Trop and Prou are associated with the Church or perhaps well-off ecclesiastics, while Peu and Moins represent the people, oppressed and downtrodden, yet still laughing and mocking Trop and Prou. To give a scriptural analogy, they are fools for Christ (1 Cor. 4:10), while their counterparts are simply fools. The play is probably the best illustration of Marguerite's "rire mystique," as defined by Ménager, and in it laughter proves superior to language.

Mocking and even sardonic laughter also features prominently in this play. When Trop and Prou first address laughter, they reveal their insecurities. Worrying about their donkey ears, Prou observes, "Car s'on voit nostre besterie, / Nous serons moquez de chacun" (Should these beastly features be seen, / We shall be mocked by one and all) (vv. 226–27). "Besterie" is a double entendre, referring as well to their stupidity. Right after this, Peu and Moins arrive laughing. Prou reacts: "Qui ha mis là ces deux marchans / Qui entre eux ne cessent de rire?" (But who brought here those two, strolling, / Who laugh together constantly?) (vv. 244–45). Unlike Trop and Prou, Peu and Moins are very pleased by their bestial features, horns, and talk about all their great qualities. They even make puns about being "cornuz" (v. 333 and elsewhere), a reference to cuckoldry, normally a symbol of humiliation. There is also the biblical reference to Moses wearing horns, a much more positive connotation.[57] As these associations multiply, laughter and playfulness govern the dialogue. As Peu remarks, "De rire ne me puys tenir" (I cannot control my laughter) (v. 338). So what exactly motivates their laughter, and what is its purpose? They say that they laugh for pleasure (vv. 404–6) and that even when they are persecuted, they laugh while thinking of their horns (vv. 415–16). When Trop asserts that he and his companion laugh as well, Peu's response is instructive: "Ouy, [vous riez] des dents, / Car du cœur rire ne sçauriez" (Yes [you laugh], with your teeth,[58] / But certainly not with your heart) (vv. 427–28). Based on Erasmus's and Joubert's observations about the *risus sardonicus*, the reference here should be obvious: while the weaker characters' laughter is innocent and generous ("de cœur"), Trop and Prou's laughter is tendentious and sardonic ("des dents"). Even when they laugh, the threat of violence is always there. The contrast here is between unrestrained laughter (Peu and Moins repeatedly describe laughing so hard they cry) and tense, counterfeit laughter (Trop and Prou remind each other of the importance of hiding or dissimulating their true nature).

The laughter of Peu and Moins is not, however, as innocent as initially portrayed. When Prou makes a distinction between the two pairs, explaining, "Nous ne sommes pas sans soucy" (We are not without worry)[59] (v. 530), the reference to the Enfants sans souci and Marot's praise of them is clear. When the laughter of Peu and Moins is directed at Trop and Prou, it is satirical and mocking. Expressing a feeling of unease that echoes Rabelais and anticipates Samuel Beckett, Trop remarks, "Je ne crains rien, fors les moqueurs" (I have no fear but of mockers) (v. 649).[60] It is even more risible that these figures fear laughter and mockery more than physical danger. Throughout the play, Peu and Moins's laughter shifts back and forth between innocent and satirical. Trop and Prou's annoyance and anger increase as they become ever more aware of the mocking undertones. As Prou complains in exasperation, "Voicy une grand' mocquerie / De nous arrester à ces foulz" (It would be a great mockery / To pay attention to these fools) (vv. 801–2). *Trop Prou Peu et Moins* exhibits the three different registers of laughter found in *L'Inquisiteur*—innocent, gently mocking, and sardonic—and again displays attempts to control or shut down laughter. Peu and Moins's laughter is profoundly unsettling to their counterparts, as if laughter could expose what those in power are trying to hide. The more the lowly duo laughs, the more their powerful adversaries express concern about having their true nature revealed. The only laughter Trop and Prou produce is the *risus sardonicus*—laughter that is bitter and aggressive.

The plays of Marguerite de Navarre discussed here are theatrical versions of *contrafactum*, the same method she used in some of her *chansons spirituelles*, whereby an evangelical message replaces the lyrics of a popular song, while maintaining the original rhyme and meter.[61] A contemporary spectator would recognize the conventions of comic theater in these plays, but the content has been radically altered. The plays exhibit both "le rire mystique" and satirical laughter. Despite their subtlety, the plays fit well within the rubric of satire, exposing as they do "the failings of individuals, institutions, or societies to ridicule or scorn."[62] The queen's satire can at times be harsh, yet ultimately it more closely resembles the "tolerant amusement" of Horace than the "bitter indignation" of Juvenal.[63] In her careful way, Marguerite de Navarre portrays the lowly people of the world, servants and children, laughing at the strong and powerful and exposing their hypocrisies, while also attempting to show them the path to true understanding. Her plays exemplify the moralizing aspects of satire, as well as the requirement of a noble form, even in the representation of "lowly" farce. The queen's aristocratic, evangelical farces are simultaneously connected to, and at a pronounced remove from, their late medieval predecessors. They provide an important insight into the evolving use of satire during this critical period, as mild chiding is replaced by a form of satire that, however gentle and careful in Marguerite's case, nevertheless questions accepted practices and offers a corrective to the status quo.

3

Artus Désiré, Renaissance France's Most Successful, Forgotten Catholic Polemicist

> Et luy [Calvin] donra tant d'escarmouches
> Par manière de mocquerie,
> Qu'à la fin aura fascherie.
> —Artus Désiré, *Grandes chroniques et annalles de passe par tout*

> Riez donc votre soûl, de ce ris sobre et saint.
> —Conrad Badius, *Comedie du pape malade*

Out of Normandy came a sort of Catholic protector, who understood better than any of his previous coreligionists how to wage this war of words fought by writing and disseminating *libelles*. In this chapter, the focus will be on this Catholic priest, for although we know very little about him, Artus Désiré contributed a great deal to the print war against heresy. As Denis Crouzet has noted in *Les Guerriers de Dieu*,

> Si l'on veut rechercher par quel biais la conscience collective a pu être immergée pleinement dans une situation prophétique, c'est sur le travail de propagande dont le prêtre Artus Désiré a été le maitre d'œuvre tout au long des années d'avant-crise qu'il faut s'arrêter. L'importance de ce travail a été complètement négligée, malgré deux récentes contributions anglo-saxonnes fort utiles. Artus Desiré fut sans doute le prophète par qui la pulsion de violence s'imposa aux "bons" catholiques. Sans la lecture des petits opuscules qu'il rédigea pour faire comprendre à tous la menace que représentait la nouvelle

religion, il est à mon avis impossible d'analyser les événements de la seconde moitié du XVIᵉ siècle.

(If one wishes to look for the means by which the collective consciousness was able to immerse itself completely in a prophetic situation, one need look no further than the propaganda efforts of the priest Artus Désiré, the master craftsman throughout the years before the outbreak of war. The importance of this work has been completely neglected, despite two recent, very useful Anglo-Saxon contributions. Artus Désiré was likely the prophet who pushed "good" Catholics towards violence. Without studying the brief works he wrote to make everyone understand the danger the new religion presented, it is in my opinion impossible to analyze the events of the second half of the sixteenth century.)[1]

The assertion that Artus Désiré has been neglected remains largely true today.[2] Yet his influence on his contemporaries was phenomenal. In the first chapter we saw Jérôme de Hangest's rather feeble response to the Affaire des placards. Artus Désiré was in many respects the first Catholic polemicist who understood how to reach a wider, more popular audience. The vast majority of his works are in verse and reasonably short, most coming in at under two hundred pages. Building on Frank S. Giese's bibliography of Désiré's works, Crouzet speculates that with 71 editions of his works produced between 1545 and 1562, this could represent a total of 60,000 to 70,000 copies in circulation, making Désiré a remarkably successful author.[3]

Our first record of Désiré dates from 1562, when he got himself in trouble. After the failure of the Colloquy of Poissy in the fall of 1561, he was part of an ultra-Catholic group that sent him as an emissary to Philip II of Spain, asking for the king's intervention on behalf of the Catholic cause in France, a clear act of sedition. Désiré's group was caught, and Désiré, who in his writings was constantly calling on the king to show no clemency to heretics in France, wrote obsequious pleas for mercy to both Charles IX and his mother, Catherine de' Medici. He was extremely fortunate, as his actions could have certainly merited death. Instead, Parlement had him make a public apology ("amende honorable") and he was sent into seclusion in a Carthusian monastery for five years.[4]

In his study on Désiré, Giese is far from generous. He describes him as follows: "Without talent, with a strictly orthodox education and no interest in classical antiquity, with a profound distrust of intellectual curiosity and no understanding whatever of the reformation, Artus Désiré lived his life untouched by any aspect of the Renaissance."[5] Giese continues,

> Désiré was one of the first to carry the fight for religious conformity and intolerance before the public, and in a language it could understand. His blind intolerance, his willful slander, and the violence of his proposals to curb the heretics, made him a fitting link between Noel Béda and the League. Further, the low quality of his arguments helps to explain the formation of that segment of public opinion which was finally roused to approve the extermination of the dissidents.[6]

I find this an overly judgmental and dated opinion. Giese does at least make the important point that, in terms of Catholic *libelle* production in France, Artus Désiré represents the bridge between Noël Béda and other Sorbonne theologians such as Jérôme de Hangest and the later Catholic League, whose vitriol would be exemplified by the incredibly effective (and also sadly neglected) polemicist Jean Boucher.[7] I cannot agree with Giese, however, that it is the "low quality of his arguments" that explains his success in combatting Protestant propaganda. There is no doubt that his work is less erudite and more populist in tone than that of many reformist polemicists, but there is also a good deal that is rhetorically similar, and it is precisely the kind of language used to reach a more mainstream audience that is the primary object of analysis for this study. Even Giese begrudgingly admits that Désiré was effective: "But despite his intellectual and artistic limitations, the fanaticism and violence of his pamphlets played some role in mobilizing opinion against the Protestants."[8]

Among Désiré's earliest writings, two works merit a combined examination: *Le Miroir des francs taupins*[9] and *Le Deffensoire de la Foy Chrestienne*. As Giese explains, the *Deffensoire* is "a reorganization and expansion of the *Miroir*, containing all the lines of the early text, and about as many more new ones."[10] Like the vast majority of Désiré's works, these are written in verse, primarily in decasyllabic meter. While the *Miroir* meanders and is somewhat difficult to follow, the *Deffensoire* is organized by chapters and much more logically structured. Of the two works' overarching themes, the one that stands out and that Désiré proposes as a solution to most of society's ills is the need to burn heretics. The different methods he uses include biting sarcasm that often gives rise to the *risus sardonicus*. In the *Miroir*, he does not waste time, asking his enemies, "Je vous demande, entre vous idiotz / Qu'on deust brusler à beaux fagotz de paille" (Among you idiots I say /

That one must burn heretics with nice bunches of straw).[11] Elsewhere he laments, "Helas mon dieu, que n'ay-je le fagot, / Et le flambeau, pour brusler ceste ordure" (Oh my God, why don't I have a bundle of sticks / And a flame, in order to burn this filth).[12] On the following page, the narrator gets even more excited at the prospect of burning heretics:

> Au feu, au feu, bruslez la malheureuse,
> Bruslez cela que jamais on n'en parle.
> Veu qu'elles sont attaintes du scandale,[13]
> Et qu'à l'erreur on les voit condescendre,
> Ne doit on pas de leurs corps faire cendre,
> Sans les pugnir par amende honnorable.

> (Light the fire, light the fire, burn this unfortunate one,
> Burn that one so that we never talk about it again.
> Given that they are overtaken by sin,
> And that into error we watch them fall,
> Should we not turn their bodies into ashes,
> Instead of punishing them with public apologies?)[14]

In the 1549 Rouen edition of the *Miroir*, "la malheureuse" is replaced by "la glorieuse." As we will see more extensively in the *Deffensoire*, women are a main target, and the change from "la malheureuse" to "la glorieuse" removes any sign of empathy for the female victim. Rather than unfortunate and miserable, she is now a haughty, prideful, and arrogant woman deserving her fiery fate. As he asks earlier,

> Je vous demande, amys, est ce pour rire,
> De veoir porter soubz les bras de ma dame
> De ce Luther la nouvelle alliance.

> (I ask you, my friends, if it's supposed to be funny,
> To see a lady carrying under her arm
> The new alliance with this Luther?)[15]

He will expand on this idea much more extensively in a later tract, but here the idea is that the participation of women is proof that this new religion is worthy of derision because it mocks the traditions of the faith. To suggest that Protestants are laughing and making a mockery of sacred customs is a rhetorical strategy to encourage a violent reaction from his Catholic audience.

In these passages from the *Miroir*, there are multiple intersections between laughter and violence. On the one hand, the execution of Protestants is not merely portrayed as palatable but encouraged enthusiastically, calling to mind the comparable enthusiasm of the Papimanes' leader Homenaz in Rabelais's *Quart livre*. There is a certain gleeful quality in Désiré's call to burn heretics, which he presents as good sport and a lot of fun. If violence is enjoyable, it can also be seen as funny, and humor and violence are inextricably intertwined in Désiré's vitriol. What is decidedly unfunny to this Norman priest ("est ce pour rire?") is that women are embracing and even flaunting heresy, carrying Luther under their arms in a semi-erotic embrace.

In the *Deffensoire*, ideas found in the *Miroir* are better organized and substantially expanded.[16] There is an interesting connection between the two titles. Obviously "deffensoire" is not a typical word choice and serves to embed in this defense the notion of the mirror, creating a sort of vernacular catechism that recalls the medieval mirror genre.[17] One of the most notable ways Désiré expands on material from the previous work pertains to women. In the dedicatory preface of the *Deffensoire*, he discusses the art of warfare and explains how, when attacking a defensive position, the best strategy is to strike the weakest fortification. Hence Protestants focus on women. He reminds his readers that the Bible makes clear how weak women are and how easily they are seduced. In the same vein, he plays up the purportedly lascivious nature of Protestants—people accept this erroneous sect because priests, monks, and nuns can be married "pour complaire à leur desir charnel et lubrique" (to satisfy their carnal and lecherous desire).[18] Thus the tone is set: the new heresy is successful because it targets weak people, primarily women, who cannot control their lustful urges.

What follows in the *Deffensoire* are nineteen relatively short chapters, each dedicated to a different Catholic practice or doctrine (interestingly, the chapter on indulgences is the shortest one), each time explaining how Protestants misrepresent the truth and corrupt the gullible; the final chapter is summative and titled simply "Autheur."[19] Désiré's audience is clearly Catholic, although he not infrequently addresses Protestants directly as "vous." And as we will see later, Désiré's *libelles* clearly made it to Geneva and provoked a strong reaction.

Because the main goal is to reinforce Catholic beliefs, much that Désiré writes is of little interest for this study. However, he inserts a liberal number of satirical insults and epithets and displays a fair amount of creativity in name-calling. He explains that Calvinists are a "gens perversans, libertins vitieux" (perverted and perverting people, lewd Epicureans)[20] and "ruraulx asniers" (country-bumpkin donkey drivers),[21] says a Protestant is "un lubrique / Un apostat . . . Un paillard heretique" (a letch, an apostate, a lustful heretic),[22] and expresses incredulity that people will believe "un asnier / Un apostat, un gros bedier" (a donkey driver, an apostate, a stupid dolt) over the Sorbonne and the Crown.[23] These heretics are "Frippiers d'enfer, de Lucifer satrappes, / Pipeurs, trompeurs de paovres creatures" (Satan's rag peddlers, Lucifer's lieutenants, deceivers, tricksters of these poor creatures).[24] Désiré's solution is as predictable as it is outrageously simple: "Que reste il plus? Faire feu de voz oz, / Et vous brusler comme gens idiotz" (What is there left to do? Make fire from your bones and burn you like idiots).[25]

For a brief moment in the *Deffensoire*, in a chapter titled "Des pasteurs et prelatz de l'Eglise," Désiré addresses the issue of pastoral corruption in the Church. It is notable that in the 1552 edition, this section is greatly reduced. This chapter also stands out because it is primarily written in pentasyllabic verse and reads much like a farce, with characters such as a "chambriere," a "commere," and so forth. It is the bawdiest part of the tract, with jokes about gluttony and adultery. He attacks lascivious monks, saying:

> Et sont gros et gras,
> Tenans leurs corps beaulx
> Chantans toujours cras,
> Comme les corbeaulx.
>
> (They are plump and fat
> Thinking that they have beautiful bodies
> Always cawing
> Like crows.)[26]

This curious chapter is marked by a mixture of levity and moral outrage. Désiré draws upon the popular, festive world of farce and carnival, lightly mocking and joking about priestly excesses, yet often veers into more sententious discourse. Altogether "Des pasteurs et prelatz de l'Eglise" is a somewhat confusing chapter, and one where the humor is much lighter and the invective kept to a minimum.

The most intriguing chapter in the *Deffensoire* is the penultimate one, titled "Des femmes theologiennes." Echoing a sentiment expressed by so many of his contemporaries, Désiré's misogynist attacks must have found a wide and approving audience. Désiré is thoroughly disgusted by the ways Protestants appropriate sacred practices that rightfully belong to the Catholic Church. That women participate is beyond the pale and elicits the strongest vitriol in his writings, other than his ubiquitous calls to burn heretics. In his attack in this chapter on Protestants in general and women in particular, he uses a common device of the *grands rhétoriqueurs*, and plays off of the stem "dur(e)," meaning "hard" or "lasting":

> Considerant la grand'ordure dure,
> Qui regne et dure, et que chascun endure
> Par grand' laidure, au sexe feminin,
> Je m'esbahy de l'immortel venin,
> Et du poison que cedit genre engendre,
> En mon esprit je ne puis bien comprendre,
> Ne bien sentir en mon entendement,
> Comme on permet si miserablement,
> Et follement, aux femmes de la France,
> Laisser porter les livres d'importance,
> Où gist et pend tout salut sainct et munde:
> Jamais n'advint un plus grand mal au monde,
> Depuis le temps que la permission
> L'on accorda de la translation.
>
> (Considering the pile of great filth
> That reigns and lasts and shall endure,
> For all its ugliness, in the female sex,
> I marvel at the lasting venom,
> And poison that this gender engenders,
> And in my mind I cannot fathom
> Nor can I come to understand
> How it is permitted so miserably,
> And so outrageously, to the women of France,
> To be allowed to carry important books,
> On which hangs both spiritual and material salvation:
> Never has such a calamity occurred in this world
> Since the time when permission
> Was given to translate [Holy Scripture].)[27]

According to Désiré, great filth has infiltrated the kingdom, and those most responsible for this contamination are women. Rather than maintaining their proper position of submissiveness and ignorance, they have the temerity to engage with and contribute to this defilement. Women are the gender responsible for producing offspring ("cedit genre engendre"), but instead of staying home and having babies, they enter the public space and spread poison. Their venom is language, specifically French, words that contaminate others. How is this possible? Because sacred texts, previously accessible only in Latin and the exclusive purview of the clergy, have been translated into the vernacular. Language and gender come together in this diatribe, as the availability of Holy Scripture in the vernacular has created the worst situation imaginable ("plus grand mal au monde"), namely that women are walking around carrying books and asserting a newfound authority derived from them. The Word of God is the domain of men; the outrage of Protestantism is that it allows and even encourages women to study Scripture.

Given Désiré's disgust over the use of the vernacular, precisely because it is accessible to women who now consider themselves equal to the theologians of the Sorbonne, it is remarkable that he is one of the first Catholic polemicists to produce works entirely in French. Much more than the Sorbonne theologians who preceded him, he tacitly acknowledges that the genie is out of the bottle and that to combat this poisonous heresy, one must use the same weapon, namely French. This is no trivial consideration, as much of the *Deffensoire* focuses on explanations of Catholic doctrine; previously, such expositions existed primarily in Latin. While expressing disgust at the translation of sacred Scripture into French, he nonetheless engages in the same praxis to reach a more general audience; one presumes that his target audience would include women, but only those with a very traditionalist understanding of their role in society.

Following the vitriolic passage quoted above, he attacks Erasmus, saying,

Et nonobstant qu'Erasme ayt voulu dire,
Que c'est bien fait aux simples gens de lire,
Il a menty, cela est contemné,
Par la Sobonne.

(Regardless of what Erasmus wanted to say,
That it is a good thing to have simple folk read,
He lied, and this has been condemned
By the Sorbonne.)[28]

For Désiré, it is precisely through these booklets or pamphlets ("livretz"), perhaps French translations of Luther's and Calvin's tracts, as well as vernacular translations of the Holy Writ, such as Marot's psalms, that the heretical poison is spread. In an extended passage of the *Deffensoire*, he mixes violent vitriol with laughter, this time the supposed laughter of haughty ladies, recalling in certain respects the *haute dame de Paris* in Rabelais's *Pantagruel*:[29]

> Qu'au lieu d'avoir des heures et matines,
> Dessus leur ventre abominable et vile,
> Portent, la saincte et sacrée evangile,
> En livres d'or penduz sur leur nature.
> Et s'il advient que par cas d'advanture,
> Leur demandez, mes dames, quel livre est ce
> Que vous portez ainsi pendu en lesse?
> Lors respondront les doulces hipocrites,
> Monsieur, ce sont les quatre evangelistes,
> Du testament composez par Marot,
> Ennemenda il n'y a pas un mot
> De superflu, tant est bien translaté?
> N'est il pas beau? C'est toute verité,
> Jamais au monde un meilleur on ne veit,
> Nous avons bien les pseaumes de David,
> Nouvellement traduictz en Françoys,
> Mais ces caphars de l'ordre sainct Francois[30]
> En contre nous sont si tresfort marriz,
> Que de despit vont dire à noz mariz,
> Que les livretz sont deffenduz en cour.
> Voyla le temps et le regne qui court:
> Voyla comment mainte Femme s'estime
> Estre sçavante en cest infame crime,
> Autant ou plus qu'un docteur de Sorbonne,
> Qui maintiendra ceste erreur estre bonne
> Jusques au feu quoy qu'on en vueille dire.[31]
> *Je vous demande amys est ce pour rire?*

(Instead of having books of hours,
Above their abominable and vile wombs,
They carry the holy and sacred gospel,
In gilded books hanging around their neck.

Artus Désiré · 63

And if it happens that perchance
You ask them, my ladies, what book is this
That you carry in this way, hanging on a leash?
Then these gentle hypocrites will respond,
"Sir, these are the four evangelists,
From the New Testament composed by Marot,
Edited so that there is not a superfluous word,
It is so well translated.
Isn't it beautiful? It is all truth,
Never in the world has one seen one better,
We have the psalms of David,
Newly translated in French,
But these hypocrites from the order of Saint Francis
Oppose us and are so distressed,
That out of spite they will tell our husbands,
That the books are forbidden in court."
Here is how the current state of affairs are:
Here is how so many women consider themselves
To be knowledgeable in this vile crime,
As much as or more than a doctor of the Sorbonne
These women who will maintain that this error is good
Until the fire of the stake, whatever one wishes to say.
I ask you friends, is this a joke? Are we supposed to take this seriously?)[32]

This extended passage brings together sexuality and textuality, as the author insists on the proximity of forbidden books and the female body. More specifically, he focuses on the reproductive parts of the female body, establishing a connection between the dissemination of heretical ideas and the means of this dissemination, females who nurture and protect these heresies near their womb. Désiré is outraged not simply by women reading books, although that is an important theme of his diatribe, but also by the perversion of the traditional female reproductive role. For religious misogynists like Désiré, not to mention most of the population at this time, married women have one primary role: the production of children. The danger of this new heresy is that it has insinuated itself through seductive texts onto the female body. The female body, instead of being used to produce babies, is being used to promulgate heterodoxy. Female arrogance and naïveté make this possible; women take pleasure in being violated by these heretical texts. His most sardonic expression is reserved for women who place themselves at the same level as Sorbonne theologians and present themselves as "femmes theologiennes." Désiré suggests that the women, rather than being horrified by this unnatural state of affairs, are laughing, openly mocking the conventions of traditional hierarchy. It is precisely this image of mocking women that is intended to generate the most violent reaction from Désiré's audience, coming as it does right after yet another reference to burning at the stake. This female insolence ridicules sacrosanct traditions and must be aggressively countered. The sacred is being mocked by the weaker sex, and women are now considering themselves as equals to men. As Natalie Zemon Davis pointed out some time ago, references to women on top are always meant to be comical.[33] Here, however, the comic effect is inextricably linked with the violence of the discourse, turning the *Deffensoire*'s humor into the sardonic laugh, where laughter serves as a pretext for aggression.

In the preface to Louise Labé's poetry, published around the same time, she implores women "eslever un peu leurs esprits par-dessus leurs quenoilles et fuseaus" (to raise their minds a bit above their distaffs and spindles).[34] A contrary admonition appears in the final passage in the *Deffensoire* and fully reveals Désiré's view of women:

> Bien mieulx vauldroit une quenouille prendre,
> Que de toucher aux livres consacrez:
> Car d'exposer les divins motz sacrez,
> La matiere est un petit par trop haulte,
> Et quelque jour cognoistrez la grand faulte
> De vostre orgueil et folle ambition.
>
> (It would be much better to take up the distaff,
> Than to touch consecrated books:
> For to expose oneself to the sacred and divine words,
> The material is much too elevated,
> And one day you will recognize the great error
> Of your pride and vain ambition.)[35]

In this misogynistic advice column, Désiré once again returns to the troubled relation between the female body and sacred texts: women should neither touch nor expose themselves to these because they are simply not equipped to deal with such lofty matters, and the only possible result is contamination and profanation of the sacred. And if there remains any doubt about Désiré's views on women, especially those who have the audacity to read and study Scripture, he concludes his chapter on female theologians with a warning to avoid "l'erreur feminine," since "une femme est pire cen[t] fois qu'un homme" (a woman is a hundred times worse than a man).[36] How would Désiré's audience have reacted to these attacks on women? Given the near universality of misogynistic views, few would have been troubled by this diatribe. For Désiré, as well as most Catholics, Protestant women were perverting the natural order of society, upending established hierarchies, and, most importantly, abandoning their traditional role of physical procreation, proliferating instead heterodox poison. Much of Désiré's language expresses horror and outrage, but there is also sarcasm and satire, nowhere more so than when he suggests that these haughty ladies are mocking sacred Catholic traditions.

In the next of Désiré's *libelles* to consider, *Les Combatz du fidelle Papiste pelerin Romain, contre l'apostat Antipapiste, tirant à la synagogue de Geneve, maison babilonicque des Lutheriens* (1550), first published in Rouen, he turns to the dialogue format that will become his signature style. The first edition contains some interesting woodcuts, primarily biblical, several of which are found in other works by Désiré printed by one or both of the du Gort brothers. A version of this tract published three years later is titled *Les Batailles et victoires du Chevalier Celeste contre le Chevalier Terrestre*[37] and is bound with a second work, *Description de la Cité de Dieu*, which was first published separately in 1550 and contains some full-page woodcuts illustrating the battle between God's faithful and Protestant heretics.

In this satirical dialogue, Désiré wastes no time returning to one of his favorite targets, women. In the prologue of the 1553 edition, a Faithful Papist laments the current state of affairs:

> Je voy en ce temps où nous sommes
> Porter aux femmes roturieres,
> Des robbes à usage d'hommes,
> Pour contrefaire les gorrieres:
> Et avec cela sont si fieres
> Qu'on les prendroit par le manteau,
> A voir leurs gestes et manieres
> Pour folles filles de bordeau.
>
> (I see in the times we are living
> Female commoners wearing

Clothes made for men,
In order to mimic gallant women:
And with this they are so proud
That one would take them, by their attire,
Seeing their gestures and manners
For crazy brothel girls.)[38]

Once again, what seems to bother our author most, and what he mocks so incessantly, is how women are acting above their station. Here one finds the carnivalesque and even gender bending of a sort, with women dressing in robes made for men ("à usage d'hommes"). The term "robbes" suggests clothing worn by men of authority, such as theologians. But Désiré compares these women to common prostitutes, taking on airs to mask their lowly and repugnant state. The primary thrust of Désiré's outrage and mockery is how the influence of Luther and Calvin in France has caused women to abandon their traditional role and adopt a more authoritative posture.

Les Combatz du fidelle Papiste is framed as a dialogue between a Papist and an Antipapist. As it begins, the former accepts with pride the "papist" insult so often used by Protestants, and with a pun defines his adversary:

Et toy qui es tu? Priapiste,
Qui laisses par ta paillardise
La saincte et catholique eglise
Pour suyvre la loy d'antechrist.

(And who are you? A Priapist,
Who, because of your lasciviousness, leaves
The holy and Catholic Church
In order to follow the law of the antichrist.)[39]

This new epithet, one Désiré will use multiple times, contrasts the faithful, righteous papist with the salacious, priapic antipapist. As we will see at the end of this chapter, Conrad Badius will also connect "papist" with "Priapist" in his play, *Comedie du pape malade*, but with the opposite effect. Each side of this polemical fight continually draws upon images of their opponents' presumed sexual excesses.

The Papist continues his tirade, condemning the unrighteous satire of his adversary: "Et te moque point des fidelles" (And do not mock the faithful).[40] Suspicions about satire and humor targeting sacred Catholic traditions are central here and elsewhere. Désiré's satire is acceptable because his target is evil; similar attacks by Protestants merit condemnation because the object of their satire is holy. The Antipapist asserts that his belief system is superior because it only emphasizes laughter ("Car elle parle que de rire"), but for his adversary this laughter is insolent and mocks sacred practices such as Lent ("manger en tout temps chair grasse").[41] In his rebuttal, the Papist relates the horrors he discovered upon visiting Geneva. He goes to great lengths to compare Calvinists to Jews, worshipping in "synagogues" stripped of all holy images and objects. The Antipapist boasts of the fun Calvinists have, free of the need to follow Catholic practices such as Lent, vespers, and so forth. Most of all, he emphasizes that they are able to laugh all the time. But Désiré portrays their mirth as wicked and mocking, a condemnable form of laughter that is irreverent and profanes the sacred. Here Désiré, like so many other religious polemicists, tries to circumscribe and control the acceptable role of humor and laughter, insisting that Protestant laughter is defilement.

The Papist also links laughter to violence, violence occasioned by his adversaries' profane mockery. In a particularly suggestive passage, the Papist exclaims,

> Mon Dieu que tu sens tes fagotz
> Et les bourréez de Paris.
> Tu prens l'evangile par ris...
>
> (My God, how you smell of burning wood
> And the kindling for the stake in Paris.
> You laughingly interpret the gospel...)[42]

This play on words recalls Gargantua's explanation of the name of Paris ("par ris"), a mildly satirical yet pleasant joke that here becomes hostile and aggressive and evokes only the *risus sardonicus*.[43] Because Protestants take a laughing attitude toward the gospel ("par ris"), the butchers and pyres of Paris await them. Laughter here is serious business indeed.

In an extended tirade, the Papist decries lowly people assuming roles reserved for the clergy, among them schoolboys who mock the sacraments ("escoliers / ... Se mocquer des saincts Sacremens"),[44] as well as country bumpkins, petty merchants, and, most offensively, iniquitous women, who want to establish a new system of belief ("gens rustiques, / Bourgeoys, Marchands, femmes iniques, / ... veullent faire loy nouvelle").[45]

In a curious juxtaposition of text and image, an engraving of a woman sitting in the countryside reading a book appears at the point where the Papist exclaims,[46]

> O la grande putrefaction
> De voir des theologiennes,
> Fauces dyaboligiennes.
>
> (O this great putrefaction
> To see female theologians,
> False diabologians.)[47]

All of these priapic pedagogues who engender Lutheran children ("Pedagogues Priapistes / Qui font les enfans Lutheristes")[48] will meet the same fate, or so hopes our Papist several times throughout the tract, once again juxtaposing levity and mockery with extreme viciousness.

> Au feu, au feu, aux heretiques,
> Que chacun porte ses bourrées,
> Afin qu'en leurs cottes fourrées
> Soient mises en poudre et en cendre.[49]
>
> (Burn, burn these heretics,
> Let everyone bring his kindling,
> So that their furred tunics
> Be turned into powder and ashes.)[50]

At the end of *Les Combatz du fidelle Papiste*, the Papist calls for France's biggest bonfire, a fire so big that from a thousand leagues away people would be able to smell the filthy smoke ("Si grand feu par villes et champs / Que de mille lieux à la ronde / On sente la fumée immunde").[51] In a polemical tract filled with sardonic invective and accusations that Protestants pervert the natural order and engender heresy, and which repeatedly asserts that they mock the sacred, Désiré's rhetorical strategy is always to lead his readers to the same conclusion: this contagion must be eradicated and collectively burned, this foreign contamination removed from the kingdom. As is almost always the case with Désiré, the author's sarcastic quips are only a prelude to incitements to collective violence.

In order to discuss Désiré's next tract, some background is helpful. In Giese's study on Désiré, he describes the events that led to its publication:

In 1553 the French reading public was treated to a sparkling and cleverly executed satire, the *Epistola Magistri Benedicti Passavanti*, composed by Théodore de Bèze, but published anonymously. Although the Catholic-Protestant theological controversy had been raging for a number of years, this pamphlet introduced a new feature into the battle: it contrasted the serenely simple virtue of Calvinists with the sodden vehemence and violence of the church leaders in Paris. According to the text, Pierre Lizet, premier président du Parlement de Paris, had sent his valet Passavant to Geneva to spy and report on the way of life he found there. Through his inept testimony and macaronic Latin, the Protestant leaders were exonerated from immorality and fanaticism, which sins were attributed instead to Lizet and his fellow Persecutors. It was presumably the publication of this work which set off, between France and Geneva, a series of sharp exchanges, which continued until the outbreak of actual warfare turned all minds to other matters. These pamphlets no longer dealt exclusively with theological questions, but, like the prototype by de Bèze, contained a large element of slander on both sides.[52]

Three years later, Désiré produced *Passevent parisien respondant à pasquin Romain*, the first Catholic reaction to Bèze's satirical tract.[53] Désiré's preface to this counterattack paints a picture of Geneva that, while patently absurd, must have made quite an impression on his French Catholic readers, for whom an ostensible eyewitness account of this strange place would have been powerful. Passavant's fierce invective against the Geneva-based faith begins here, as he describes Geneva and its leaders to his friend Pasquin (an obvious reference to Bèze's pasquinade):

> Et je t'asseure que pas un seul de leurs venerables prescheurs, et paillards de leur eglise ne voudroient seulement toucher du doigt le feu pour maintenir leur doctrine et loy: ains en leurs banquetz, et apres que ilz sont saoulz, Calvin, Farel, et Viret, les premiers de leur eglise, s'en mocquent: et disent de ceux qui se font brusler, qu'ilz font comme les moutons, qui se jettent d'eux mesmes dedans la riviere, suyvant leurs compagnons,[54] qui sont allez les premiers, et au devant. Si tu veux prester audience (comme est ton ordinaire) je te diray le tout de ce que j'ay veu et ouy de ces venerables, par l'espace de dixhuict moys, jamais ne faillant à une de leurs assemblees, pour mieux pouvoir congnoistre leur impudence et asseuree arrogance contre Dieu et son Eglise.

(And I assure you that not one of their venerable preachers and lechers of their church wants to even touch the fire with his finger in order to maintain their doctrine and law: but during their banquets, after they are drunk, Calvin, Farel, and Viret, the leaders of their church, mock such behavior: they say that those who are burned at the stake do so like sheep who throw themselves into the river, following their companions who went first and led the way. If you want to hear about it (as is your custom), I will tell you everything I saw and heard from these venerable people, over the course of 18 months, never missing one of their assemblies, in order to be able to better understand their impudence and bold arrogance against God and His Church.)[55]

If there is a difference in how Catholics and Protestants attacked each other, it has been observed that Catholics attacked people and Protestants assailed sacred objects.[56] As we will see in the next chapter, Protestant mockery of the Eucharist in works such as the *Satyres chrestiennes* obviously horrified Catholics.[57] Meanwhile, French Catholic persecution of Calvinists, including a growing number of executions in France, contributed a new group of martyrs for the Protestant faith, eventually immortalized in Jean Crespin's *Livre des martyrs* (1554). In Désiré's salacious look into life in Geneva, along with the well-established tropes of Calvinists as lecherous and debauched (when not pale and emaciated), what is most striking is the sardonic portrayal of the church leaders' ostensibly cynical attitude toward Calvinist martyrs, a group that would be considered wholly sacred by Calvinists.

We have already seen extensive examples of Désiré's penchant for encouraging the burning of heretics in France, but now he provides us with another fictitious scene to bolster his argument. In a rhetorical move that completely desacralizes the sanctified discourse of martyrdom, Désiré paints a picture of drunken church leaders, who would not lift a finger, let alone allow it to get burned, to support their own cause, ridiculing those who have sacrificed their lives for the faith and calling them sheep. The Protestant faithful who give their lives for the cause are portrayed as imbeciles and, more shockingly, their leaders are shown to be callous and uncaring about the fiery fate of their followers. This level of sardonicism does not have a precedent in Désiré's writings. We have already encountered Désiré's jubilant wishes for the death of heretics in France. Now, in an act of rhetorical ventriloquism, he portrays the Calvinist leadership as unconcerned about the lives of their coreligionists being executed in France. Was this his attempt to reach wavering French Calvinists?

Continuing in a gossipy tone, our polemicist projects sacrilegious levity and mockery onto his adversaries. In a rather loaded question, Pasquin asks, "Et dy moy donc touchant à leurs ceremonies exterieures, pour mieux voir et congnoistre leurs badignages et mocqueries de dieu, et des sainctz sacremens de son Eglise" (So tell me about their liturgy, in order to better see and understand the ways they jest and mock God and the holy sacraments of His Church).[58] Passavant tells him that the Calvinists sit in church and mock the pope and the king and that noblemen sit there without reacting. The reformists insist that good works do not matter and take money from the poor that they use for themselves. All of this condemns Calvinists precisely because they laugh at and make a mockery of what a good Catholic holds most sacred.

Recognizing the effectiveness of the polemics of Pierre Viret, whose writings we will explore extensively in the next chapter, Désiré takes aim: this teacher from Lausanne may be a grammarian, but he is no theologian.[59] He mocks Viret's role as a satirist, explaining that when Geneva needs help, no one is better suited for this sort of work: "Et d'avantage par l'occupation qu'il prend, quand il faut faire quelque menée et trahison contre quelque bon et simple personnage, car l'avarice, trahison, et flaterie, luy sont plus propres, que de prescher: il semble mieux un badin en chaire, qu'un prescheur, sans contenance, et moins de doctrine" (And more so through the occupation he has, when it is necessary to produce some sort of plot or betrayal against some good and simple person, because avarice, betrayal, and flattery suit him better than preaching: he seems more like a pulpit clown than a preacher, with no composure, and even less doctrine).[60] The key epithet here, and one that he repeats five pages later, is "badin en chaire."[61] This requires a bit of parsing to appreciate better the sardonic humor in this mock title. The *badin* is a key figure in contemporary farces and comic plays, one immediately recognizable to Désiré's audience as the fool (or at times the *faux-naïf* who is actually the trickster).[62] Désiré is unmasking the learned Viret, mocking his satirical discourse and suggesting that he is no more than a clown or a trickster, performing antics in the pulpit and lacking the gravitas of the Catholic clergy.

Besides an extended attack on Viret and other Genevan leaders (he refers to Théodore de Bèze as an adulterer who has married a prostitute), the main focus of *Passevent parisien respondant à pasquin Romain* is a city filled with licentious, ungodly behavior. Genevans are referred to as "Epicuriens et Atheistes."[63] Moreover, in addition to avarice, not to mention debauchery, their most audacious offense is *laughing* at their own sacrilegious behavior. After recounting a final tawdry, outrageous tale, our Parisian Passavant concludes, "Et de telle histoire ilz en font leur passetemps et risée" (And from such a story they entertain themselves and laugh).[64] The supposed laughter of the Genevans is the final proof of their evil nature. While Désiré's salacious description of Geneva is meant to provoke disgust, it also produces laughter, as when he mocks Calvin's most popular polemicist, Viret. As always, Désiré's teeth are bared, and the only laugh his humor generates is the *risus sardonicus*. He does employ sarcasm, wordplay, and other elements of comedy in this *libelle*, but the menacing quality of the discourse so overshadows these that the humor quickly turns to anger and outrage.

Two years later, Désiré returns to the topic of Geneva, providing his readers again with two different imaginary exposés of the headquarters of Calvin's recently founded faith. One of these is *Les Regretz, complainctes, et lamentations, d'une damoiselle, laquelle s'estoit retiree à Genesve pour vivre en liberté, avec la convertion d'icelle estant à l'article de la mort* (1558), written as a continuation of the *Passevent parisien*. This pamphlet recounts the tragic story of a woman who converts to Calvinism and flees to Geneva, where the conduct of the reformists horrifies her to the point of death. Fearing damnation, she asks her daughter to set up an interview with Calvin to persuade him to abjure. The interview, unsurprisingly, does not go well, and after she dies, she is thrown into a ditch, where dogs tear her body apart. There is really nothing humorous to be found here, other than Pasquin's darkly comic comment that being eaten by dogs is better than being buried in a Protestant cemetery.[65]

The same year Désiré published a much more elaborate *libelle*, again providing an ostensible firsthand account of life in Geneva, the *Grandes chroniques et annalles de passe par tout,*[66] *chroniqueur de Geneve, avec l'origine de Jean Covin, faucement surnommé Calvin* (1558). In this dialogue, Passepartout relates to Master Pierre du Quignet his misadventures in Geneva, explaining that he spent eighteen months investigating the city.[67] This pamphlet was successful enough to produce a Calvinist response the same year from Jacques Bienvenu, the *Response au livre d'Artus Desiré, intitulé: Les grandes chroniques et Annales de Passe-partout.*[68]

Some have doubted Désiré's authorship of the earlier *Passevent parisien* because of the absence of violent discourse. In this *libelle*, however, our author returns to his favorite topic, the need to burn and hang more heretics in France. He also provides an auto-reference to the *Passevent parisien*, with our new eyewitness Passepartout asking his interlocutor,

> N'as-tu point veu la grand' Chronique
> Qu'en a fait un bon catholique,
> Qu'on nomme Guillot[69] Passevent,
> Qui passe par là bien souvent
> Pour voir leur manière de vivre?
> N'as-tu point veu ce plaisant livre
> Qu'il a fait de leur pauvre vie?
>
> (Have you not seen the great Chronicle
> That a good Catholic wrote,
> Who is called Guillot Passavant,
> Who passes through there [Geneva] often
> To see their way of living?
> Have you not seen that pleasant book
> That he wrote about their poor life?)[70]

Right before this he asks his companion,

> Ne sçais tu rien de ces faulx cris,
> De ces paillards, de ces badins,
> De ces apostatz Christaudins,[71]
> Que à Geneve sont alez,
> De peur qu'avoient d'estre bruslez?
>
> (Do you know nothing of the fake cries
> Of these depraved people, these fools
> These Christian apostates,
> Who went to Geneva,
> For fear of being burned at the stake?)[72]

At the start of *Grandes chroniques*, two key elements are introduced: intertextuality and invective. As with so many pamphlets of this period, this one begins by calling the reader's attention to previous texts, providing a framework and context for the latest offering. This sequel promises to be even more revealing, providing readers with an extended exposé that goes beyond the Parisian Passavant's previous account. Passepartout promises further revelations about these depraved fools in Geneva, a group of lawless people who have come to this foreign city because they both fear French law and desire to realize their most debauched fantasies. Désiré's goal is to belittle and dehumanize Calvinists, making his readers more comfortable with and enthusiastic about his proposed violent solution for dealing with Calvin's coreligionists.

Added to the mix is a repeated lament that the king is either not sufficiently aware of the problem of heresy in France or failing in his duty to prosecute these heretics.[73] As Passepartout complains early on,

> Nous debvons bien estre esbahis
> De voir par tout nostre pais
> Tant d'heretiques respandus,
> Sans estre bruslez, ne pendus.
>
> (We must be quite astounded
> To see throughout our country
> So many heretics moving about,
> Without being burned or hanged.)[74]

The problem, as presented here, is that no one is taking the law seriously; on the contrary, people are making a mockery of orthodoxy. As he ruefully notes, "Chascun ne s'en fait plus que rire" (Each [of these heretics] does not worry and only laughs).[75] For Désiré, a death sentence is the only sensible way to deal with such blasphemous laughter. Far from being tragic, such death should provoke retributive laughter, thus castigating heretics' laughter. Désiré highlights repeatedly the audacious mockery and blasphemous satire of his religious adversaries precisely so that his own readership will react in support of his violent proposals.

A key passage that offers a useful explanation of how these two elements—satire and violence—work together comes when Passepartout describes Calvin to his friend:

> Mon amy, c'est un diable d'homme
> Qui à bien priser ne vaut rien:
> Car s'il void quelque bon Chrestien
> Qui face un signe de croix,
> Le malheureux à haute voix
> L'appellera chasseur de mouches,[76]
> Et luy donra tant d'escarmouches
> Par manière de mocquerie,

Qu'à la fin aura fascherie.

(My friend, he is a devil of a man
Who, to value properly, is worth nothing:
Since if he sees any good Christian
Who makes the sign of the cross,
This miserable man out loud
Will call that person a vain fellow,
And will create such a verbal skirmish
By means of mockery,
That in the end there will be trouble.)[77]

In a metonymic construction, Désiré explains why both Calvin and by extension Calvinists are "worth nothing." In this description, Calvin performs an act of symbolic violence, lashing out at the simple ritual of a "bon Chrestien." Rather than respect the man's pious act, Calvin feels compelled to pile on insults and "mocquerie," which will end in a physical assault. It is hard not to extrapolate and read this as a condemnation of the propaganda offensive launched by Protestant writers, who each year were churning out an ever-increasing number of mordant attacks on Catholic beliefs and practices. In Désiré's description, Calvin reveals their motives: hatred and contempt for good Christian folk who should be outraged by such irreverent and scornful behavior. The only appropriate response to Protestant satire and vitriol is lethal violence, as our Norman priest makes clear here and elsewhere. Protestant mocking laughter aimed at sacred rituals must ultimately be silenced, but in the meantime, Désiré fights fire with fire, aiming his own mordant satire here at the spiritual leader of this Protestant sect.

A key passage in the *Grandes chroniques* blurs the lines between pamphlet and play, as the performative aspects of theater are brought to bear in an anecdote. Passepartout recounts a tragic farce (the word "farce" is even used in the story)[78] in which a lady in La Rochelle seeks revenge on her male servant who refuses to convert to the reformed faith.[79] She conspires with her *chambrière* to plant a silver finger bowl on the servant and accuse him of theft, forcing her husband to dismiss him. The husband does not fall for the trick, so next she turns to her neighbor, who agrees to swear the servant is the thief. This time the servant is let go, and if the story ended there, it would be a religious version of a stock farce, with scheming wife, chambermaid, and neighbor (all women) pitted against the male servant and husband. However, the end of the tale is heavily moralistic and tragic:

the neighbor's guilt is so extreme that she falls fatally ill but before dying confesses her sin and reconverts to Catholicism. Just as we saw with Marguerite de Navarre's theater, Désiré is able to use a stock theatrical format, easily recognizable to his readers, and add on his own religious and polemical layers, turning a conventional farce into a mordant, ideologically charged satire.

The *Grandes chroniques* contain another evocation of performance, this time pitting two types of performances against each other (recalling in certain respects Panurge's humiliation of the *haute dame de Paris* during a religious procession).[80] In the tract, Maistre Pierre describes how outrageous it was that sacred processionals in Paris to implore the Almighty for rain were disrupted by Protestants behaving like buskers and street performers.

> Mais trouvois tu pas bien estange [*sic*] …
> Voir gens masquez, et comme en guerre
> Sonner tabourins et auboys:
> Et blasphemer à haute voix
> Par les grands rues de Paris:
> Et qui plus est, par un mespris
> De sainctes congregations,
> Se moquer des processions
> Et faire cent mille insolences?

> (But did you not find it strange
> To see masked people, as if in war
> Sounding drums and horns:
> And blaspheming out loud
> On the main thoroughfares of Paris:
> And moreover, through scorn
> Of the holy congregations,
> Mocking the processions
> And producing a hundred thousand rude remarks?)[81]

This stark juxtaposition is an effective way to horrify Désiré's Catholic audience. Protestants are portrayed as warlike but also like lowly street performers, who do not hesitate to commit blasphemy and sacrilege, mocking the sacred. How to deal with such shocking satirical performances? "Si on en faisoit brusler, / Les autres meschans se tairoient" (If we burned some of them, / The other wicked ones would shut up).[82]

In the final section of the *Grandes chroniques*, Désiré directly addresses the printing trade. He refers to Robert Estienne, the famous printer who had to flee to Geneva in 1551 and was burned in effigy in Paris. Désiré laments the production and circulation of heretical tracts, crying out:

> Helas! Qu'il y a d'imprimeurs
> Semblables à ce meschant là:
> Qui sont respandus çà et là,
> Tant par les villes et citez,
> Que par les universitez:
> Desquelz nous provient de grans maux
> Encore des plus principaux
> Malheureux, et sacramentaires,
> Qui sont de mauvais caracteres
> Contre les sainctz de Paradis.
>
> (Sadly, there are printers
> Like this wicked man [Robert Estienne]:
> Who spread throughout here and there,
> As much in towns and cities,
> As in the universities
> From whom come to us great evils
> Still among the main leaders,
> Those who are sinister, and sacramentarians,
> Who are bad characters
> As opposed to the saints of Paradise.)[83]

This is an interesting portrayal of the Protestant book trade. Désiré correctly identifies printers as agents of change, spreading heterodox ideas throughout the kingdom.[84] At this time Geneva is printing and distributing the greatest number of polemical tracts and establishing itself as a major center of print production in Europe.[85] Our Norman priest is doing his part to combat this, using the same weapon as his adversaries and with tremendous success. Passepartout tells his friend that because of his wickedness, Robert Estienne is now destitute in Geneva and no longer has a printing press, details that are untrue[86] but serve to highlight how Désiré frames this battle of words—"the saints of Paradise" must dominate, while wicked writers and printers like Estienne must fail.

A year later, Désiré once again returns to Geneva with *Les Disputes de*

Guillot le Porcher[87] *et de la Bergere de Sainct Denys en France contre Jehan Calvin* (1559). In this dialogue, a supposedly naïve shepherdess (she in fact plays the role of the *badin*, or *faux-naif*) comes to Geneva to talk to Calvin. She begins by explaining why she has come to meet him:

> Monsieur Calvin qui avez grace
> De prescher le sainct evangile,
> Et d'orner vostre langue grasse
> Plus que ne fist jamais Virgile,
> Pour ouyr vostre esprit agile
> Où la grace de Dieu repose,
> Je suis venue en ceste ville
> Apprendre de vous quelque chose.
>
> (Sir Calvin, you who have the grace
> To preach the holy gospel,
> And to decorate your foul mouth
> More than Virgil ever did,
> To hear your agile mind
> Where the grace of God resides,
> I came to this city
> To learn something from you.)[88]

Although her words seem complimentary, one can detect irony and sarcasm, as when she refers to his "langue grasse."[89] Further, emphasizing his rhetorical prowess is an insult, since it suggests a gift for manipulating language, a verbal manifestation of insincerity. Comparing him to Virgil is also an interesting choice. Rather than comparing him to a Christian saint or some important religious figure, she intentionally chooses a pagan poet. While she says she wants to learn from Calvin, it is clear she has already figured out Geneva's charlatan-in-chief.

Calvin is not fooled and immediately calls her out as a papist, seduced by some "Docteur Sorboniste."[90] At this point Guillot le Porcher (swineherd) shows up and takes on Calvin directly. The extended analogy he uses throughout the dialogue is predictable: he has come to find out why his pigs have left the pure water of the fountain (a reference to Christ as a fountain found in John 4:14) "Pour venir boire en ce dit lac, / De l'eau bourbeuse orde et vilaine / Qui est plus puante que tac" (to come drink in this lake / Of filthy, muddy, and foul water / That stinks worse than rot).[91] Everyone who has come to Geneva has done so looking for the freedom to live a dissolute lifestyle where they eat meat on Fridays and during Lent and where former monks sleep with prostitutes. Unsurprisingly in a work by Désiré, Guillot and the shepherdess suggest that the best solution is to burn these swine.

Désiré uses his long-established populist rhetoric to produce a mordant contrast between haughty Calvin and the simple swineherd Guillot, much as Marguerite de Navarre did in *Le Mallade* between the supercilious doctor and the modest chambermaid. At one point, Calvin interjects,

> Et par mon serment c'est pour rire
> De veoir un porcher ignorant
> Qui veut enseigner et instruire
> De ce pays le predicant.

> (I swear this is a joke
> To see an ignorant swineherd
> Who wants to teach and instruct
> The preacher of this country.)

To which Guillot replies,

> J'ayme trop mieux mon ignorance
> Et ma simplicité de cœur
> Que je ne fais ton arrogance
> Fondée en schismes et en erreur.

> (I like so much more my ignorance
> And my simplicity of heart
> Than I do your arrogance
> Founded on schisms and errors.)[92]

Désiré portrays Calvin laughing at Guillot's simplicity. Such mocking laughter is meant to anger and incite his readership, and is another example of the *risus sardonicus*. Guillot's counterargument mirrors that of the author: Désiré has been widely criticized by both contemporaries and later critics for a simplistic, unsophisticated style that does not compare favorably to reformist *libelles*, some of which we will examine in the next chapter. Here both the author and his protagonist Guillot embrace their own plainness and mock the pretensions of their humanist-trained adversaries. This suggests something about Désiré's target audience. His polemical works are not intended for scholars and humanists; he is writing for commoners, perhaps even the illiterate who could hear his dialogues read aloud or used in sermons. The overall tone in *Les Disputes de Guillot le Porcher et de la Bergere de Sainct Denys en France contre Jehan Calvin* is angry vitriol; the humor is the extreme satire of the sardonic laugh.

Let us conclude our discussion of Désiré's polemical works with a curious anthology titled *Le Contrepoison des cinquante deux chansons de Clement Marot, faulsement intitulees par luy Psalmes de David*, produced in 1560. At this point Marot had been dead for sixteen years. While the much better-known dispute between Sagon and Marot has received a fair amount of critical attention, this one-sided dispute has not.[93] Moreover, while Marot's translation of the psalms would become a mainstay of Calvinist worship, as well as a *cri de guerre* on the battlefield during the French Wars of Religion, it is perhaps unsurprising that Désiré's attempt to produce a Catholic "remedy" for Marot's psalms has remained in obscurity. And this despite the fact that a year after producing this aggressive parody, he published a set of sincere psalms as a Catholic counterpart to the Calvinist psalter.[94]

As Jacques Pineaux points out in his introduction to a facsimile reproduction of the *Contrepoison*, Désiré noted as early as 1550 the danger of Marot's psalms to the faithful, writing in his *Combatz du fidelle papiste* that the psalms are

> . . . si tresmal Marotté[95]
> Que le sens du texte a osté
> Par un grand et scandaleux crime.
>
> (. . . so terribly Maroticized
> That [Marot] removed the sense of the text
> By a great and sinful crime.)[96]

As Pineaux notes, Marot's translation of the psalms was not simply an expression of Protestant piety but also a forceful instrument of propaganda. To counter this, Désiré sought to reassure his Catholic readers, beginning each of his psalms with the incipit from the Vulgate. As Marot had done with some of the psalms he translated, matching their rime and meter with that of popular songs, Désiré also used *contrafactum*, taking the rime and meter of Marot's popular hymns and replacing the text with his own. As Pineaux concludes in his introduction to the *Contrepoison*, the strength of the Protestant reaction to Désiré's psalms points to their efficacy.[97]

In his dedication to the Duke of Savoy, Désiré explains his intention to combat the poison spread by Marot's psalms. Pineaux refers to the Duke of Savoy's own efforts to oversee a war of *libelles* against Geneva.[98] At the end of the dedication, never one for subtlety, Désiré makes an ostensibly humble request:

> Et de ma part je supply humblement
> Nostre Seigneur, qu'il vous doint telle grace
> Que vous puissiez exterminer la race
> Des Chiens mastins obstinez et mauvais
> Afin que tous nous puissions vivre en paix.
>
> (And for my part I humbly beg
> Our Lord, that he provide you with such grace
> That you are able to exterminate the race
> Of these obstinate and wicked mastiff Dogs
> So that we may live in peace.)[99]

Désiré's response to Marot's psalms is merely an intermediary step. While in this *libelle* he satirizes a work sacred to Calvinists, ultimately he encourages action, namely the eradication of heretics in both France and Geneva; the Duke of Savoy, to whom the *Contrepoison* is dedicated, held nominal dominion over Geneva. Savoy had only been restored to the duke, Emmanuel Philibert, with the Peace of Cateau Cambrésis the year before.[100]

The second of the *chansons* begins with a fantasy in which the kings of the world will unite to destroy these heretics, followed immediately by this reference to divine, wrathful laughter:

> Entre eulx diront derompons et brisons
> Leurs faulses loix dont tromper nous pretendent,
> Au loing de nous jectons et mesprisons
> Les Apostatz, par lesquelz ilz nous tentent,
> Lors Jesus christ qui les haultz cielz habite
> Des malheureux se rira de là hault
> Et confondra la nation mauldicte
> Qui en sa loy grandement erre et fault.
>
> (Among them [the kings of the earth] they will say, let us break apart
> Their false laws with which they aim to trick us,
> And let us scornfully sweep away

The apostates, who are used to tempt us,
Then Jesus Christ who inhabits the highest heaven
Will mock these wretched people from on high
And will confound the cursed nation
That in its law greatly errs and goes astray.)[101]

This is a striking passage in that it portrays not so much divine wrath as divine laughter. In this extended fantasy, Désiré imagines the leaders of the Catholic world uniting to crush the heretics, with Christ as a spectator of this gruesome performance, delighting in and laughing at the cruel fate of these "malheureux" apostates. Christ's laugh, as portrayed here, is the *risus sardonicus*.

Rhetorically, this godly laughter is a righteous counterpart to the iniquitous laughter of Désiré's religious foes. In *Chanson XIV*, he returns to the theme of the blasphemous satire produced in Geneva:

Ha malheureux, qui vous estudiez
A vous mocquer de la doctrine bonne
Des sainctz Prelatz et Docteurs de Sorbonne
Lesquelz sont tous sur l'eglise appuyez,
Et alliéz.
O qui et quand justice eslevera
Son bras puissant pour vous jecter au feu?
Lors Jesuchrist nostre souverain Dieu
Son peuple juste adonc esprouvera,
Et gardera.

(O miserable ones, who spend your time studying
How to mock the holy doctrine
Of saintly prelates and Sorbonne doctors
Who are all sustained by and allied with the Church.
O who will it be and when will justice raise
Its strong arm to throw you into the fire?
Then Jesus Christ our sovereign God
Will at that time test and protect
His righteous people.)[102]

For Désiré, violent retribution will be the natural result of aggressive Calvinist satire. He portrays Protestant mockery as blasphemy against God's chosen people, guaranteeing that they will meet a violent end. Mockery of sacred doctrine, such as transubstantiation, provokes Catholics to a form of sacred, divinely sanctioned violence. This would prove true not only in Désiré's polemical parody but in reality as well.

In *Chanson XVIII*, he addresses the issue of clemency toward Protestants. As one might surmise, Désiré finds any act of generosity toward Calvinists outrageous because these heretics are ungrateful, even scornful, toward those who would help them:

> Delivrez sont des prisons par tesmoings
> Faulx et meschans, dont leurs cœurs inhumains
> Sont resjouys, nous jectant regardz maintz,
> Par grand risée.
>
> (Delivered are they from prison by witnesses
> False and wicked, whose inhuman hearts
> Rejoice, throwing us many looks,
> With great laughter.)[103]

Désiré emphasizes the purported laughter of his religious enemies, for it is precisely the reason they cannot be trusted or forgiven. This laughter must be silenced in the most draconian way possible. Going one step further, and returning to a shocking theme from the *Passevent parisien*, in *Chanson XXVI* he once again suggests that when a heretic is executed in France, his coreligionists in Geneva are amused:

> Les Paillardz se resjouissent
> Et gaudissent
> Voir leurs semblables brusler
> Aux lieux et places publiques.
>
> (These dissolute people rejoice
> And celebrate
> To see their coreligionists burn
> In public squares and places.)[104]

The *Contrepoison* provides yet another example of the hybrid use of humor and violence, laughter and brutality. Désiré's rhetorical strategy is as straightforward as it is effective with his Catholic readership: rather than being repulsed by violence against Protestants in France, Catholics should take righteous pleasure in it and even find such punishments amusing.[105] Why? Precisely because their adversaries are not in fact sincere; their professions of piety are undermined by their sarcasm and satire; not only do they mock the sacred, but they are so cynical that they find the execution of fellow Calvinists in France cause for joyous celebration. For Désiré, Protestant satire, which by 1560 was widely disseminated in France, is proof of their culpability. No true believer would be so irreverent as to laugh at revered doctrine and beliefs. Such laughter is the ultimate form of blasphemy and justifies the eradication of this "race." In all of these parodic psalms, perhaps the most striking image is that of Christ in heaven, looking down at the slaughter of Protestant heretics and laughing. Désiré's satire is castigating when taking aim at Protestants, and he simultaneously castigates Protestant satire itself throughout his corpus.

Artus Désiré represents a critical bridge between the relatively inept responses of the Sorbonne in the early years of these polemical exchanges and the firebrand tactics of the Catholic League in the latter part of the century. Désiré was ridiculed and then ignored until the late twentieth century, when Denis Crouzet offered an important reassessment. Subsequently treated more favorably by critics such as Jeff Persels, Antónia Szabari, and Chris Flood, Désiré deserves further reassessment and renewed interest. As Crouzet notes, after citing one of Geise's unfavorable characterizations of Désiré,

> ce qui peut sembler aujourd'hui une étroitesse d'esprit avait, entre 1545 et 1562, une finalité précise qui était de l'ordre de la persuasion: il s'agissait, par un discours systématiquement schématique et totalitaire, de construire une image répulsive de l'adversaire et de tenter de maintenir, par l'angoisse eschatologique et par la violence des dénonciations, les chrétiens dans la vraie Église.

(what seems today to be a narrow mentality had, between 1545 and 1562, a precise purpose that was about persuasion: using a schematic and totalitarian discourse, it was a question of constructing a repulsive image of the adversary and attempting to sustain, through eschatological agony and the violence of denunciations, the Christians of the true Church.)[106]

Désiré's goal was simply to persuade, using the brashest and most aggressive tactics possible. To borrow Crouzet's phrasing, the "colossal" number of Désiré *libelles* in circulation testifies to their popularity, even if we do not necessarily understand it.[107] Few of Désiré's tracts are readily accessible today,¹⁰⁸ but they were best sellers with far-reaching impact. His pamphlets were published in Rouen, Paris, Lyon, and elsewhere and went through multiple editions, placing tens of thousands of copies into circulation. His populist rhetoric evidently struck a chord and certainly caused Geneva to take notice and to try to combat his influence, as we will see in the last part of this chapter. Of the *libelles* produced during this time, his most successful display the common touch and were accessible to an audience beyond the elite and educated. While he would win no prizes for literary sophistication, that is not the goal of propaganda, and Désiré was one of the Catholics' most persuasive propagandists.

The final example in this chapter provides the most compelling illustration of the porous boundaries between written tracts and plays. Conrad Badius, who published many *libelles*, also wrote, had performed, and published a play, the *Comedie du pape malade*, in which a character representing Artus Désiré plays a key role. Among other insights, the play provides proof that Désiré made quite an impression on his Genevan adversaries. Conrad Badius was the son of the famous printer Josse Badius, who played a major role in publishing the 1555 Geneva edition of the Bible in French, the first to provide the verse divisions still used today. Conrad Badius is best known for the dozens of works he published, many of them polemical. He was an important player in the network of sometimes itinerant printers who circulated reformist materials in France. In 1562, the year after his play was published, he died of the plague in Orléans, having left Geneva to participate in the first French War of Religion.¹⁰⁹

Badius's play offers a fantastical description of the circulation of *libelles* and the ways in which opposing sides (as well as the occasional brave moderate) propagated their ideas through print. Two aspects of the play are particularly intriguing. This is the only play I know of that so explicitly depicts the world of pamphleteers; it stages the production and dissemination of polemical works and features several pamphleteers, including Artus Désiré, as characters.¹¹⁰ (Judging by the sheer number of references to Désiré, it is clear this Catholic polemicist was extremely effective at irritating his Calvinist adversaries.) One of the main subjects of the play is the propaganda battle between Protestants and Catholics in France. As the pope complains,

Entr'autres griefs j'avois ma fille France
Qui m'a tousjours porté obeissance,
Et m'a été en tous endroits fidele

> Sans se monstrer en un seul point rebelle,
> Qu'un tas de gens sorciers et enchanteurs
> Partis de là, et bien subtils menteurs,
> Par leur babil en erreur ont tiree
> Et de dessous mon aile retiree.
>
> (Among other problems I've had there is my daughter France
> Who has always been obedient to me,
> And has in all respects been faithful
> Without rebelling in any way;
> A bunch of sorcerers and enchanters
> Having left from there [Geneva], these very fine liars,
> By their nonsense have pulled her into error
> And removed her from under my wing.) (vv. 335–42)

The theme of the pope's extended complaint is language and how words are used and manipulated to convince people to leave the Catholic faith. In a Protestant play, the pope's lament is of course intended ironically, but the presence of Catholic polemicists as characters underscores Protestant concerns about the propaganda wars. While the Catholic response to Protestant propaganda had been rather ineffectual in the 1520s and 1530s, by the 1540s and 1550s, Catholic polemicists like Artus Désiré were reaching a much wider audience and more effectively responding to Protestant attacks. At one point, the character representing Désiré refers to his notorious *Passevent parisien respondant à Pasquin romain* (v. 1292). All the Catholic polemicists in the *Comedie du pape malade* are conniving, arrogant, greedy liars who act like bumbling fools and play supportive roles to the main characters, the pope and Satan. All are portrayed as ridiculous and say things that would evoke scornful laughter from the Geneva audience that saw the play performed in 1561.[111]

Another intriguing aspect is that the framing, in particular how the play begins and ends, illustrates how religious partisans like Conrad Badius sought simultaneously to exploit and to contain forms of laughter. The beginning paratextual material is particularly instructive in understanding how Badius attempts to guide and control his audience. The published version of the play begins with a preface, "Au lecteur fidèle," which starts, "Le proverbe du Comique Payen [Terrence] . . . dit que Vérité engendre haine" (The proverb of the Pagan Comic [Terrence] . . . says that Truth produces hate).[112] Acknowledging from the start that his work is polemical and will be seen as offensive by some, and using the rhetorical device of *captatio benevolentiae* in a way that recalls Rabelais's prologue to *Gargantua*, Badius implores his audience, "Ne vous offensez donc point, ô Lecteur, de la liberté que je prends" (Do not be offended, dear reader, by the liberties I take). As he continues, however, his tone becomes much more strident:

> Car le temps de lumière est venu qu'il faut que la vie ignominieuse de ce monstre infernal, et de tous ceux de sa secte, soit decouverte.... Ne vous ébahissez donc si en ce temps que Dieu veut rétablir les ruines de son Israël il se trouve des gens qui découvrent les énormités de cette abominable église Romaine, lesquelles sont venues au comble, et sont montées devant Dieu, qui a en sa main sa vengeance toute prête pour exterminer cette grande paillarde, qui a enivré tout le monde du vin de sa paillardise, regnant par tyrannie sur le siège de Dieu, duquel il faut maintenant qu'elle soit précipitée en ignominie et confusion perpetuelle.
>
> (For the time of light has come and it is necessary that the dishonorable life of this hellish monster, and all those of her faction, be revealed.... Do not be surprised therefore if, in this time when God wants to reestablish His ruined Israel, there are people who discover the heinousness of this abominable Roman church, those who have reached their limit, who have risen up before God, Who has ready in His hand His vengeance to exterminate this great whore, who has intoxicated everyone with the wine of her wickedness, ruling through tyranny on the throne of God, from which she must now be cast headlong in dishonor and eternal confusion.)[113]

This passage underscores the Calvinist motto, *Post tenebras lux*. But there is no subtlety in the "truth" Badius wants to share with his audience. Aggressive polemics dominate, ensuring that the target audience will be limited to the Protestant faithful who reject the "abominable église Romaine." At the end of preface, he tries to soften his tone, explaining, "j'écrivais pour les simples" (I wrote for simple people),[114] but even that phrasing is ideologically charged, as reformists frequently praised the simplicity of their own writings in contrast with the obtuse language of Catholic theologians.

The next section of the *Comedie du pape malade* is the "Argument," which sets the scene: "Le Pape, prochain de la mort, ... / Consolé par sa mommerie / (J'entends Prêtrise et Moinerie)" (The Pope, near death, ... / Consoled by his band of ragtag actors / (I mean the Priesthood and Monkery)) (vv. 1, 5–6). This image of the dying pope consoled by his "mommerie" sets the tone for the play and also creates a sort of mise en abyme. The sarcastic term *mommerie* emphasizes the disparity between high-minded piety and lowbrow hijinks, presenting the pope and his entourage as street performers—crude, obscene, and full of mischief. This intentional blasphemous depiction is the primary source of humor in the play. However, as I have noted elsewhere, ridiculing your religious adversaries and their practices is extremely problematic, given that you in turn will face similar attempts to satirize your own sacred beliefs and customs. If the pope and his cohorts can be represented as hucksters and mountebanks, so can Calvin and other Protestant leaders, creating an underlying tension in this and other polemical works. The conclusion of the "Argument" illustrates the serious nature of laughter in this context:

> Lors Dieu avec sa vérité
> Vivra en toute éternité
> Au milieu de sa pauvre Église
> Que tant on outrage et méprise,
> Faisant cesser ses cris et pleurs
> *Et changeant en ris ses douleurs.*
>
> (Then God with His truth
> Will live for all eternity
> In the midst of his poor Church
> Which has been so insulted and scorned,
> Ending her cries and tears
> *And changing into laughter her suffering.*) (vv. 37–42; emphasis mine)

Protestant suffering will eventually be turned into laughter, a common trope in evangelical and reformist writings, as we saw in Marguerite de Navarre's plays. Despite the bitterness and sardonic laughter found in the *Comedie du pape malade*, the ultimate goal is to achieve the transformed, psalmic laughter of the converted and the saved.

A prologue immediately follows the "Argument." Here Badius moves further to narrow his intended audience and circumscribe the use of laughter. As the prologue announces, "Soyez tous bienvenus, si vous n'êtes pas Papistes" (You are all welcome here, if you're not papists) (v. 8). More interesting is how the prologue addresses the issue of laughter:

> Sus sus donc Huguenaux, que l'on vo' voie en place,

> Pour voir si vous avez si maigre et triste face
> Qu'on bruit, et si complots dressés pour vous détruire,
> *Quand il en est saison vous empêchent de rire.*
> *Je n'entends pas d'un ris profane et sans science,*
> *Ains partant du repos de bonne conscience,*
> Qu'ôter on ne saurait, pour tourment q' l'on fasse,
> À ceux qui ont reçu de Jésus Christ la grâce.
> *Riez donc votre soûl, de ce ris sobre et saint.*
>
> (Here now, Huguenots, let us look at where you are seated,
> To see if you have as thin and sad a face
> As it is rumored, and if the conspiracies raised to destroy you,
> *When in due time they keep you from laughing.*
> *I'm not talking about a vulgar and ignorant laugh,*
> But one that comes from peace of mind,
> So that one cannot remove it, no matter what torture is used,
> For those who have received Christ's grace.
> *Therefore laugh your fill, with this sober and holy laugh.*) (vv. 13–21; emphasis mine)

This is one of the most intriguing references to laughter I have found in my research, although it is not an isolated one. Badius is trying to explain the positive use of laughter, while cautiously distinguishing which forms of laughter are acceptable. He says he seeks to lighten the burden of his audience through laughter, but certain forms of laughter are not acceptable, such as laughter that is "profane et sans science." But the laughter aroused by this militantly ideological play could hardly be characterized as lighthearted. This disdain for "un ris profane" is tricky, since there is much in this play that is scatological and "sans science." The simple people ("les simples"), the larger audience he seeks to reach, include those who lack the "science" of humanist training. This tension is pushed further at the end with his paradoxical formulation, "Riez donc votre soûl, de ce ris sobre et saint." The word *soûl* evokes gluttony and excess, yet the drunken laughs Badius hopes to provoke are also supposed to be sober and saintly. There is of course a positive history in evangelical humanist discourse regarding drinking and drunkenness. One need only recall Rabelais's writings on this topic. However, this is also perhaps the best illustration of where the *risus sardonicus* leads, namely to the point where laughter is so restrained and constrained that it almost stops being laughter. This is what Badius is calling for here in terms paradoxical to the point of self-contradiction. The genie is already out of the bottle, and polemicists on both sides are already quite adept at satirical insults and scatological humor far removed from the sober piety presumed to govern their lives.[115]

Throughout the *Comedie du pape malade*, with the pope, Satan, clergymen, and a supporting cast of miscreant pamphleteers, there is much that is vulgar and profane; as George Hoffmann describes it, humor in the play could "quickly slid[e] into ejaculatory, excessive laughter."[116] However, to mitigate its own excesses, the play proposes a sort of deus ex machina solution at the end with the arrival of two allegorical figures, Vérité and L'Église. Satan has just finished talking about the pope when Vérité announces herself. Even the versification switches. Until this point, octosyllable meter has dominated; when Vérité speaks, the meter switches to decasyllable, indicating a change in register from low to high.[117] Once Vérité has finished her speech, L'Église offers the final moral gloss in heptasyllabic verse. This conclusion serves to cordon off and control crude laughter, allowing the play to end on a sententious note. It recalls the rather abrupt endings of farces and morality plays (when the audience is invited to go for a drink or a meal) but is certainly more elaborate and has a very different purpose. Even though there is much in the *Comedie du pape malade* that is not serious, the doctrinal pronouncements at the end function as a sort of close-off valve, turning the audience's attention away from the scatological coarseness that occupies a large part of the dramatic action and reasserting the central importance and seriousness of faith.

This play's mixture of invective and sententious discourse contains a variety of types of humor. There is the hopeful and innocent laughter of the converted, but there is also the negative laughter of the *risus sardonicus*. Performing the pope's death onstage in a comedy is an example of this. As Persels notes, comparing the *Comedie du pape malade* to plays of the 1520s and 1530s, "Gone is any attempt at reconciliation; the hopeful, gentle, evangelizing corrective of a Marguerite de Navarre is now replaced by the defiant, martial rhetoric of a besieged minority with an established and growing history of martyrdom."[118] At the eve of the outbreak of the Wars of Religion, the partisan humor of writers such as Désiré and Badius is so strident and aggressive that it restricts possibilities for laughter, as the jokes and barbs often serve as mere pretexts for violent denunciations.

4

Geneva's Polemical Machine

Comme il y en a aucuns, qui ont des froides risées,
lesquelles il semble advis qu'on leur ayt arraché du gosier par force.
—Jean Calvin, preface to Pierre Viret, *Disputations chrestiennes*

Artus Désiré's efforts, along with those of other Catholic contemporaries, were focused on combating the increasing stream of polemics coming out of Switzerland and being disseminated throughout the French kingdom. This chapter centers on a crucial period of this production, from the 1540s to the start of the 1560s, a time marked by heightened religious tensions in France and increased activity and proselytizing efforts by Calvin's church. During this period, Geneva, the most popular destination for an ever-growing number of French exiles, was investing enormous time and capital publishing tracts and other religious materials, as well as polemical works destined for their French compatriots. The chapter on this period in Robert Kingdon's *Geneva and the Coming of the Wars of Religion in France* is titled "The Flood Tide: Books from Geneva." As Andrew Pettegree noted, in an essay paying homage to Kingdon, this activity "turned what had, until this point, been a publishing backwater, into one of the most influential, or notorious, centres of print culture in Europe."[1] Kingdon's observation that "these books must be given partial credit for the revolutionary temper that helped produce war in 1562" seems appropriate, and this chapter buttresses that view.[2] My aim is to uncover some of the ways the Geneva church used humor in its proselyting and propaganda efforts, both to provoke French Catholics and encourage the Geneva faithful to mock and scorn their Catholic persecutors. I will focus on Pierre Viret and Théodore de Bèze, contemporaries of Conrad Badius, highlighting pamphlets that have not been studied extensively.³

Calvinist pamphleteer Pierre Viret has been called the most popular writer of the French Reformation.⁴ A prominent Reformist preacher and teacher (he taught for several years at the Reformist Academy in Lausanne and spent his last years at the academy established in Orthez by Jeanne d'Albret, Marguerite de Navarre's daughter), Viret was also a prodigious writer and defender of the Geneva-based faith and produced more than fifty works over the course of his career. No one besides Calvin himself published more pages than Viret. Some of his works were translated into several languages, and many of his writings went through multiple editions. Outside the world of religious studies, however, Viret is all but forgotten now, and modern editions of his works are almost nonexistent. He was a close associate of Calvin, who wrote a preface offering qualified support for what is perhaps Viret's best-known work, his *Disputations chrestiennes* (1544).⁵ Calvin's reservations about Viret's polemical writings underscore a key tension during this period, with satire and laughter on one side and piety and reverence on the other.

Always the pedagogue, Viret had a knack for reaching a large public, and his writings were generally more accessible than those of many of his fellow Reformists.⁶ A well-trained humanist, Viret wrote religious and polemical tracts replete with biblical and classical references, including allusions to satirical writers such as, surprisingly, Lucian, portrayed by religious polemicists on both sides as an atheist who mocked religious belief.⁷

A useful place to start is with a tract Francis Higman has called Viret's first important work, *De la difference qui est entre les superstitions des anciens gentilz et payens, et les erreurs et abuz qui sont entre ceux qui s'appellent chrestiens* (1542).⁸ Published two years before his notorious *Disputations chrestiennes*, this pamphlet sets out many of the satirical themes that Viret would return to throughout his career and also takes up many of the same mercantile comparisons we saw in Marcourt's *Livre des marchans* in chapter 1.

The goal of *De la difference* is to ridicule Catholic belief by connecting it to past pagan practices, and thus in the first section Viret draws several unfavorable comparisons to religions from antiquity, mocking those ancient pagans who would "adorer les herbes, comme aux oignons, et semblables choses, et les bestes brutes pareillement, comme Cocodriles, Cygoignes, et autres telz monstres" (worship herbs such as onions and the like, and brutish beasts as well, such as crocodiles, swans, and other such monsters).⁹

The setup for the coming joke is clear: first Viret gets his reader to laugh at the absurdity of pagan customs and beliefs, and then comes the inevitable punchline, as he suggests that Catholic practices are equally ridiculous. He uses idolatry to link the two and spends a fair amount of time expounding biblical interdictions and pagan practices, using the well-established trope of linking *créature* (creature) with *Créateur* (Creator) and arguing that Catholics wrongly replace the *Créateur* with *créatures*. By 1542, this was already a well-established attack line for Protestants.

Viret enlivens the attack and introduces a familiar topic, monasticism, within a new context, idolatry. Monasticism had of course been ridiculed for centuries, and Rabelais's monastic satire in *Gargantua* is particularly memorable. But the target is usually the gluttony and inutility to society of monks.[10] Here, however, Viret makes the connection between monasticism and idolatry through a comical vestimentary analogy. First he makes a joke that is only visible on the page; after listing the colors of the habits of various orders, he mocks the monk who believes that having "une corde pour saincture" (a rope for a belt/sanctity) makes him more agreeable to God.[11] With their numerous costumes and robes that make them feel conspicuous, Viret says, monks create for themselves a "nouveau dieu," who takes pleasure "Comme des hommes mortelz feroyent à veoir des momons, batteleurs, folz, badins, et joueürs de farces desguisez en divers habitz, pour jouër leur personnage" (like mortal men would do watching actors, buffoons, jesters, fools, and performers of farce disguised in all manner of costumes to play their character).[12] Here the reader is a mocking spectator to whom the monks' ostensibly saintly garb is just a farcical costume that renders them risible.

Viret's *De la différence* is lengthy, but in these first pages he lays out his entire satirical argument, deriding the sacred offices and practices of Catholicism by upending them. Pagans are idolaters because they worship things such as plants and animals rather than God. They try to render material what should remain spiritual. To a mid-sixteenth-century Christian audience, this would be both absurd and laughable, evoking the sort of scornful, condescending snigger that characterizes the *risus sardonicus*. It is nevertheless curious that instead of immediately attacking obvious Catholic corollaries to pagan practices, such as saint-relic or Marian worship (the subtitle of the pamphlet reads, "de la vraye manière d'honnorer Dieu, la Vierge Marie, et les Sainctz"), Viret first focuses on monastic vestments. The monk's robe is a clever choice, because it is not only a symbol of the monk's vows and commitment but also the locus of his authority and, by extension, that of the Catholic Church.

Equating reverence for the monastic habit with pagan worship of idols is made possible by a second analogy, more familiar to Viret's readers than Egyptian or Greek religious practices, namely the world of street performers and buskers. This is a much more effective strategy and one that appeals to a wider audience than educated humanists and theologians. The actors and *badins* of the day, who disguised themselves with donkey ears and other outlandish accoutrements, were both lewd and funny. Street performers represented the lowest of lowbrow entertainment, and their appeal to the masses was often based on crude humor.[13] Their repertoires were full of obscene jokes and sexual innuendo, jarring in juxtaposition to the idealized austerities of monastic life. Viret calls his readers' attention to how costume and disguise remove people from their "natural" state. Ultimately, his analogy between monks and street performers does in fact connect monks with gluttony and lasciviousness, or *paillardise* ("bawdiness"), a favorite word for Viret and other religious polemicists. With their phallic props, performing farces filled with gluttony and lust, performers embodied the spirit of *paillardise*. Viret draws upon the performative aspect of costume, blurring boundaries, conflating the sacred with the profane in order to desacralize and satirize the former. He portrays monasticism as nothing more than a performance, inauthentic and ultimately masking lasciviousness. The paradox is that while street performers' costumes highlight bawdiness, in Viret's discursive performance, monks' vestments disguise it.

In *De la difference*, Viret uses the city of Rome to make the connection between Catholics and pagans. He associates the capital of the ancient pagan empire with the modern-day papal court in a very unflattering way, anticipating Joachim Du Bellay's similar division in *Antiquitez de Rome* (1558). Referring to a scurrilous version of the myth of Rome's foundation by Romulus and Remus, one that goes back as far as Plautus and Livy, Viret mordantly observes,

> comme leurs histoires tesmoignent, ont esté nourriz et allaictez d'une loupve: ils ont pensé que cela leur seroit plus grand honneur, si toute la terre estoit pleine de bastardaille, et de filz de putains, nourriz non pas de femmes de bien, mais de loupves (car les Latins appellent loupve une paillarde.)

(as their history makes clear, [Romulus and Remus] were breastfed and nourished by a she-wolf ["loupve" or "lupa" in Latin]; they thought that this would be the greatest honor, if all the world were filled with bastards, sons of prostitutes, fed not by noble women, but rather by prostitutes ["loupves"] (for the Romans called a prostitute a she-wolf).)[14]

Drawing upon burlesque retellings of the foundation myth of Rome, while playing on the double meaning of "loupve" or "lupa," Viret's real target is the current leader of Rome, the pope. The pope's authority rests on the New Testament passage where Christ designates Peter as the founder of Christianity, becoming for Catholics the first Bishop of Rome.[15] Replacing this foundational story with a bawdy retelling of the pagan foundational myth of Rome is outlandish and highly satirical. Replacing a saint with a prostitute produces a satire intended to undermine the prestige and foundational power of the Roman Catholic Church.

Throughout the treatise, Viret offers example after example of Catholic practices that make a mockery of true devotion. These practices are not only erroneous but also an affront to the Almighty. To take one instance, in discussing Lent Viret takes aim at Ash Wednesday, observing,

> il leur paindra une grande croix au frond avec ses cendres et puis s'en reviendront tout charbrouillez, comme s'ilz sortoyent de la forge d'un mareschal, et puis se riront et moqueront l'un de l'autre. Ne sont-ce pas de belles farces que nous jouons devant Dieu? Et si cecy n'est farce et mocquerie de Dieu, je ne scay que c'est, se mocquer de Dieu.

> (he paints a big cross on their forehead with ashes and they come back all covered in charcoal, as if they were coming out of a blacksmith's forge, and then they laugh and mock each other. Are these not splendid farces that we perform before God? If this is not a farce and a mockery of God, then I do not know what it means to mock God.)[16]

Again, theater and theatrics, and in particular the theater of farce, are brought to the fore and a sacred ritual is upended and recast as a comic spectacle that offends God.

As we will see even more in his *Disputations chrestiennes*, in *De la différence* Viret employs many classical and even biblical antecedents to justify his use of crude humor and satire in attacking Catholicism. In one salient passage, he evokes the Greek philosophers Heraclitus and Democritus, the pair known for weeping and laughing at society's deplorable state. In the same passage, Viret also implicitly refers to the Old Testament prophet Elijah and the priests of Baal (among other possible Old Testament personages), a reference that he makes explicit elsewhere:

> Il fauldrait beaucoup d'Heraclitus pour plourer suffisamment ceste grande misere et malediction qui est cheuté sur les hommes. Et beaucoup de Democritus pour se rire et moquer de leur sotise et folie incredible, qui est d'autant plus digne de moquerie, qu'elle semble plus avoir d'apparence de sagesse, et que ceux qui l'ont introduicte et la maintiennent encore à present, ont plus grande persuasion de leur sçavoir, sagesse et justice. Ce n'est pas sans cause que les Prophetes s'en rient et moquent si souvent, pour monstrer plus clairement la vanité et frenaisie de ces malheureux idolatres.
>
> (It would require many Heraclituses to sufficiently bemoan this great misery and curse that has befallen humanity, and many Democrituses to laugh and to mock their stupidity and unbelievable folly, which is all the more worthy of mockery, as it presents itself as wisdom, and those who introduced and maintain it still today are greatly convinced of their knowledge, wisdom, and justice. It is not without reason that the prophets laugh and mock so often, in order to show more clearly the vanity of these unfortunate idolaters.)[17]

In this syncretic defense of satire, Viret references both the sardonic mockery of Democritus and the scornful ridicule the prophet Elijah heaped on the priests of Baal in a biblical passage that is key for a Christian justification of seemingly unchristian satire.[18] In Viret's own writing, one finds a penchant for Democritus's approach to society's ills, an approach much like Montaigne's in his *Essais*.[19] In the next *libelle*, we will see Viret develop much more extensively his eclectic defense of satire, a defense that is fraught with tension, as the author is constantly switching registers between anger and laughter, between theological seriousness and crass mockery.

One final passage from *De la difference* contains another notable justification for Viret's sardonic laugh. He asserts, "Nous avons le conseil du Sage, qui dit: Respons au fol selon sa folie, afin qu'il ne luy semble, qu'il soit sagesse.[20] Les choses sont aucunesfois si folles et si absurdes, qu'elles ne sont pas dignes de confuter par raison, mais seulement d'estre moquées." (We have received the advice of the Sage [Solomon], who says, Answer fools according to their folly, or they will be wise in their own eyes. Sometimes things are so foolish and absurd that they are not worthy of being rebutted rationally, but should simply be mocked.)[21] This is a tricky position to maintain, and one that Viret himself frequently contradicts in his writings, as he uses a plethora of rational arguments to rebut Catholic positions. These are juxtaposed with moments of verbal excess, where language is no longer constrained by theological considerations, and where vitriolic satire comes to dominate the discourse.

Viret's *Disputations chrestiennes* (1544), published two years after *De la difference*, originally appeared in three volumes totaling over nine hundred pages and is Viret's best-known and most developed satire. Viret, like countless other humanist-trained writers, was very partial to the dialogue format. Here four interlocutors take different positions and discuss a variety of issues pertaining to Catholicism, particularly purgatory and the treatment of the dead (last rites, funerals, requiems, etc.). Reading these long dialogues, one is struck by their pedagogical quality—Viret is always trying to teach, and when he makes satirical attacks, he quickly returns to pious matters and focuses on questions of doctrine.

The *Disputations* begin with two prefaces, the first by Calvin, who expresses great hesitancy about satire. He begins by citing Horace's ideal of *dulci et utile*, opening the possibility of entertainment and amusement in the context of religious instruction.[22] Calvin sees those who produce jokes ("faceties" is the word he chooses) as running two potential risks:

> Car un homme qui veut user de faceties se doit donner garde de deux vices. L'un est, qu'il n'y ayt rien de contraint, ou tiré de trop loing. Comme il y en a aucuns, *qui ont des froides risées*, lesquelles il semble advis qu'on leur ayt arraché du gosier par force. L'autre est, de ne point decliner à une jaserie dissolue, laquelle en latin se nomme scurrilité, en nostre langage, plaisanterie. Ainsi de tenir le moyen, c'est, de savoir bien à propos, et avec grace, et par mesure parler joyeusement, pour recréer tellement qu'il n'y ayt rien d'inepte, ou jetté à la volée, ou desbordé, ce n'est pas une vertu commune ou vulgaire.

> (Someone who wants to make jokes needs to watch out for two vices. One is that it is too forced, or that it is too outlandish. For example, there are some *who have cold laughs*, which seem almost torn from their throats. The other danger is not to fall into dissolute gossip, in Latin

referred to as buffoonery, in our language, a joke. Thus one needs to hold to the middle, to know how to express oneself joyfully with equity, grace, and restraint, to entertain in such a way that there is nothing that is inept, rash, or over-the-top, as not everyone knows how to pull this off.)[23]

This is a curious caveat. One is left wondering what exactly "cold laughs" represent, but they seem connected to the *risus sardonicus*. Calvin gets at the heart of the matter when discussing tensions surrounding the use of satirical humor in the context of religious conflict. First, he suggests that jokes in the tradition of Horace's lighthearted satires are acceptable, while the more aggressive and hostile satirical tradition of Juvenal is not. But even lighthearted satire should avoid anything too scurrilous. Calvin is attempting to define the rules of the game for satire while recognizing the challenges involved and the ways in which humor and satire cannot be easily contained. His censorious views foreshadow the intolerance toward humor and satire that he expresses in his *De scandalis* of 1550, a text he had been thinking about since 1542 and in which he equates certain forms of satire with irreligion.[24]

In this preface, however, Calvin does offer several defenses of Viret's satirical work. First, he downplays the importance of the humor in the treatise. He acknowledges that Viret's method includes a certain type of laughter ("forme de risée") but maintains that religious doctrine is the main focus, and the humor is present merely as an accessory ("comme un accessoire").[25] He warns against turning sacred things into objects of laughter ("on ne les [les choses sacrées] tourne en risée").[26] On the other hand, there are practices and beliefs so ludicrous that it is impossible not to laugh at them: "Mais en descrivant les superstitions et folies dont le povre monde a esté embrouillé par cy devant, il ne se peut faire qu'en parlant de matieres si ridicules on ne s'en rie à pleine bouche" (But in revealing the superstitions and follies that unfortunate souls have been caught up in, one cannot help but burst out laughing when talking about such ridiculous things).[27] He connects this to biblical tradition, alluding to Old Testament prophets such as Elijah:

> en racontant des resveries si sottes, et des badinages tant ineptes, nous usions de moqueries telles qu'ilz les meritent. Quand nous en ferons ainsi, ce sera à l'exemple des Prophetes: lesquelz en traictant la simple verité de Dieu, parlent avec une majesté, qui doit faire trembler tout

le monde: mais en blasmant les resveries des idolatres, ne font nulle difficulté d'user de risées, pour monstrer combien elles sont ridicules.

(In discussing such stupid ideas and such feckless nonsense, we use the mockery they deserve. When we do so, we are following the example of the Prophets, who in treating God's simple truth speak with a majesty that makes the world tremble, but in impugning the ideas of idolaters, they have no problem using laughter to show how ridiculous these ideas are.)[28]

The idea is one that Viret and other Calvinist polemicists insist on repeatedly: there are certain religious practices in Catholicism that are so outrageous and ludicrous that it is impossible to treat them rationally or with restraint. They must be exposed and derided. This is, however, a slippery slope, as Calvin himself acknowledges at the end of his preface: "Mais j'ay allegué ceste comparaison seulement pour monstrer que ce n'est pas donner occasion aux Lucianiques et Epicuriens et autres contempteurs de Dieu, de vilipender la religion Chrestienne, ou l'avoir en mespris, quand on se moque des corruptions d'icelle" (But I have offered this comparison simply to show that this is not to allow lovers of Lucian, Epicureans, and other despisers of God to malign the Christian faith or to scorn it just because the corrupted elements of the religion are being mocked).[29] How does one satirize certain Christian religious practices without mocking Christianity? This represents a serious challenge and helps explain the growing misgivings about humor as new and more vicious forms of humor and satire were unleashed.

Especially when compared to later satirical works coming out of Geneva, Viret's *Disputations* are rather tame. In his own preface, Viret begins by discussing language, explaining that he chose to write in French instead of Latin to reach more people, in particular poor, ignorant folk who do not know Latin ("les povres ignorans").[30] There are certain ways in which this assertion is valid, and his works were broadly disseminated, but one cannot help but note the vast erudition, biblical and classical, in his dialogues. There is often a populist flavor to his critiques (he portrays wealthy and gluttonous priests intentionally keeping the people ignorant), but it is somewhat overshadowed by extended theological explorations and an endless stream of supporting *exempla* that reveal impressive humanist training. Still, the *Disputations* are written in French, and multiple citations from the *Aeneid* and other classical works are translated into the vernacular. The only Latin used is presented sarcastically, with priests mumbling set phrases from the Catholic liturgy that highlight their corruption and ignorance.

In making fun of his Sorbonne adversaries' use of scholastic-inflected Latin, Viret offers a description that strongly recalls similar satires in the *écolier limousin* episode in Rabelais's *Pantagruel* (1532) and Geoffroy Tory's *Champfleury* (1529):[31]

> Dieu sait quelle escorcherie ilz tiennent, et comme ilz escorchent le latin, tellement qu'ilz ne parlent ne latin ne françois: mais voulant fuyr tout ce que leur semble vulgaire, afain qu'ilz soyent estimez plus grans orateurs, forgent un langage tout nouveau, et mesprisent les bons motz françoys, pour mendier et desrober ceux des langues estranges.

> (God knows what butchery they perform, as they disfigure Latin so much that they speak neither Latin nor French. Wanting to avoid anything that seems common to them, so that they will be considered great orators, they forge an entirely new language, and scorn the use of good French words, preferring to beg and steal from foreign languages.)[32]

This emphasis on plain, unadorned prose that avoids Latinate constructions reflects Calvin's own insistence on using clear and succinct French, and this anti-Ciceronian rhetorical style was to have an important influence on later French prose.[33]

Viret follows this with a critique of other writers and their readers that echoes Calvin's previously stated concerns. He attacks those who prefer reading dirty books, so-called "livres de paillardise."[34] Later, he strengthens this critique, saying that one must be able "trier l'or du milieu de la fiente, et separer la poison de la bonne viande" (to sort out the gold from the dung, and separate the poison from the good meat).[35] As he elaborates his position, he mordantly observes that there are those who wish to

> escrire seulement des folies, plaisanteries, farceries, jeux et passetemps, comme badins, morisqueurs, farceurs et plaisanteurs.... mais plusieurs ne se contentans point d'estre badins entre les hommes font encore pis. Car ilz ne s'adonnent qu'à scurrilité, et leur semble qu'ilz ne pourroyent assez delecter les hommes, si leurs deviz ne sont tous pleins de propos de ruffiens, et de maquereaux, de vilanies et blasphemes.

> (write only nonsense, jokes, farces, and empty banter, acting like tricksters, pranksters, and deceivers.... But many, not satisfied with being charlatans, do worse.... They indulge in offensive language, seeking at all cost to delight their readers with sayings that are filled with the iniquitous and blasphemous language of ruffians and pimps.)[36]

Whatever Viret's intentions are here, there is real irony in his protest as he seeks to distinguish his own writing from that of others. Despite Viret's purportedly pious purposes, the *Disputations* and some of his other works could also be labeled "livres de paillardise," as they contain a fair amount that could easily be deemed vulgar and crass. It is hard not to read both Calvin's and Viret's defense of this particular satire as splitting hairs, drawing distinctions that are not immediately evident.

In his preface, Viret also draws upon the work of two of the most prominent classical satirists, Lucian and Diogenes, with a rather elaborate exploration and defense of Lucian in particular. This presents distinct challenges, as both classical figures could be seen by contemporaries, especially in the latter part of the sixteenth century, as blasphemous atheists.[37] The fundamental problem that many polemical writers encounter is how to navigate the uses of satire in the context of Christian belief. Writers like Viret insist that their own satirical output is justified and go to extreme pains to show why this is so, but they invariably condemn the satirical writings of their adversaries. Viret's discussion of writers who try to imitate Lucian's satirical style is unintentionally amusing. He notes,

> ains semble qu'ilz se soyent totalement adonnez à l'imitation de Lucian, homme sans dieu et sans religion, moqueur et contempteur de Dieu et des hommes. S'il est question de passer le temps, de se rire, jouer et gaudir des superstitions et idolatries, des bigotz caphars et hypocrites, et de tous les estatz du monde, il ne nous faut ja cercher autre auteur, et n'avons point besoing de ces nouveaux Lucianistes, qui ne sont que ses petis disciples.... Car s'il faut faire comparaison du langage, ilz n'aprochent point de son eloquence.

> (But it seems that they have completely given themselves over to imitating Lucian, a man without God or religion, a mocker and despiser of God and of people. If it is a matter of spending one's time laughing, playing and making fun of superstitions and idolatrous thoughts, bigoted deceivers and hypocrites, and of all the ways of the world, we do

not need to find another author, and we do not need these new writers imitating Lucian, who are but his feeble acolytes. . . . If you compare their styles, these imitators are nowhere near his level of eloquence.)[38]

On the one hand, according to Viret, one should not imitate Lucian, a godless man who scorned religion. On the other hand, Viret's contemporaries who do try to imitate Lucian doubly fail, because Lucian is a much better writer. This is a rather odd position for a Christian polemicist to take. Viret's adversaries are not only guilty of blasphemous pronouncements; they are also guilty of bad writing.

Recognizing the tenuousness of his position, he offers the following justification of Lucian, while further denigrating Lucian's modern-day imitators: "Car quelque meschant et ennemy de Dieu et de toute religion qu'il [Lucien] ait esté, toutesfois nous ne pouvons nyer, qu'il n'ait esté savant homme, grand orateur et philosophe, et qu'il n'ait escrit beaucop [*sic*] de choses bonnes et trop meilleurs que ne font ceux cy" (For although Lucian was evil and an enemy of God and of all religion, nevertheless we cannot deny that he was an intelligent man, a great orator and philosopher, and that he wrote a lot of good things and better than those who imitate him).[39] This is not unlike countless other justifications by Christian humanists who insist on the importance and value of pagan models, even when they are at odds with the beliefs and practices of Christianity. Like others, Viret references Saint Augustine's assertion that Christians should borrow what is useful from pagan philosophers.[40] What Viret is ultimately doing in this preface, after giving negative examples of satirical or scandalous writing, is asserting his own right to produce Lucianic writing. The implicit message is that his own satirical style is *dulci et utile*, worthy of both the Lucianic tradition and Christian principles. This is a fine line to draw and exposes the underlying tensions and contradictions of this polemical treatise.

If the first half of Viret's preface is concerned with what is unacceptable writing and reading for pious Christians, the second half is occupied almost entirely with a defense of his own writing against those who might find it offensive or insufficiently serious. As he asserts,

> Combien que je me moque des abuz, erreurs, heresies, superstitions et idolatries de l'eglise de l'Antechrist . . . je ne me moque de chose qui ne soit digne, non seulement de moquer, mais de la haine et abomination de tout le genre humain: et que je ne descouvre pas seulement les abuz, sans monstrer quant et quant le vray usage des choses.

(No matter how much I mock the abuses, errors, heresies, superstitions and idolatries of the Church of the Antichrist... I only make fun of things that merit not only contempt, but also the hatred and outrage of the entire human race; and moreover, I do not simply reveal the abuses without also showing the true way that things should be done.)[41]

His argument is twofold and recalls Calvin's. If Viret satirizes Catholic practices and beliefs, it is because they merit scorn, if not outright hostility. Furthermore, his ridicule is pedagogical—instead of simply deriding Catholic practices, he offers alternatives and correctives, what he and his religious cohorts would call true doctrine.

Viret then attacks those who would condemn his writing: "Parquoy il me semble que ceux qui ont les oreilles tant delicates, et ne peuvent seulement endurer un petit mot joyeux contre l'idolatrie et superstition... ne sont pas juges equitables, mais de jugement trop corrompu et perverty" (This is why it seems to me that those who have such delicate ears that they simply cannot endure a little playful remark against idolatry and superstition... are not fair judges, because their judgment is so corrupt and perverted).[42] This strong language is surprising, coming as it does after his own condemnation of scurrilous writing. Here he suggests that censorship or censorious attitudes can be misdirected or simply wrong. This is rather heavy-handed moralizing—Viret instructs his readers not to laugh at or enjoy certain forms of satire or particular types of jokes, yet not to be censorious toward Viret's own satirical writing. Such is the nature of writing dominated by religious concerns. Like Calvin, Viret supports his position with biblical examples, referring to Paul's injunction to be fools for Christ's sake (1 Cor. 4:10), as well as the example of Elijah mocking the priests of Baal (1 Kings 18:27). More generally, he observes that even "la parolle de dieu n'est pas tellement severe et tetrique, qu'elle n'ait ses ironies, farceries, jeux honnestes, brocardz, et dictons convenables à sa gravité et majesté" (the word of God is not so clear and harsh that it does not contain its ironies, tricks, wholesome playfulness, quips, and sayings suitable to His gravity and majesty).[43] This foreshadows Montaigne's more far-reaching observation in "De l'experience" that even truth has its limits.[44] Allowing for such ambiguous and polysemous possibilities in the word of God is a challenging position, one that Viret seems to understand as he reaches the end of his preface. How does one make light of beliefs and practices sacred to Catholics without ultimately undermining Christianity?

Viret concludes his preface by once again distinguishing his own Lucianic style from that of his adversaries, using a canine metaphor and including an unflattering, misogynistic characterization of whimsical writers who lack his own seriousness of purpose:

> Il [Dieu] ne veut point de ces petits chiens plaisanteaux, pour estre en delices aux dames, mais veut des bons mastins, et de gros levriers qui ne sont point pour porter à la manche, mais pour abbayer et chasser le loup du parc. Parquoy s'il y a des personnages *qui mordent en riant,* ilz donnent à entendre qu'ilz ne prennent pas grand plaisir à telz jeux, mais qu'ilz voudroyent bien avoir autre passe temps, et occasion de parler de meilleurs [sic] matieres. Toutesfois ilz monstrent à ceux qui ayment les passe temps, et qui y prennent plaisir, comme Democritus à se rire et moquer des folies et resveries des hommes, qu'il n'est ja besoing qu'ilz aillent cercher autre matiere. La court de l'Antechrist leur en donne assez, et de plus digne de rire, et en laquelle on se peut mieux jouer sans offenser Dieu, si on le faict de telle affection et de telle modestie, qu'en ces dialogues. . . . Tant y a, qu'il me semble, que je n'ay pas escrit chose qui puisse porter dommage à la religion Chrestienne.

> (He [God] does not want these pleasant little dogs which delight ladies, but rather wants good mastiffs and sturdy greyhounds which are not made for carrying on your sleeve, but are made for barking and chasing the wolves away. This is why if there are those *who bite while laughing,* they make it known that they do not take pleasure in such games, but that they would like to have other pastimes, and the chance to speak about more important matters. Still, they show those who enjoy leisure and take pleasure in it, like Democritus, who laughs and makes fun of the follies and fanciful ideas of men, that they need look no further. The court of the antichrist provides them with enough material, and it merits their laughter. One can poke fun at it without offending God, if one does it with the same level of affection and modesty as one finds in these dialogues. . . . Such as it is, it seems to me that I have not written anything that could damage the Christian faith.)[45]

This conclusion contains one of the most direct references in Viret's work to the *risus sardonicus,* laughter that bites. It recalls Erasmus's classical references that liken this particular form of laughter to animals showing their teeth and appearing to smile but biting instead. In Viret's Horatian-style defense of his own writing (*dulci et utile*), he is asserting that the usefulness of his work is precisely in its bite. Others may produce pleasant and amusing material, but they are not manly enough; their work lacks sufficient mordancy, as they produce literary lapdogs fit only for women. Viret's sardonicism is justifiable because it attacks Catholic dogma; humor employed for other reasons is weak and inferior. The underlying question is an important one: Once people start making fun of certain religious practices and beliefs, where does one draw the line? How is it possible to ridicule people and customs considered sacred without eventually having the whole religious edifice crumble? It is ironic that staunch believers like Viret actually create the opportunity for future writers such as Cyrano de Bergerac and Voltaire to satirize the whole framework of Christianity. While much of this concluding section of Viret's preface to the *Disputations* derides comic writing deemed too effeminate, the final phrase—"il me semble, que je n'ay pas escrit chose qui puisse porter dommage à la religion Chrestienne"— somewhat desperately insists on the saintliness of his satirical project.

Overall, the preface of the *Disputations chrestiennes* constitutes one of the finest and most elaborate defenses of satire of the period. Viret displays his vast erudition in addressing the main issues surrounding the use of humor and satire in religious polemics. The dialogues themselves are rather straightforward and seem somewhat tame, especially compared to later works by others. Viret sets the stage, as he does in other dialogues, with four characters: Hilaire, Eusebe, Theophile, and Thomas. There is a performative quality to their conversation, but in the same way that the action in French Renaissance theater, especially tragedy, can stall because of overly verbose soliloquies, there are times when the conversational quality disappears altogether and sententious monologues dominate. The main targets in these six dialogues are the concept of purgatory, referred to as the "purgatoire Platonique, poetique et Papistique" (Platonic, poetic, and papist purgatory) in the second dialogue,[46] and Catholic last rites and masses for the dead.

In the first dialogue, the characters are making fun of saints' legends, including a miraculous resuscitation compared to Christ's raising Lazarus from the dead. Hilaire reveals the same anxiety found at the end of Viret's preface. After mocking the *Golden Legend*, he adds, "Je ne nye pas sa resurrection [Lazare], mais je nye tous ces mensonges adjoustés à l'histoire evangelique" (I do not deny the resurrection [of Lazarus], but I deny all of these lies that have been added to the gospel story).[47] The characters mock the extravagant claims in the hagiographies, yet this particular moment draws attention to the parallels between these claims and those in the Bible. Epistemologically, attacking certain miraculous claims of Catholicism while simultaneously affirming the veracity of other miracles is a slippery slope and leads inexorably to the questioning of all such assertions.

Elsewhere in the *Disputations*, characters discuss how Catholics cleanse souls in purgatory as people wash their clothes or the dishes.[48] Viret's main contention, and one that he develops extensively, is that purgatory is a pagan concept that Catholics appropriated. He quotes Virgil's *Aeneid* extensively, in French translation, to support this claim. Mocking the idea of holy water, Viret cites Diogenes's mocking his contemporaries for engaging in similar aquatic purification rituals. Viret also employs a culinary metaphor that will be developed much more fully in later Protestant works and that recalls Rabelais's anti-monastic satire. The characters discuss an imaginary kitchen where priests and monks gorge themselves and feed lies to the public. Another target of their derision, as already seen in other reformist works, is clerics' clothing, with monks and priests portrayed as cross-dressers. The characters play off the ambiguity of the French word *robe*, meaning both robe and dress, to denigrate priests and monks for their ostensibly feminine garb, proof that "ilz sont effeminés, et dignes d'estre tenuz pour femmes" (they are effeminate, and deserve to be mistaken for women).[49]

Intriguingly, the six dialogues that constitute Viret's *Disputations chrestiennes* end with a sarcastic poem in decasyllabic verse, parts of which one could imagine being sung in a tavern. It is prefaced with a comment about insincere emotions and laughter. Thomas remarks, "Vous disiez, en parlant des lamentations que les prestres font après les mortz, qu'ilz font des piteux à-lentour d'eux, quant aux grimasses exterieures, et qu'ilz s'en rient en leur cueur" (You were saying, in talking about the display of grief that the priests put on after someone dies, that they make themselves out to be the most pitiful in their laments and exterior grimaces, while in their hearts they laugh).[50] This inversion of the *risus sardonicus*, with a portrayal of feigned sorrow masking contemptuous laughter, leads to the final poem:

> Moynes, Nonnains, prestres, et maquereaux,
> Bastardz, putains, deschirons noz cheveux,
> Car maintenant sont esteins les forneaux,
> Qui tant nous ont nourris gras et pompeux.
> Bien nous pouvons tenir pour malheureux
> Car le bon temps qu'avons eu est passé.

> Mort est celuy qui nous a amassé
> L'argent duquel faisions Gaudeamus.
> Helas il est maintenant in pace.
> Parquoy chanter nous faut autre Oremus.
>
> (Monks, nuns, priests, and pimps,
> Bastards, whores, let's pull out our hair,
> Since now the ovens are extinguished
> That kept us so well nourished and full of ourselves.
> We can consider ourselves unfortunate
> Because the good times that we have had have passed.
> The one [Purgatory] is dead who helped us pile up
> The money with which we offered our "Let us rejoice" [gaudeamus].
> Alas, he [Purgatory] now rests in peace.
> This is why we need to find other forms of "Let us pray" [oremus].)[51]

The characters, assuming the voices of clerics, lament the loss of Purgatory, which had served them so well and kept them well fed, as they were paid to pray for the dead. Lumping nuns and priests together with prostitutes and pimps sets the sardonic tone, and the kitchen theme returns as the monks regret the loss of their all-you-can-eat buffet, paid for by their liturgical performances. These religious hustlers must now find a new scheme ("chanter nous faut autre Oremus") to maintain their lavish lifestyle. At the end of this lengthy polemical work, Catholic clergy take the stage and sing their burlesque pastiche of the Latin sung during the liturgy. Here and elsewhere, Viret works to link the holy offices of the Catholic Church with the lowbrow world of street performances. By doing so, he is trying to evoke a particular type of laugh from his readers, a mordant laugh provoked by pillorying his religious adversaries.

Eight years and several treatises later, Viret produced *La Physique papale* (1552), a series of five dialogues featuring the same four characters as in his *Disputations chrestiennes*. The *Physique papale* has been seen as a precursor to the *Satyres chrestiennes de la cuisine papale* (discussed next), attributed in the past to Viret, although more recent scholarship suggests the author was Théodore de Bèze.[52] In the *Physique papale*, Viret draws upon and develops further the gastronomically themed satire so popular among reformists, as the characters sarcastically explore what they call the "philosophie de cuisine" of the Catholic Church.[53] Like the *Disputations chrestiennes*, the *Physique papale* is a highly learned work, and again there are passages from the

Aeneid, as well as from Ovid's *Metamorphoses*, and references to Plutarch and Cicero. The overarching argument against certain Catholic beliefs is the same: Purgatory, holy water, and other beliefs and practices are appropriations of pagan ideas, and because of their syncretic, impure practices, Catholics are idolaters.

In this so-called "philosophie de cuisine," the kitchen dominates as the locus of the greed and gluttony that motivate Catholic clergy.[54] Viret focuses on Mardi Gras and Lent, comparing them to pagan practices. As so often happens, his comparisons not only denigrate the Catholic Church but also show the pagan version to be superior. In the case of the Bacchanalia and Saturnalia festivals, Viret's characters insist that even the pagan Romans wearied of the debauchery and moderated their habits. Deriding Lenten practices, Theophile states that at least the Romans were not hypocrites: "Ilz ne faisoyent pas des Caresme-prenans, et ne se crevoyent pas de manger et de boire. Ilz ne se débordoyent pas en toutes dissolutions, pour aller le lendemain mettre un petit de cendre sus leurs frontz, comme qui voudroit jouer une farce, et se moquer de Dieu et des hommes." (They did not act like it was Mardi Gras, and did not burst with food and drink. They did not get carried away with all manner of indulgence, and then go the next day and put a little ash on their foreheads, like those who would perform a farce and mock both God and men.)[55] This comment reflects an important theme in Viret's work: the performative, theatrical aspect of Catholicism. Lenten ritual is here compared to a comic play, in which a performance of abstemious piety masks voracious indulgence. For Catholics the ash cross put on foreheads on Ash Wednesday is a symbol of contrition and renewed commitment to Christ. Here the ash cross is part of a farcelike performance, comparable to the flour and makeup on the faces of street performers. There are several references to farces, as well as *morisques*, an exotic sort of dance or performance, and *moueries*, terms from the world of street performance and theater.[56]

In one passage, this line of attack reaches the Catholic Mass, represented as a farcical rendition of Christ's Last Supper (the characters are discussing Easter traditions). Theophile, describing Catholic clerics, declares:

> Vous vous monstrez bien semblables aux petis enfans, en cela, qui maintenant pleurent, maintenant rient: et declairez manifestement, que toutes voz mines et voz pleurs ne sont sinon jeux, farces et moqueries. Vous faites encore un petit la bonne mine, le matin de Pasques, pource

que vous vous administrez et recevez la cene, en vostre façon. . . . Et puis le disner passé, durant toutes les festes de Pasques: il ne est plus question, sinon de rire et jouer et gaudir. La chaire mesme, en laquelle la predication se fait, en laquelle voz prescheurs veulent encore plus contrefaire la gravité des Prophetes . . . n'est elle pas toute convertie en farce? Car alors messieurs les Caphars, qui ont presché le Caresme, en recompense des larmes et des pleurs qu'ilz ont faitz jetter aux dames, en préchant, non pas tant la passion de Jesus Christ, que celle de la vierge Marie, et les lamentations d'icelle, leur baillent des bouquetz, et racontent des petites sornettes et contes joyeux, pour faire rire, et éveiller les auditeurs, qui sont tant soulz, qu'ilz n'en peuvent plus.

(You act a lot like little children, crying one instant and laughing the next, and you clearly show by this that all your facial expressions and your tears are merely games, farces, and mockery. You do a bit the same on Easter morning, when you administer and receive communion, in your way. . . . But then the meal has passed, and during the rest of the paschal feasts, there is nothing but laughter, playing, and enjoyment. The pulpit itself, from which the preaching takes place, with which your preachers still want to counterfeit the solemnity of the Prophets . . . is it not all turned into a farce? ["toute convertie en farce?"] For these hypocritical priests who have preached Lent, as a reward for the tears they got the ladies to shed in preaching not so much the Passion of the Christ, as that of the Virgin Mary and her sorrow, they offer them bouquets and share with them tall tales and funny stories, to make them laugh and to awaken those listening who are so drunk that they cannot do anything else.)[57]

This description focuses on performance and insincerity—because the preachers' actions are insincere, with their feigned expressions like theatrical masks, the ostensibly sacred rituals they officiate should not be taken seriously. What Catholics portray as solemn is actually risible, and the rites Viret's treatise describes are farces. The justification for this satirical attack on the sacred lies in the close juxtaposition of laughter and sorrow. Just like actors who switch between tragic and comic roles, priests are adept thespians who switch immediately from sorrow to mirth, the latter negating the gravitas of the former. Rather than the host being transformed ("convertie") into the body of Christ, the entire performance of Mass is instead "toute convertie en farce." Instead of the communion wafer being "toute convertie" into the body of Christ through transubstantiation, here the pulpit on which Mass is held, "la chaire" (a pun suggesting both the pulpit and Christ's flesh), is converted into a stage for farce ("n'est elle [la chaire] pas toute convertie en farce?").[58] Once again, ritual is lampooned and recast as mere spectacle, with its insincerity and deception proof of its corruption.

This anti-Catholic satire is supported by a common misogynistic attack used by Protestants, namely that Catholics place too much importance on the Virgin Mary and not enough on her Son. This is a far cry from early Protestant rhetoric, which made the proto-feminist argument that women should have access to Scripture. Instead, the priests described here are overly focused on women (placing excessive attention on the Virgin Mary, talking to their female parishioners, getting them to cry, and giving them flowers while their drunken husbands sleep) in a way intended to elicit a disdainful guffaw based on gender stereotypes. Viret's audience is supposed to laugh at these Catholic clergymen precisely because they shower too much attention on women, both contemporary and biblical.

In the subsequent discussion in the *Physique papale*, this satirical outburst is followed by a counterpoint—Thomas asks the question: Are people not allowed to laugh? Theophile insists that people should certainly enjoy themselves and that no one finds more enjoyment than the servants of God, but "Ilz ne se resjouyssent pas en se moquant de Dieu" (they do not enjoy themselves by mocking God).[59] Thomas then turns to Hilaire, who cites Johannes Oecolampadius's *De risu paschali*, a book the German reformer published in 1518, attacking the use of lighthearted stories and anecdotes during Easter sermons. This complaint is central to Viret's argument: the sacred loses its efficacy and even its meaning when combined with laughter and humor. Laughter in the *Physique papale* is treated as serious business, and the use of it in the context of religious liturgy is blasphemous. Viret raises suspicions about humor and laughter even as he tries to evoke a particular form of sarcastic laughter from his readers. Still, the pamphlet provides some lighthearted moments, with jokes about Hilaire's name and its etymological connections to hilarity. Humor is present throughout this polemical tract, but disrespectful humor or irreverent levity, such as that of Catholic priests, is questioned and criticized; only the scornful smirk of the converted is permitted.

The last pamphlet to consider in this chapter is perhaps the best-known reformist satire from this period, the *Satyres chrestiennes de la cuisine pa-*

pale (1560). It was published anonymously in 1560 by the printer Conrad Badius, two years before the outbreak of the first War of Religion in France. Badius actually had to spend three days in prison for publishing the pamphlet before he had received permission from the Geneva Consistory.[60] This important *libelle* appeared at the beginning of a three-year period marked by the publication and circulation of an unprecedented number of polemical works from Geneva printers (1560–62).[61] The *Satyres chrestiennes* are part of an interesting subgenre of polemics that could be classified as "papal indigestion," a reformist tradition that goes back in French at least as far as the *Farce des theologastres* discussed in chapter 2. In the sixteenth century, representations of eating and drinking are almost never innocent and are often ideologically charged and ripe with interpretive possibilities. The most famous example is perhaps Montaigne's "Des Cannibales," though Rabelais offers an abundance of material as well.[62]

Théodore de Bèze, the likely author of the *Satyres chrestiennes de la cuisine papale*, knew and collaborated extensively with Pierre Viret. In his very useful critical edition of the *Satyres chrestiennes*, Charles-Antoine Chamay points out that the author of this polemical tract was well-versed in Marot's satirical verses and psalm renderings, Rabelais's tales of Pantagruel and Gargantua, and the world of popular culture, especially the theatrical world of farce, *sottie*, and *sermon joyeux*.[63] There is a clear performative quality to the pamphlet, and one can imagine certain scenes being acted out on a stage. One can also imagine it being read aloud in the same way Rabelais's work was read to François I.[64] The culinary theme and gluttonous images recall in particular Rabelais's work, especially his verbal pyrotechnics, although as Bernd Renner has noted, none of the positive or ambivalent associations with the scatological elements of gastronomy (or more specifically the gastrointestinal) are found here.[65] To put it succinctly, all the shit in this pamphlet is bad shit.

The title of the pamphlet alone captures a fundamental tension in the use of humor and satire in the context of contemporary religious debate. "Satyres chrestiennes" is a perfectly syncretic expression; Roman satire, notably the satires of Horace and Juvenal, was readily available for the first time in sixteenth-century France. The author of this pamphlet is well informed about Horatian and Juvenalian satire, and the pamphlet contains several explicit references to both. Satire is a pagan genre that expresses values that are in important respects at odds with Christianity, yet these are "Christian satires."[66] Here and elsewhere during this time period, one finds polemicists struggling with the contradiction of trying to maintain a pious position while simultaneously attacking religious enemies using decidedly unchristian means.

It is notable that the "Preface to the reader" of the *Satyres chrestiennes* devotes a fair amount of attention to this problematic issue and attempts to delineate a theologically acceptable justification for mockery and laughter in ways that recall both Calvin's and Viret's prefaces to the *Disputations chrestiennes*. As the author describes this challenge, in an uneasy attempt to justify past indulgences not unlike his current satire, he says, "Mais ayant jetté ma veuë sur certains escrits facetieux, et toutesfois chrestiens aussi tost nostre Bon Dieu m'a tant fait sonder les secrets de sa parole, que tout incontinent j'ay eu horreur de l'abysme où peu au paravant je m'estoye precipité" (But having taken a look at certain kinds of writings which could be considered facetious, yet still Christian, soon enough the good Lord helped me to discover the secrets of His word, so that suddenly I was horrified by the abyss into which I had earlier thrown myself).[67] The qualifiers in this statement are important: he does not fully indulge in facetious or satirical literary traditions, only certain ones ("certains escrits facetieux"), which are still "Christian," meaning respectable. His confession underscores the strain between comic and religious traditions, as the writer now seeks to combine the two in his "Christian" satires. In trying to bridge the gap between satire and religious belief, he references Horace's *Satires* and asks the question,

> Qu'est-ce... qui empesche que celuy qui rit ne die verité? Ainsi donc je suis venu d'un rien à un tout, comme en riant. Et de faict, il est certain que les diverses accoustumances des hommes, et les diverses natures font que la verité se doit enseigner par divers moyens, de sorte que non seulement elle peut estre receuë par demonstrations et graves authoritez, mais aussi sous la couverture de quelque facetie.
>
> (Who is to say that the person who laughs does not also speak the truth? Thus I have come from nothing to everything, even while laughing. And in fact, it is clear that people's different habits and their diverse natures make it so that the truth must be taught by different methods, so that not only can truth be received by demonstrations and serious authorities, but also under the guise of a joke.)[68]

This passage resonates with Viret's preface to *Disputations chrestiennes*.[69] Bèze is trying to maintain a delicate balance—humor can be disrespectful and even blasphemous, but it can also be a truth-teller. It can uncover contradictions, ironies, and hypocrisy. It can open to ridicule objects and practices previously considered holy. In the context of religious polemics, however, humor is a two-edged sword and can be difficult, if not impossible, to manage. In any system of belief, once certain practices or beliefs are attacked, finding a stopping point can prove tricky. Once writers and dramatists debase beliefs and customs that their religious adversaries consider holy, with the express intent of rendering them profane and therefore risible, preserving the notion that certain practices and beliefs are off-limits becomes increasingly difficult. Bèze, the likely author of this pamphlet, reveals discomfort about discussing theological issues (and theological disagreements are at the heart of this pamphlet) in a humorous way, highly aware of the divisions being erected between high and low, between belief and laughter.

This *libelle* does pay tribute to Rabelais throughout, with more explicit references to this author known for his irreverent treatment of supposedly lofty matters than to any other. The elaborate descriptions of voracious monks preparing and consuming a seemingly endless list of delectable foods recalls Frère Jean and his merry band of cooks in chapter 40 of the *Quart livre*. Given the amount of anti-monastic and anti-Sorbonne satire in Rabelais's works, it is unsurprising to find so many references to him, as well as stylistic similarities. Still, it should also be remembered that Calvin condemned Rabelais's writings in 1550 in his *De scandalis*, accusing him of obscenity and irreligion. This underscores an important observation Chamay makes in his introduction to the *Satyres chrestiennes*: "les *Satyres chrestiennes* attestent de manière exemplaire qu'en matière d'écriture, Genève peine à définir des règles et des interdits. Notre auteur accumule jeux de mots grivois et basses plaisanteries." (The *Christian Satires* show in exemplary fashion that in matters of writing, Geneva was really struggling to define rules and establish what was off-limits. The author here piles on bawdy wordplay and crude jokes.).[70] This pamphlet is a germane example of how satirical and sardonic uses of humor increase at the same time that suspicions about their uses (and usefulness) grew, which might help explain why Bèze, the future leader of the Genevan church, chose to leave his name off the pamphlet.

In this tract, mocking jokes about Catholics are combined with an effort to define the humor of the opposing side as offensive and even sacrilegious. For example, in the third satire (there are eight total), priests and monks are described as "Mocqueurs de toutes et de tous...content[s] de plaire aux pucelles, / Et nous servir de faceties...souls-de-rire" (Mockers of both women and men,...happy to please the young women, / and offer us jokes), and always "filled (or drunk) with laughter."[71] For Protestants, Catholic laughter is hypocritical and derisive, making a mockery of the truly sacred. Protestant polemicists constantly question priests' seriousness in performing their liturgical duties, asserting that these are merely feigned performances and that the priests are more interested in levity and vulgar pursuits. While Bèze's incendiary comments depict Catholic laughter as rude, obscene, and ultimately blasphemous, what is far more notable in the *Satyres chrestiennes* is the type of humor he himself uses to mock Catholics, humor that is sardonic and at times violently offensive. For example, the fourth satire attacks the monastic tradition:

> Ces couvents du monde retraits,
> Sont de ce manoir les retraits,
> Et cuvier à buer les linges
> De ces singesses et ces singes
> Abominablement puans.

> (These convents removed from the world,
> Are the outhouses of this world,
> And a washtub in which to scrub the linens
> Of these monkeys male and female
> Who [or which] stink horribly.) (vv. 2–6)

The conflation of "retreats" ("retraits," places removed from the world) and "toilets" (also "retraits" in French) is of course meant to be both funny and offensive, as is the rhyme of "linges" (dirty laundry) and "singes" (monkeys). In the fifth satire, there is a reference to "salted rat tongues" (langues de rats salés) (v. 310), with puns on "rats" (rats) and "ras" (shaved), meaning "tonsured," and also on "salés" meaning "salted" but with echoes of "salacious." The third satire labels priests' sermons "predicacations" (v. 514, emphasis mine), combining sermon with excrement ("predication" and "caca"). All of these are highly unflattering images intended to be aggressively funny.

Bèze portrays the Catholic Church as pagan in origin and structure and the papacy as a sort of comic theater. In a brazen appropriation, the Roman goddess Proserpina, wife of Hades, took on the name of the Papacy,

Et sous fards de laide beauté

Se feit clamer la Mere Eglise.
De là vient qu'elle se desguise
D'un beguin, qui trousse à merveilles,
De l'ASNE les grandes aureilles,
... Et din dan dan dit la clochette;
A son col tourne sa cornette,
Sur son col met un grand gaban;
A son chapeau pend le ruban,
Qui denote qu'on ne si frotte.

   (And hiding under the makeup of ugly beauty
Proclaimed herself Mother Church.
Thus it is that she disguises herself
With a bonnet that hides
The big donkey ears,
... and ding, dong, ding goes her bell;
Around her neck she wears a *cornette*,
She wears a big coat with a hood;
From her hat hangs a ribbon
Which indicates that you're not supposed to rub it.) (Satire I, vv. 142–46, 149–53)

There are several explicit references in this passage to the world of comic theater, including to Pierre Gringore's pro-Gallic *Le Jeu du Prince des Sotz et de Mère Sotte*, commissioned by Louis XII in 1512 to attack Pope Julius II.[72] As Jelle Koopmans has amply demonstrated, in the medieval theatrical tradition and elsewhere, there were many connections between fools and devils.[73] Connecting the stage character of the fool with the papacy is in many respects nothing new, yet the explicit representation of the pope dressed as a character out of a farce elicits laughter. Such an image recalls the sort of entertainments that one finds throughout the Middle Ages in such carnivalesque activities as the *messe des fous*, which took place around Christmas time and during which hierarchical roles of the priesthood were reversed with peasants dressed as priests, donkey ears were donned, facetious *sermons joyeux* in kitchen Latin were preached at the pulpit, and cross-dressing was a popular comic activity.[74] In this post-Reformation world, however, such representations of the world upside down are ideologically charged and rather than a temporary suspension of the status quo, Geneva pamphleteers are militating for the adoption of a new form of Christianity and arguing for the elimination of the papacy, thus radicalizing the reversal and increasing its mordancy.

The passage cited above denigrates and mocks the pope's holy vestments. For example, the reference to him/her wearing a "cornette," a piece of clothing already unfashionable at the time and comparable to today's academic hood, is particularly notable. A contemporary reader would have likely caught the reference to the *Farce de la cornette,* a salacious and bawdy play that mocks societal conventions and hierarchies by ridiculing an elderly man who presents himself as a patriarchal figurehead but who is in fact utterly inept.[75] Bèze represents the pope as an actor dressed in drag (normally it would be a male actor disguised as a female character, but here the transvestism goes in the opposite direction), grotesquely displaying "laide beauté" and donning the costume of the *sot* or fool. Again, the strategy is to replace one form of performance, liturgy, with another, comic theater, in which the pope appears as a salacious buffoon.

Crassly debasing the sacrosanct is the primary comic device throughout the *Satyres chrestiennes*. Catholic clerics are referred to as "vrais disciples de Pathelin" (true disciples of Pathelin), the most famous scoundrel in medieval comic theater.[76] The pope is repeatedly called "Mere Sotte" (Satire VII v. 10), the name of a well-known character in the *sottie* plays and that also evokes the traditional feminine metonymical designation of the Church as "Mere Eglise." Priests and monks throughout the pamphlet try to mask their gluttony with Lenten performances, and always, when something should be treated as sacred, these churchmen laugh. In the sixth satire, the setting is another papal banquet where, in ways meant to arouse the reader's scorn, priests continue to remind each other of the need to laugh. As one monk remarks, hypocritically critiquing Lent,

> Garde-nous de melancholies,
> Car trop mieux vaut rire et danser
> Que tousjours ainsi grimacer.
>
> (Let's avoid melancholy,
> Since it's much better to laugh and dance
> Than to always thus be frowning.) (vv. 371–73)

In response, everyone decides to laugh. In the following satire, priests talk about making their parishioners laugh, mocking their own kitchen Latin ("latins de cuisine" vv. 37–38). The pamphlet portrays all of the priests' laughter in purely negative terms, while generating another kind of laughter at the expense of these blundering fools and lascivious gluttons, the bitter and sardonic laughter whose aim is to destabilize and undermine the gravitas and authority of the Catholic hierarchy.

Invective dominates this pamphlet, but nothing is more extreme than its treatment of the Catholic Eucharist, which the failed Colloquy of Poissy the following year showed to be the fundamental irreconcilable difference between French Catholics and Huguenots. In the *Satyres chrestiennes*, the Catholic Lamb of God of the Mass (AGNUS) is turned into an anus.[77] More offensive still is an attack on the digestive aspects of the Eucharist, in response to a highly literal question that Thomas Aquinas had answered centuries before[78] but which Protestant polemicists bring up anew: If the communion wafer is literally the body of Christ, then what happens when you digest it? In the end, according to Catholic belief, do you not defecate the divine? As the pamphlet asks,

> O belle science
> Pour estre sauvé à son aise
> Mangeant son Dieu, ne luy desplaise!
> Mais en fin, docteur tres subtil,[79]
> Ce doux Dieu que deviendra-il?
> Il faut bien qu'il demeure au ventre,
> Ou sorte par ailleurs qu'il n'entre.
> Paradis doncques en effect
> Sera le ventre ou le retraict.

> (O beautiful wisdom
> In order to be saved at one's ease
> By eating his God, may it not offend him!
> But finally, great learned one,
> This sweet God, what becomes of Him?
> It must be either that He remains in your stomach,
> Or exits by some orifice other than the one He entered.
> Paradise is thus in effect
> Either your stomach or the toilet.) (Satire V, vv. 525–33)

Catholic heaven is thus a latrine and transubstantiation provides nothing more than an extreme case of indigestion. What sort of laughter does such scatological humor evoke? It is the aggressive guffaw of the zealots, the *risus sardonicus*. There is a telling line in the third satire that encapsulates this particular form of humor. Speaking in the context of carnival and carnivorous delicacies, describing how the priests slaughter the sheep ("agneaux" is a gruesome pun combining carnivorous gluttony with the slaughter of innocent congregants), there is the following wordplay: "Tost apres en font boucherie. / Yci faut que ma bouche rie" (Shortly after they butcher them. / Here my mouth must laugh) (vv. 102–3). The homophony between "boucherie" and "bouche rie" is a potent example of the *risus sardonicus*.

In the works of pamphleteers like Viret and Bèze, the generous humor of Rabelais's *Pantagruel* and *Gargantua* has disappeared, replaced by comedy in the service of militant partisanship and demagoguery.[80] Polemicists like Viret and Bèze sought to strike a precarious balance, one that worried Calvin, between acceptable and unacceptable forms of satire and humor. In this effort they seemed to recognize that the floodgates were being opened and that in the future Christianity itself would come under attack by writers using the same satirical strategies employed by these deeply committed believers.

5

Abbeys of Misrule on the Stage

Nul de nous n'en est estranger.
Ils ont faict en nostre pays
Se qu'il convient qu'ilz soyent haÿs:
Vela le poinct de nos leçons.
—*Le Maistre d'escolle, la mere et les troys escolliers*, vv. 100–103

In this chapter, the focus is on two of the most popular *sociétés joyeuses* in France: the Conards de Rouen and the Parisian Basoche. These confraternities made up of young men and with a reputation for mischief were dubbed Abbeys of Misrule by Natalie Zemon Davis.[1] Before looking at their theatrical productions, it is helpful to provide some context for each group.

For the Conards, it is important to understand, as best we can, how they fit into the city of Rouen, a city that was strongly affected by the Reformation. By several measures, Rouen could be considered France's second most important city after Paris. It was the administrative capital of Normandy, the seat of one of the largest archbishoprics in France, and a major center of manufacturing and trade.[2] At midcentury, its population was somewhere between 71,000 and 78,000. The next largest city, Lyon, had a population of 58,000 in 1550; other provincial cities ranged between 20,000 and 40,000. Strategically located on the Seine between Paris and the English Channel, it was France's busiest port in the sixteenth century. Rouen was where ships were offloaded and their cargo transferred to barges or wagons bound for Paris. As such, it was a cultural crossroads that attracted merchants and diplomats from England, the Netherlands, Spain, and elsewhere. With the city's climate of active exchange, Luther's writings were not long in arriving in Rouen, with the first evidence of Lutheran "contamination" discovered as early as 1524. By 1530, Martin Bucer referred to Normandy as "little Germany."[3]

Based on the records of Rouen's governing bodies, one can detect in the half century leading up to the Wars of Religion "a strong undercurrent of fear of popular violence."[4] While the growth of Protestantism in Rouen was strong, Protestants remained a minority. In Geneva's records one finds that the number of emigrants arriving from Rouen was higher than from any other French city. By 1560, there were at least 10,000 Protestants in Rouen, a number that reached as high as 16,500 by 1565, a substantial figure representing 15 to 20 percent of the city's population.[5] Beginning in the 1540s and most notably in the 1550s until the outbreak of war, Protestants made their presence known and created many disturbances throughout the city, in response to what they perceived as Catholic superstitions and idol worship. As Henry Heller notes, "Calvinists became increasingly bold in their attacks. In May, 1545, they desecrated some sixty-five images and statues in the cemetery of St. Maur. About the same time they attacked an image of the virgin which was the traditional focal point of ecclesiastical processions."[6] When the Cardinal de Bourbon (the man the Catholic League would later insist was the rightful heir to the throne after Henry III's death in 1589) made a rare appearance in Rouen in 1561 (he had been archbishop of the city since 1550), he was ridiculed with "a thousand insults." Someone had attached to his pulpit a broadsheet showing a flock of geese, the prize traditionally awarded to the king of liars during popular festivities.[7] With this increase of anti-Catholic activity in Rouen came a strong counterresponse. Rouen became notorious for its burning of heretics, and the city took several measures during this period to suppress heresy.

In this first section of this chapter, I would like to discuss a selection of *moralités* performed by the Conards, Rouen's notorious Abbey of Misrule. In trying to understand the composition and function of this group, Dylan Reid's "Carnival in Rouen" is particularly helpful. Reid highlights the fluid identity of the group: "The *Conards* have been described as youths, lawyers, and nobles; as standard-bearers of popular dissatisfaction, as tools of a wealthy urban oligarchy, and as incipient Protestants."[8] Like other similar societies, their primary responsibility was to organize carnival celebrations. Their golden age, when they appeared to be most active, was from around 1530 to 1560. Henry Heller asserts that by midcentury the Abbey had 2,400 to 2,500 members and was dominated by the sons of the city's elite.⁹ As Reid points out, one of the best records we have is *Les Triomphes de l'Abbaye des Conards*, which provides an elaborate description of their activities surrounding Mardi Gras in 1541. He offers the following description of their procession the Sunday before Lent, alleged to have had two thousand participants:

> It began with the Funeral of Commerce, who was carried on a black litter strewn with white tears, accompanied by children bearing candles and by his offers and servants, such as Credit and Hazard. The household and council of the Abbot followed, preparing the way for the Abbot himself, who rode surrounded by his cardinals. All were dressed in splendid costumes of red damask, with trains of green taffeta carried by children. The magnificent Abbot wore a miter encrusted with jewels, and rode a mule harnessed with gold trappings.¹⁰

There were elaborate costumes and masks, dancing, allegorical performances, *tableaux-vivants*, and people handing out satirical leaflets. Celebrations continued throughout Monday and Tuesday, with a banquet and a variety of performances. It is worth noting that the carnival procession began and ended with references to Rabelais: in the initial parade, someone carried a sign that said, "Alcofribas le disoit bien" (Alcofribas said it well), Alcofribas being the pseudonym used by Rabelais when he published *Pantagruel* and *Gargantua*; at the concluding banquet they had someone read from *Pantagruel*. As Reid points out, this indicates the sophistication of the group, as well as their penchant for satire,¹¹ and is interesting as further proof of the strong connection between Rabelais and carnival, as well as providing an example of his work being read aloud to a socially mixed audience in a carnival setting.¹² The Conards' elaborate carnival processions made such an impression that when Henri II visited Rouen in 1550, he specifically requested they participate in his royal entry. They paraded for him and performed the *Farce des veaulx*.¹³

One of the most debated issues surrounding the Conards and other Abbeys of Misrule is whether they were subversive or part of the establishment.¹⁴ Reid has argued that in the case of the Conards, this is a bit of a false dichotomy, and that they were, in fact, both—they were known for and even got in trouble for their satire and indecorous antics, but they were also an important part of the establishment in Rouen, what Reid classifies as the "middling class" of merchants, craftsmen, and artisans.¹⁵ For our purposes, it is worth noting that two key members of the Conards, Noël Cotton and Isaac Jehan, were reprimanded in 1542 for distributing scandalous pamphlets. Two decades later, they had become key leaders of the Huguenots in Rouen. Cotton was executed in 1562 for his leading role in the Protestant rebellion.[16] Other members of the Conards took the opposite side of the conflict. Heller, in suggesting that the Conards were pseudo-Protestants, points to evidence in some of the plays examined in this chapter of attacks made on the Church. Of the play *L'Église, Noblesse et Pauvreté qui font la lessive*, Heller asserts that it is "marked by a revulsion against the burning of heretics, a practice for which Rouen had become notorious."[17] As we will see, however, the Conards produced other plays whose satire is aimed directly at Protestants. Tracing their progress from a unified group to their eventual disbandment, Reid concludes, "This communality [of the Abbey of the Conards] would be shattered by religious divisions and economic changes later in the century, and the loss of this communality would be a decisive factor in the eventual demise of the Abbey itself at the beginning of the seventeenth century."[18] Benedict points out that by the eve of the outbreak of the first War of Religion, in part in reaction to Calvinist attacks on the Conards' antics and mummeries, the group showed itself to be stridently Catholic, much like the Basoche we will examine in the second half of this chapter.[19] In examining four morality plays performed by the Conards, one can begin to see signs of religious division, as the plays present a variety of satirical targets and religious views.

Between 1535 and 1545, the Conards performed in Rouen six morality plays found in the La Vallière manuscript, which dates from between 1564 and 1571.[20] This manuscript is primarily known as a valuable resource containing a number of farces and *sotties*. Until now, despite Jonathan Beck's helpful critical edition of the six *moralités* contained in the manuscript, little scholarly attention has been devoted to these plays, which is surprising given the impact they may have had. In Beck's introduction, he points out the dangers of such performances, citing a case in Libourne in 1555, in which actors were arrested and threatened with torture. In 1540, a group in Paris performing a morality play on the topic of the corruption of the church met a worse fate: according to a witness, five of them were thrown into the Seine and drowned.[21] Beck draws an important distinction between traditional *moralités*, where the purpose of the play is to celebrate a saint or in very general terms exalt virtue and condemn vice, and what Émile Picot originally referred to as *moralités polémiques*, such as the ones studied here, which are much more openly satirical and ideologically charged.[22]

These short polemical plays are fascinating for their heterogeneity in a city where Protestants made huge inroads in the 1540s and 1550s but where Catholic opposition remained strong. Beck quotes Imbart de la Tour, who observed, "dès le début de l'agitation luthérienne, la polémique monte sur les tréteaux" (from the start of the Lutheran agitation, polemics took to the stage).[23] Beck also makes the important point that "Prédicateurs (prêtres, moines surtout) et enseignants (professeurs, régents, maitres d'école, instituteurs) haranguant les foules pour garder ou gagner des partisans atteignent facilement *en un jour* une audience plus vaste que ne le font tous les livres imprimés à Paris en un an (au nombre exact de 88 en 1501, de 332 en 1549)" (Preachers (priests, monks especially) and teachers (professors, regents, schoolmasters, teachers) exhorting the crowds to keep or win over partisans easily reach in one day a larger audience than the books published in Paris do in a year (to be exact, from 88 in 1501, to 332 in 1549)).[24] These and other plays examined in this book were extremely effective at reaching a more popular audience, most importantly those who could not read. The plays here show various ways derisive humor could be used in a populist context to generate religious anger.

Of the six *moralités* in the La Vallière manuscript, I will focus on four, two anti-Catholic and two virulently anti-Protestant. Such heterodoxy suggests the possibility of more than one group of Conards performing in Rouen or at least argues for a more nuanced view of this famous *société joyeuse*.[25] It is clear the group was becoming more religiously diverse and was in some ways a microcosm of Rouen itself during this time of radical change.

All of these plays are very short, around 200 to 300 lines. The first one to discuss, referred to earlier, is *L'Église, Noblesse et Povreté qui font la lessive* (The Church, Nobility and Poverty Who Do the Laundry). The 1541 procession of the Conards included a mimed adaptation of the play.[26] This play is anticlerical and has clearly evangelical, even Protestant leanings. The populist theme of the Third Estate against the First and Second dominates the dialogue. The Church, a character, is arrogant, worldly, and powerful and begins by singing a bawdy song and then bragging about her corruption. Next comes Nobility, who also boasts about her ability to do whatever she wants with impunity. Finally, Poverty speaks, lamenting her frail, powerless state.[27] At one point, after the others heap scorn on her, Poverty says she can no longer keep quiet and sarcastically mocks the Church's abuses and hypocrisy. The play's humor is primarily scatological, with multiple jokes about the malodorous laundry that Nobility and the Church make Poverty wash, in particular the Church's soiled clothes.

The action features a *bâton*, the stick that is the ubiquitous weapon of farce, and Nobility and the Church use it cruelly. In a refrain repeated four times, Poverty complains: "Noblesse bat sans estre bastue d'ame" (Nobility beats others without being beaten by anyone). Poverty of course is not allowed to retaliate: "Sy je m'en venge, en prison—lieu infame— / Il me fera soubdainnement loger" (If I get revenge, in prison—horrid place— / He will swiftly place me).[28] At the conclusion, Nobility and the Church beat Poverty after she complains about having to do their laundry without compensation. She ends her lament with a xenophobic, populist-inspired question: "Suys je payenne ou Sarasine?" (Am I a pagan or a Saracen?)[29] Her outrage is clear; a good Christian woman, she is treated worse than a godless foreigner. Throughout this play, the physical comedy and hijinks of farce are recast in a religiously charged context, where the satire is more acerbic and the laughter evoked is bitter and resentful. The play mixes this laughter with harsh satire and physical violence, in a germane example of the *risus sardonicus*.

Our next play is also of reformist inspiration, *Le Ministre de L'Église, Noblesse, le Laboureur et le Commun* (The Minister of the Church, Nobility, the Plowman and Everyman). Again the three estates are personified, with the Plowman and Everyman together representing the poor, rural and urban. At the beginning, the Minister and Nobility decide the three of them should play "Capifol," a medieval game comparable to "blind man's bluff," in which the blindfolded person is hit and must guess his assailant. Nobility prepares straws to draw; Everyman picks the long one and is beaten. Each time he correctly guesses his attacker, the Minister and Nobility tell him he is wrong. As the blows increase in severity, so does Everyman's critique of the Church and the nobility. Finally, Everyman's frustration reaches the breaking point and he explodes:

> C'est bien babillé!
> Le povre Commun est taillé,
> Bastu, robé, et mutillé,
> Pillé, tribouillé, barbouillé;
> Et s'y se plainct de tel effort,
> On luy dira que c'est à tort!
>
> (Such babbling!

Poor Everyman is cut up,
Beaten, robbed, and mutilated,
Plundered, roughed up, smeared;
And if he complains about this attack,
He is told that he is wrong.)[30]

Then the Plowman is beaten. Here the satire becomes more blatantly partisan. When the Minister asks him about whom he is complaining, he replies,

Des faulx prelas,
Et des faulx prescheurs,
Qui de mal dire sont amateurs,
Et preschent par leurs traditions
De faulces expositions.

(False prelates,
And false preachers,
Who are very good at speaking ill,
And preach by their traditions
False interpretations.)[31]

This reference to "faulx prescheurs" and "faulces expositions" is a clear attack on the Catholic clergy and their "traditions." Near the end of the play, the Plowman and Everyman strike a more stoical note. The Plowman says to his friend, "Commun, suyvons Monsieur Sainct Pol: / Prenons confort en desplaisir" (Everyman, let us follow sir Saint Paul / Let us take comfort in affliction).[32] Both of these passages suggest Protestant influence, especially the reference to Saint Paul, which likely alludes to the start of Paul's second letter to the Corinthians.[33]

The play ends abruptly on a happy note, with the characters laughing, singing, and inviting the audience to play this merry game. The foregoing violence, with the powerful beating the powerless into submission, certainly undermines this mirthful conclusion. It is hard not to read the laughter here as rueful and resentful. As the Plowman bitterly complains near the end of the play, "Au foyble on veoyt porter le fort" (We see the weak carry the strong).[34] What stands out in this carnivalesque play, and what sets it apart from many similar ones, is a reversal of the dynamic typical of such comic plays. Whereas usually a character of higher social standing is humiliated by a character of lower status, here those of lower social status are blatantly attacked by those in power. There is laughter and merriment here, but there is an overarching sardonic edge to the humor. Although at the end the characters express the same sort of resigned acceptance one finds at the end of many of these comic plays, what has just transpired onstage is a scathing condemnation of the excesses of the first two estates, with particular venom aimed at the priestly class. The play ends more positively because the lower figures have found their own voices and openly express disillusionment with their situation. This is certainly more radical (and more dangerous) than what one typically finds in traditional comic plays.

The penultimate *moralité* is *Hérésie, frère Simonie, Force, Scandale, Procès et l'Église* (Heresy, Friar Simony, Force, Scandal, Lawsuit, and the Church). This is an anti-Protestant play that also argues for reform within the Church. At the beginning, five different characters want to get into the Church, but they do not have the right key to open the door. (Heresy has an "iron key from Germany"; Simony has a "silver key," etc.) The most obvious allegory here is that Lutherans, represented by Heresy, are not allowed to enter because they lack the proper key or authority. When the Church enters, she offers a fairly long lament, with a refrain repeated four times: "L'Eglise n'a plus de support" (The Church no longer has any support). She complains about how the other characters harm her, and as they try to enter, she rebuffs them. At a certain point her language grows more violent, such as when she is going over the different types of keys offered, and concludes by naming her favorite key: "Clef d'un grenyer plain de fagos / Pour les rediger tous en pouldre!" (The key from a loft filled with bundles of wood / To reduce them all to powder!)"[35]

Hérésie, frère Simonie, Force, Scandale, Procès et l'Église contains numerous obscene puns, as well as a fair amount of violent discourse. There are lewd jokes about how Friar Simony wants to enter from behind. Force is a character reminiscent of the braggart, cowardly soldier (*soldat fanfaron*) in farce,[36] and instead of a key he has a sword. When the Church draws her own sword, he panics (as do the others), creating the most comic scene of the play. While the classic cowardly soldier sketch is funny, here the comic effect is tempered by the menace of real violence at the end of the play. Laughter is abruptly silenced as the Church, directly addressing the audience, says that for now she will be merciful but that people need to get in line or there will be harsh consequences: "Vous en avés bonne avertance" (You have been warned).[37] This is yet another example of how a fairly anodyne form of popular entertainment is recast in a much more acerbic context, where the stakes are higher and the danger is real. There is certainly nothing to laugh about in the play's conclusion, with its ominous warning to those who do not bend to the Church's will.

The final morality play to discuss in this chapter, *Le Maistre d'escolle, la mere et les troys escolliers* (The Schoolmaster, the Mother, and the Three Students), provides the strongest illustration in this group of *moralités polémiques* of humor and satire that provoke a sardonic laugh. While it is labeled a *farce joyeuse* in the manuscript, there is little joy to be found here. As Beck argues in the introduction to this play, theater is not merely a reflection of society; it can also militate for change and incite people to do things.[38] In this case, the play encourages people to kill Protestants. The action begins with a mother coming to a school to ask the teacher where the students are and what they are learning. First the teacher assures her, "Car bonne doctrine et science / A mes escolliers veulx montrer" (Because good doctrine and learning / To my students I want to show). When she asks again where the students are, the Magister's response suggests violence: "Je les ay envoyés sur les champs / Coriger un tas de meschans" (I sent them into the fields / To correct the behavior of a bunch of miscreants).[39]

Shortly after, the students return, having roughed up some heretics. They all use laughably bad Latin, reminiscent of other farces, especially *Maître Mimin étudiant*, and one of them offers a crude explanation of why they hate heretics:

> Nul de nous n'en est estranger.
> Ils ont faict en nostre pays
> Se qu'il convient qu'ilz soyent haÿs:
> Vela le poinct de nos leçons.
>
> (None of us is unaware.
> What they have done in our country
> Which is why it is appropriate that they be hated:
> That is the point of our lessons.)[40]

This xenophobic justification, labeling Protestants as foreigners who have come to destroy the kingdom, is typical of Catholic polemics during this time. The students also list the offenses of Protestants, who refuse to respect Lent or worship saints. The students make indelicate puns that accuse Protestants of sexual perversion, using terms like "abitavit" (v. 142) ("habite à vit," meaning they "live on dicks") and "habitaculum" (v. 145) ("habite au cul," meaning they "live on ass"). This wordplay is both vulgar and funny, but the surrounding discourse is too sententious to allow the audience to laugh for long. If Protestants are ridiculed, it is only so they will be hated more. At the conclusion of *Le Maistre d'escolle*, the teacher is asked what they should do. His response is chillingly simple: "Qu'on les brulle, sans efigie!" (Let us burn them; and not in effigy!)[41] After this brutal ending, they sing a song. The only laughter possible in this play is the *risus sardonicus*, cruel laughter motivated by partisan hatred.

The plays performed by the Conards show how forms of popular entertainment could be readily adapted for religious and ideological aims. In a presage of future violence, these polemical morality plays exhibit many of the underlying tensions of the competing beliefs in Rouen and elsewhere in France. They also reveal the heterodoxy of a city that remained strongly Catholic yet contained a sizable Protestant minority. While pamphlets could reach a far-flung readership, polemical plays with audiences numbering in the hundreds could produce powerful and immediate effects, quickly stirring emotions and potentially serving as a call to arms.

We end this chapter with a look at a play performed in 1564 (a year after the end of the first War of Religion) by the Basoche, a famed Parisian legal society with a history of performances going back at least to the early fifteenth century. This polemical morality play, *Moralité de Mars et Justice*, came at a time in France when tremendous changes were occurring in the types of plays being performed and even their venues. Humanist-inspired plays that drew heavily on the classical genres of tragedy and comedy were supplanting genres such as farce, *sottie*, and *moralité*. Five-act comedies were replacing short comic plays, and professional Italian acting troupes were arriving in France. Two symbolic events are often referred to in explaining the demise of medieval theater: the Paris Parlement's decree banning the performance of *mystères* in 1548[42] and, in 1549, the publication of Du Bellay's *La Deffence, et illustration de la langue françoyse*, in which he calls on French playwrights to restore the "ancienne dignité" of classical comedy and tragedy, whose position had been usurped by "Farces et Moralitez."[43] By 1564, there were fewer examples of religious polemic in comic plays, as tragedy was becoming the primary vehicle for such material. Notably, one finds almost no references to France's religious conflict in either the comedies or the tragedies produced by members of the Pléiade, such as Ronsard's cohorts Jodelle and Grévin. Plays like those that we have examined were disappearing, and in this final one, while one finds vituperative polemics, the humor is more melancholy than mordant.

Like the Conards, the members of the Basoche were primarily younger, single men, who at times got themselves in trouble for bad behavior, but the Basoche had a more clearly defined membership, as it was a legal society. As Stephanie Lysyk explains, "The Basoche [was] designed to ease the law clerk's entrance into legal practice and to provide an interim set of social affiliations for young men positioned between the successive power structures of the family and the profession."[44] Many cities in France had Basoche societies, but the Parisian was the oldest and best known. Even within Paris, there were multiple Basoche groups, but the most important was the Basoche du Parlement.[45] They regularly performed farces and other theatrical pieces, as well as *causes grasses*, "a type of mock trial in which all the weight of standard courtroom procedure and jurisprudence was brought to bear upon a frivolous and often risqué complaint."[46] They had a reputation for hijinks and shenanigans, but they were also very much a part of the establishment and regularly received financial support from the Parisian Parlement for their various activities. The Basoche's performances were typically held in the *grand'salle* of the Palais, the same place where legal cases were heard,[47] and were celebrated in the writings of authors such as Rabelais and Marot for their joyful exuberance.

While the Basoche's performances often caused problems (much of what we know about these is based on legal records), the society was typically required to submit the text of a play to the Parlement two weeks before a performance, and they were prohibited from making fun of the Crown or public figures, a prohibition that would later include religion.[48] These merry pranksters were also enforcers of the status quo, a position that is made clear in *Mars et Justice*. In the very Catholic capital city of Paris, France's most famous performers took to the stage to decry the current state of affairs, placing the blame squarely on the Protestant menace. *Mars et Justice* follows the typical conventions of a polemical morality play, with allegorical figures bemoaning the present situation, although Jean-Claude Aubailly and Bruno Roy maintain that the play is instead much more like a *sottie* and compare it to the *Sottie pour le cry de la Basoche* (1548).[49] Regardless, what is important for this study is that the views expressed are militantly Catholic, lamenting the harm done to the city and the country and placing the blame on French Protestants and their nefarious foreign allies.

Mars et Justice begins with Mars, the god of war, talking about how he loves conflict and bloodshed. He is quickly joined by the Minister, a Protestant seeking his help. The Minister complains that he is not able to practice his religion and that he and his coreligionists are threatened by both water (drowning) and fire (burning at the stake) (v. 25). Mars, acting the role of friend and confidant, tells the Minister, "Sans la guerre, prescher tes freres ne pourront" (Without war, your brothers will not be able to preach).[50] From the start, the play makes a direct connection between Calvinist proselytizing and armed conflict. The Minister is willing to harm the kingdom to protect his heretical beliefs and is avaricious as well. In a scene intended to offer a Catholic audience a partisan explanation of the motives behind Protestant vandalism and iconoclasm during the first War of Religion, Mars urges the Minister to turn to violence so he can enrich himself by pillaging churches.

Unsurprisingly, at this juncture a third character, the Merchant, joins the alliance. Given that the first pamphlet examined in this book was Antoine Marcourt's *Livre des marchans*, there is a certain symmetry to be found in this last play, where Marcourt's Protestant polemics are reversed and now it is the Calvinists who are rapacious. The two warring camps are now set, with Mars, the Minister, and the Merchant on one side and, on the other, Rouge Affiné (a partner of the Basoche), Bec Affillé (Sharpened Beak), and Decliquetout (Blabs Everything) all aligned with Justice. However, the first alliance is unstable and rife with potential treachery—the Merchant is very uncomfortable working with a heretic, but the Minister is financing the war from which he profits. Such is the distrustfulness and disingenuousness of this alliance that at one point the Merchant tells Mars to kill the Minister. The conflict itself is of short duration, and after Mars wreaks havoc, the Minister pays him off. The play ascribes the basest motivations to the Protestants, who, far from fighting to defend their beliefs, are shown to be treacherous, duplicitous, and greedy.

At this point in *Mars et Justice*, there is an interlude of approximately a hundred verses, in which the remaining characters ask one another what they have been doing. Rouge Affiné notes it has been two years since they have been able to stage a play, likely a result of the disruptions of war.[51] Rouge Affiné asks about the Prince des Sotz, the leader of the Enfants sans souci, and who had likely gotten in trouble with Parlement. Also during this interlude there are references to various collegians, groups that also produced many plays in Paris and were often at odds with the Basoche, as comments in this section make clear. Collegians were more likely to have Reformist sympathies, while the Basoche remained fiercely Catholic. At one point, Rouge Affiné makes a joke at the expense of the collegians, asking, "Mais que sont devenuz les veaul[x] / De Beauvais?" (But what has happened to the dimwits of Beauvais?)[52] The Collège de Beauvais was one of the colleges of the University of Paris where collegians performed farces and other plays.

At the end of this interlude, an important change occurs: the verse switches from lofty alexandrines to lowly octosyllabic verse, the traditional meter of farce.[53] The action of the play has ended, and yet *Mars et Justice* will continue for another three hundred lines. As Aubailly and Roy note, this second part "semble avoir été surajoutée pour atténuer par un rire franc la virulence partisane du début de la pièce" (seems to have been added to the play to lessen through a hearty laugh the partisan virulence of the play's beginning).[54] This further confirms the play's unusual hybrid nature. The last section of *Mars et Justice* is a stream of reminiscences by the characters, recalling a host of scabrous stories, primarily about marital infidelity, the stuff of typical farces or *causes grasses*, filled with deceptive wives, cuckolded husbands, and scheming lovers. It even ends like a typical farce, with Rouge Affiné telling the others, "Allons disner car il est temps. / Que nous prenions noz passetemps" (Let's go eat because it's time / For us to enjoy ourselves).[55] This is a strange addition to this sententious play, but it recalls the original reputation of the Basoche. It is odd, after all, for a group long known for its irreverent antics and playful spirit to stage a censorious *moralité polémique*.[56] This appendage at the end of the performance seems a wistful reminder of the former spirit of the Basoche, now lost under the rubble of war. At the end of *Mars et Justice*, there is laughter, but it is ruefully nostalgic and detached, recalling rather than acting out such mirthful misbehavior. With opposing religious forces in France leading the country to all-out civil war, the once lighthearted and mischievous Basoche created a work that contains very little humor and is instead dominated by ideological stridency. In certain respects, *Mars et Justice* shows how laughter has been cordoned off, even if, in the last section, the performers turn to the past, mournfully evoking a time when laughter was unrestrained and not so dangerous.

6
Ronsard the Pamphleteer

> Vivent sans chastiment, et à les oüyr dire,
> C'est Dieu qui les conduist, et ne s'en font que rire.
> —Ronsard, *Continuation du Discours*

This book's symbolic starting point is the notorious Affaire des placards of 1534; its end point is the most famous Catholic polemical attack against Calvinists, the famed poet Pierre de Ronsard's *Discours des miseres de ce temps*, a series of pamphlets produced between 1562 and 1563 that elicited a strong response from his Genevan adversaries. Before turning to these pamphlets, it is helpful to provide a larger context, identifying key events in Paris in the period leading up to the first War of Religion, which broke out in April 1562, shortly before Ronsard published his first polemical tract, *Discours des miseres de ce temps*.[1] To do so is to recount historical events that have been examined, described, and debated countless times. While there are many sources to turn to, one of the most helpful is Barbara Diefendorf's seminal work on Paris during this time, *Beneath the Cross*. Her chapter "The Intensification of Religious Hatreds, 1557–1562" is particularly useful in providing us with a sense of the increasing Catholic hostility toward Protestants.

After the death of the boy-king François II in 1560, his mother, Catherine de Medici, took a more tolerant view of Protestants and actively sought to curb persecution of them. During François II's brief reign, the ultra-Catholic Guise brothers had exerted enormous power, in part because the king was married to their niece, Mary Stuart. Ronsard was a strong supporter of the Guises, writing several poems praising them. With François II's death and the establishment of Catherine's regency (Charles IX was only ten when his brother died), Catherine asserted her independence from the Guises, even allowing Protestants to preach at court. There were even rumors that Charles IX might convert, which might have been part of the inspiration behind Ronsard's publication of *Institution pour l'Adolescence du Roy* in 1562, a work that follows the Erasmian tradition of providing humanist-inspired advice to the young king but that also contains a reference to the dangers of Calvinism.[2]

In Paris, religious tensions were getting progressively worse, with several events that presaged the eventual St. Bartholomew's Day Massacre. During this time, Paris was filled with fear and suspicion, and as Barbara Diefendorf notes, "The potential for disaster is evident when we realize that, while Parisian Huguenots were being taught to suffer persecution as proof of their faith, Parisian Catholics were being urged to be avengers in the name of an angry God."[3] The first large-scale religious riot occurred on 4 September 1557, the so-called Affair of the rue Saint-Jacques. Student priests in the Collège du Plessis on the rue Saint-Jacques had spotted a group of three or four hundred Calvinists worshipping at a private residence across the street, and a large, angry crowd gathered. Many Protestants made their escape (Calvinist noblemen often carried weapons), but the mob attacked others, and when city officers arrived they arrested 130 Protestants, mostly women and children.[4] This event was to be followed by many similar ones, small and large, in subsequent years.

In 1561, during the first year of Catherine de Medici's regency, a number of royal decrees were issued on toleration, all of them deeply resented by Parisian Catholics. At the same time, Calvinists were getting more assertive, requesting permission from the Crown to build their own churches. In September 1561 the Colloquy of Poissy began, arranged by Catherine de Medici in hopes of finding common ground between Catholics and Protestants. After six weeks of increasingly futile discussions, it was brought to an end. Ronsard had been in attendance and heard his Calvinist rival Théodore de Bèze speak. Meanwhile, Protestant proselytizing in the capital was increasing, much to the consternation of the vast majority of the city's Catholic residents. Catherine was even providing Protestants with protection for their meetings. Still, violence was increasingly common in Paris. As Diefendorf details,

> On 12 October, angry Catholics closed the city gates against the large number of people that had gone out to hear Calvinist preachers in the

northeastern suburbs. Several persons were grievously injured as the Calvinists attempted to fight their way back into the city. A week later, the king sent orders that the Parisians were to turn in their arms at the Hôtel de Ville. Here was another blow to the Catholic population: Calvinist noblemen were seen attending the assemblies of the new religion in arms; their services were guarded by officers of the watch; and yet the people of Paris, who prided themselves on their political and religious loyalties, were to be denied the right to self-defense.[5]

This situation only heightened Parisian Catholics' paranoia and fear. In December 1561, Huguenots vandalized the Église Saint-Médard in Paris, eliciting a harsh reaction from the populace, stirred up by the increasingly polemical attacks of Catholic preachers.

On 17 January 1562, the Crown issued the Edict of Saint-Germain, or Edict of January, calling for limited tolerance of Huguenots. Catholic reaction in Paris was strong, and many registered protests. Although the Edict forbade Protestants from worshipping inside the city's walls, it was unacceptable to Parisian Catholics. The beginning of March brought the Massacre of Vassy, when the duc de Guise and his troops slaughtered dozens of Protestant worshippers. When Guise arrived in Paris on 16 March, he was welcomed as a hero. He deliberately entered through the Porte Saint-Denis, traditionally used for royal entries, to give an impression of power and authority. And, indeed, he was greeted royally and met by an impressive entourage of nobles, city officers, and bourgeois. The crowds that lined the streets to watch shouted their joy—and their hatred of the Huguenots.[6]

Guise was accompanied by 1,500 armed soldiers and immediately ran into the prince de Condé and Théodore de Bèze, who were coming back from a sermon with five hundred cavalrymen. In the following days, multiple skirmishes occurred between soldiers loyal to Guise and those loyal to Condé, and shots were fired. There was the very real possibility of Catholics and Protestants massacring each other.

On 20 March, a bloody riot erupted when Catholics attempted to disinter a corpse that had been buried with Calvinist rites the night before at the Cemetery of the Innocents. Parisian Protestants were increasingly convinced they would meet the same fate as the victims at Vassy, and many started to arm themselves. During Easter week, which began on 22 March, further clashes occurred. Finally, the city's new governor, the cardinal de Bourbon, convinced both Guise and Condé to leave the capital; Condé and his troops left on the twenty-third, and Guise left the following day. On 6 April, the king came back to the city and issued a new declaration, exempting Paris and its suburbs from the Edict of January. As Diefendorf concludes,

> This special exception, which was repeated in every edict of toleration or pacification down to the Edict of Nantes, was prompted by the protests of the city's civil and religious authorities. More important, it was forced upon the king by the unruliness of the Parisian populace. A sign of the failure of the politics of moderation, it represents a clear victory for the Parisians in their struggle against the new religion.[7]

Condé met up with Coligny in Orléans, and by April, the first War of Religion had begun. While Paris did not suffer physically during this war, there were psychological effects on Parisian Catholics, whose fear and suspicions toward Calvinists greatly increased during the conflict.

Soon Catholics would have an unexpected champion in the war of words that paralleled the armed conflict. In May or June 1562, Pierre de Ronsard, the famed lyric poet and leader of the Pléiade, did something wholly unexpected—he wrote a pamphlet, *Discours des miseres de ce temps*, assuming a new persona and addressing an audience in certain respects quite different than the one that listened to and read his poetry. This work would be followed the same year by the *Continuation du Discours des miseres de ce temps*, presenting a symmetry with his earlier *Amours de Cassandre* and *Continuation des amours de Cassandre*. At the beginning of the following year, he published his *Remonstrance au peuple de France*, and then, clearly upset by the Protestant response to his pamphlets, he published a *Response de P. de Ronsard Gentilhomme Vandomois, aux injures et calomnies, de je ne sçay quels Predicans, et Ministres de Geneve, Sur son Discours et Continuation des Miseres de ce Temps*. As Malcolm Smith has observed, these poetic tracts had a greater influence than any of the other works of Renaissance France's famed poet.[8]

Until that point in his career, Ronsard's poetry had been almost entirely lyrical, secular, and profane—filled with pagan mythological references and epicurean themes and devoid of Christian references. Yet in the *Discours des miseres de ce temps*, the poet refashioned himself as an arch-Catholic defender of the faith. Ronsard entered an arena of literary production that had been growing both in the number of works circulated and in polemical intensity during the previous few decades. Ronsard's suddenly prominent role in the propaganda war of pamphleteers, the *lutte des libelles*, was the sixteenth-century equivalent of a movie star or a pop musician becoming a political activist, with similar results. Many Catholics were excited to have someone so famous take up their cause; Protestants mocked the hypocrisy of an irreligious and dissolute court poet taking up a moral cause.

Of this series of pamphlets, Malcolm Smith comments that "la doctrine des réformés est réduite, parfois, en slogans, les chefs de la Réforme apparaissent en portraits satiriques et un humour génial se laisse apercevoir même dans la polémique la plus brûlante" (Protestant doctrine is reduced, at times, to slogans, the leaders of the Reformation appear in satirical portraits, and brilliant humor is on display even in the most scorching polemics).[9] He later observes, "Dans les *Discours*, Ronsard distille un ton de conviction, une atmosphère de sympathie et de collusion avec son lecteur, un humour attrayant" (Ronsard infuses into the *Discours* a tone of conviction, an atmosphere of collusion with his reader, and seductive humor).[10] While much has been written about the polemics and the religious and political views in the *Discours*, their humor has received scant attention.[11] Unsurprisingly, the type of humor that dominates both in Ronsard's *Discours* and in a Calvinist response I will also examine is sardonic satire.

Before addressing Ronsard's series of polemical pamphlets, it is helpful to step back a few years to 1559, when he published his *Second livre des meslanges* after the death of Henry II.[12] At the end of this work, he engages in a dialogue with a fellow poet, Louis des Masures, who had converted to Protestantism. In this "Discours de Louis des Masures Tounisien à Pierre de Ronsard," Des Masures laments his exile, recalling better times in the court of François I and blaming Envy: "Son regard de travers ne reçoit aucun ris, / Sinon de voir mal heur, ou quelques gens marris" (Her twisted look receives no laughter, / Except to see misery or aggrieved people).[13] Here we find a foreshadowing of the invective that will follow, where laughter comes only at the expense of others. We have already seen examples of schadenfreude in polemical exchanges between Artus Désiré and Geneva. In this chapter, more than anywhere else in this book, we will find powerful examples of it, providing another dimension to the sardonic laugh. As we have seen throughout, Freud's notion of tendentious humor that comes at the expense of an absent other (or others) features prominently in Catholic and Protestant polemics. In the case of Ronsard, beginning with the *Discours de Louis des Masures* and reaching its apex in the back-and-forth between the poet and his Genevan adversaries, this tendentiousness becomes at times highly personal, adding an element of schadenfreude to the sardonic laugh.[14]

The next year saw the publication of Ronsard's *Œuvres* (1560), which included two elegies at the end, the *Elegie à Guillaume des Autels* and the *Elegie à Des Masures*. In both, Ronsard decries the increasing dissemination of polemical pamphlets. His *Œuvres* were published right after the Amboise conspiracy, when a group of Protestants attempted to kidnap the young king, François II. People in France blamed this botched conspiracy on Jean Calvin and Théodore de Bèze, who until then had counseled Protestants in France to submit to persecution.[15] From the beginning, Ronsard lays the groundwork to justify his future participation in the *lutte des libelles*. As he asserts in the beginning of his *Elegie à Guillaume des Autels*:

> Car il fault desormais deffendre noz maisons,
> Non par le fer trenchant mais par vives raisons,
> Et courageusement noz ennemis abbatre
> Par les mesmes bastons dont ils nous veullent battre.
> Ainsi l'ennemy par livres a seduict
> Le peuple devoyé qui faucement le suit,
> Il fault en disputant par livres le confondre,
> Par livres l'assaillir, par livres luy respondre,
> Sans monstrer au besoing noz courages failliz,
> Mais plus fort resister plus serons assailliz.

> (For we must henceforth defend our homes,
> Not by sharp-edged iron but by lively arguments,
> And courageously defeat our enemies
> With the same sticks with which they want to beat us.
> So it is that using books the enemy has seduced
> The people led astray and who falsely follow the enemy,
> We must attack with books to confound our enemy,
> With books assault him, with books respond to him,
> Without showing if needed our strength broken,
> But resist more strongly the more we are attacked.)[16]

Ronsard offers here a strong justification for the much lower and direct style of the pamphleteers, a remarkable shift for a celebrated court poet who built his reputation on humanist erudition and recondite paraphrasis. (One recalls that in 1553, the year after the publication of his *Amours de Cassandre*, Ronsard produced a second edition with commentaries by his friend Marc-Antoine Muret to explain the numerous classical references.)

He both disparages Protestant pamphlets and recognizes their efficacy. As others have noted, Ronsard was struggling to adopt a poetics with the kind of transparency he previously derided in poets such as Marot.[17] The poet who had fashioned himself as a lyrical prophet whose poems were inspired by divine furor was now moving toward the direct and simple style proven so effective by his Protestant foes. Ronsard's tone here is alarmist, providing the justification that this textual onslaught must be met on its own terms and defeated. It is because of this danger and the damage it has already caused that Ronsard will take up verbal arms and, as he will phrase it a couple of years later, use his "plume de fer sur un papier d'acier" (iron pen on steel paper).[18]

At the end of the *Elegie à Guillaume des Autels*, Ronsard turns to a personified Mother France in a nativist xenophobic discourse that will feature prominently in his pamphlets:

> France, de ton Malheur tu es cause en partie,
> Je t'en ay par mes vers mille fois advertye,
> Tu es marastre aux tiens, et mere aux estrangers,
> Qui se mocquent de toy quand tu es aux dangers:
> Car la plus grande part des estrangers obtiennent
> Les biens qui à tes fils justement appartiennent.

> (France, for your Misfortune you are in part to blame,
> I have through my lyrics warned you a thousand times,
> You are a cruel mother to your own children, and a mother to foreigners,
> Who mock you when you are in danger:
> For the majority of foreigners receive
> The goods which rightly belong to your sons.)

He continues his lament:

> Tu te mocques aussi des profetes que Dieu
> Choisit en tes enfans, et les fait au meillieu
> De ton sein apparoistre, à fin de te predire
> Ton malheur advenir, mais tu n'en fais que rire.

> (You also mock the prophets that God
> Has chosen among your children, and causes them in the middle
> Of your breast to appear, in order to prophesy
> Your coming misfortune, but all you do is laugh.)[19]

Here he presents laughter as tendentious and scornful, as a kingdom that accommodates foreign heretics mocks and laughs at its own people. Ronsard is also adopting the rhetorical stance favored by Catholic polemicists such as Artus Désiré, insisting that Protestantism is a foreign contagion not to be tolerated in the kingdom. Ronsard laments that France is neglecting her own in favor of foreigners.

In his *Elegie à Loïs des Masures*, Ronsard presents a mocking portrayal of Luther, explaining where "the Calvinist cult" ("la secte Calvine") takes its inspiration:

… d'où seroit animé
Un poussif Alemant, dans un poesle enfermé,
A bien interpreter les sainctes scriptures,
Entre les gobelets, les vins et les injures?

(… From where would be inspired
A torpid German, in a stove-heated room,
To correctly interpret the Scriptures,
Among the goblets, wine, and insults?)[20]

Here Ronsard is playing on national stereotypes: Germans are not to be trusted because they are drunkards. He sarcastically invites his Catholic audience to laugh at the Reformation's founder, a boozer so vile that when not drinking, he is trading insults with others. (Note the assonance of "vins" and "injures.") Much as Protestant invective sought to debase practices and offices sacred to Catholics, here Ronsard reduces Luther, the founder of a religious movement, to a comical caricature.

Two years later, Ronsard fully developed attacks of the kind prefigured in these elegies when he published the *Discours des miseres de ce temps*, dedicated to the queen mother, Catherine de Medici. Conrad Badius's *Comedie du pape malade* (see chapter 3) had mocked an assortment of Catholic pamphleteers with allegorical names. Without a doubt, Ronsard's pamphlets, if published earlier, would have earned him a central role in that play. Based on the initial Protestant reaction to Ronsard's attacks, one can imagine various allegorical names used to describe the Vendômois—le Glorieux, l'Athée, le Dissolu, or perhaps simply le Prêtre, a sobriquet Calvinists did indeed use against Ronsard, mocking the pious pretentions of this profane poet.

Gustave Cohen described these four pamphlets as sections of a "retable satirique sculpté pour l'autel de Catherine [de Médicis] et des Guises" (sa-

tirical altarpiece sculpted for Catherine de Medici's and the Guises' altar).[21]
There are several comical and satirical aspects to consider. Ronsard's initial *Discours* draws upon the Juvenalian satirical tradition and is a jeremiad lamenting the discord brought about by foreign Protestants. He begins with an extended metaphor, describing France as a ship at sea needing guidance, as does the young Charles IX. Ronsard implores the queen mother to ensure that the young prince be devout and maintain the faith of his ancestors rather than change to a foreign one (vv. 35–40). He implores the queen:

> La France à jointes mains vous en prie et reprie,
> Las! Qui sera bien tost et proye et moquerie
> Des princes estrangers, s'il ne vous plaist en bref
> Par votre autorité appaiser ce mechef.
>
> (With hands clasped France begs you and begs you again,
> Alas! France who soon will be both the prey and object of mockery
> Of foreign princes, if it does not please you in short
> By your authority to bring an end to this harm.)[22]

Catherine de Medici may be the official recipient of Ronsard's *Discours*, but the French people are clearly his intended audience, and here he plays on fears of foreigners, suggesting that if the queen does nothing to stop the spread of heresy, foreign leaders will make a mockery of France (recalling his earlier concerns about foreign pamphleteers mocking the Catholic faith). He overlooks the fact that leaders such as Calvin, Viret, and Bèze were all French. Ronsard will take care of these menacing foreign polemicists through his writing, but he calls on royal authority to do the more serious work of extirpating heretics from France. The pamphlet ends on a plaintive Juvenalian note—authority is lost, everything is now allowed, and the world is upside down, the kingdom led astray by the error of a foreigner ("l'erreur d'un estranger"), namely Luther (see vv. 175–90).

Composed in either October or November 1562, Ronsard's second pamphlet, the *Continuation du Discours des miseres de ce temps*, is much more mordant and sardonic. He begins with this memorable appeal to the queen:

> Madame, je serois ou du plomb ou du bois,
> Si moy, que la nature a fait naistre François,
> Aux siecles advenir je ne contois la peine,
> Et l'extreme Malheur dont nostre France est pleine.
> Je veux maugré les ans au monde publier,

D'une plume de fer sur un papier d'acier,
Que ses propres enfans l'ont prise et devestue,
Et jusques à la mort vilainement batue.

(Madame, I would have to be made of lead or wood,
If I, whom nature caused to be born French,
For future generations did not recount the pain,
And the extreme Misfortune of which our France is full.
I want, despite my years, to publish to the world,
With an iron pen on steel paper,
That France's own children grabbed her and ripped her clothes off,
And wickedly beat her to death.)[23]

Right from the start, Ronsard focuses on violence committed against his country, preparing the way for the verbal violence that he himself will unleash in this pamphlet. France has been cruelly attacked by a foreign religion; Ronsard must respond and set the record straight for future generations.

In the next twenty verses, Ronsard makes two references to Protestant laughter, laughter he characterizes as cruel, the *risus sardonicus*. Continuing the allegory of a foreign aggressor violating mother France, he notes acerbically, "Puis en le [le corps] voyant mort il se rit de ses coups, / Et le laisse manger aux mâtins et aux loups" (Then seeing this dead body he laughs at his blows, / And lets it be eaten by mastiffs and wolves).[24] It is notable that beginning with the 1578 printing Ronsard makes an important change to verse 17, replacing "se rit" with "se sourit," replacing laughter with a smile.[25] This curious modification speaks to changes in what forms and expressions of laughter were acceptable; it suggests that Ronsard was trying to tone down the sardonic laughter in his work. A few lines later, he once again brings together laughter and violence, as he deplores the brigands who "Vivent sans chastiment, et à les oüyr dire, / C'est Dieu qui les conduist, et ne s'en font que rire" (live without punishment, and to hear them say it, / It is God who leads them, and they do nothing but laugh).[26] The extreme indignation here is caused not only by this foreign adversary's violence but, more importantly, by the laughter and merriment of these sadistic invaders. Like the dog and horse in Erasmus's description of the sardonic laugh, they bare their teeth not to laugh but to bite. Both Calvinist laughter and violence are described as bestial, underscoring Protestants' subhuman status. Ronsard condemns Protestants' mocking laughter because it is associated with violence; it is not hard to see a connection here to the Protestant satires widely disseminated in France. Ronsard's satire is violent too, of course, and he quickly lashes out against his religious enemies, highlighting the death and destruction Protestants have wrought in France and concluding with a sarcastic question, "Appelez vous cela Eglises reformées?" (Is this what you call reformed Churches?)[27]

Starting in line 95, Ronsard directly addresses his greatest adversary, Théodore de Bèze. He implores,

> Ne presche plus en France une Evangile armée,
> Un Christ empistollé tout noircy de fumée,
> Portant un morion en teste, et dans la main
> Un large coustelas rouge du sang humain.
>
> (Stop preaching in France an armed gospel,
> A pistol-carrying Christ all darkened with smoke,
> Wearing a helmet on his head, and in his hand
> A large cutlass reddened with human blood.)[28]

While the image of Jesus packing heat can be seen as funny, this is something much more sardonic and biting. It is meant to be absurd but also ugly and disturbing. Ronsard is credited with inventing the sarcastic term "Evangile armée" (armed gospel) to describe the hypocrisies of a faith that claims to adhere to the New Testament while committing acts of violence and destruction.[29]

Soon after, however, he turns to a more playful, comic image, one Protestants had often used to desacralize Catholic leaders and ceremonies. Addressing Geneva's preachers, Ronsard says,

> Et vos beaux Predicans, qui fins et cauteleux
> Vont abusant le peuple, ainsi que basteleurs,
> Lesquels enfarinés au mi-lieu d'une place
> Vont jouant finement leurs tours de passe passe.
>
> (And your handsome Preachers, who, sly and cunning
> Go around abusing the people, just like jugglers,
> Who, their faces covered with flour in the middle of a square
> Go around slyly playing their sleight of hand tricks.)[30]

Here Ronsard uses the exact simile previously employed by Protestant polemicists such as Bèze and Viret and turns the tables, suggesting it is the

Protestants who are like street performers, covering their faces in flour and playing tricks. Calvinists, rather than being devout believers, are con men who prey on the innocent. Ronsard takes the theatrical image further when he suggests that the leaders of Geneva are like playwrights putting on a tragedy who, fearful of ridicule, send in the "nouveaux aprantis" to do the job.[31] Descriptions such as these highlight the theatrical, performative quality of this and other polemical pamphlets.

One of Ronsard's lines of attack is making fun of the diversity of opinions among the various Protestant faiths, proof of their capriciousness. At one point he suggests they go find a different audience in the New World, rhyming "Canibales" with "Calvinales" (vv. 235–36).[32] Then he asks about the kind of change this strange new Calvinist faith has wrought on people:

> Faittes moy voir quelqu'un qui ait changé de vie
> Apres avoir suivy vostre belle folie?
> J'en voy qui ont changé de couleur et de teint,
> Hydeux en barbe longue, et en visage feint,
> Qui sont plus que devant tristes, mornes et palles,
> Comme Oreste agité des fureurs infernalles.
>
> (Show me someone who has changed their life
> After having followed your seductive folly?
> I have seen those who have changed their color and complexion,
> Hideous with a long beard, and with a deceiving face,
> Who are always sad, gloomy, and pale,
> Like Orestes being tortured by hellish furies.)[33]

This is an image Ronsard will return to later, when he takes aim at Calvinists' physical appearance, mocking them for looking pale and depressed, sporting long beards, and bemoaning the world around them. He depicts Protestants as fundamentally unhealthy and sickly. The suggestion to his Catholic audience is to beware, as one is taking a serious health risk, not to mention giving up all happiness, by choosing this faith. The physical portrait he creates here is also intended to provoke a mocking, sardonic laugh, as his religious adversaries are reduced once again to a comical caricature.

Shortly after the *Continuation du Discours des miseres de ce temps*, Ronsard writes his *Remonstrance au peuple de France*, which he tells us later he composed in three days during the pseudo-siege of Paris, which lasted from 25 November to 10 December 1562.[34] In the *Remonstrance*, he attempts to control laughter by connecting Protestant satire with blasphemy. As we have seen before, he simultaneously castigates satire while also producing his own castigating invective. He begins with a Job-like lament, wondering why God has not intervened and bitterly commenting on how the Catholic faith is being denigrated:

> Certes si je n'avois une certaine foy
> Que Dieu par son esprit de grace a mise en moy,
> Voyant la Chrestienté n'estre plus que risée,
> J'aurois honte d'avoir la teste baptisée,
> Je me repentirois d'avoir esté Chrestien,
> Et comme les premiers je deviendrois Payen.
>
> (Admittedly, if I did not have such strong faith
> That God by His good grace instilled in me,
> Seeing that Christianity is treated as nothing more than a joke,
> I would be so ashamed to have had my head baptized,
> I would repent for having been a Christian,
> And like those from Antiquity I would become a Pagan.)[35]

The key here is his use of "risée," suggesting that the effect of Protestant satires has been to reduce Christianity to a joke. Faced with such blasphemous efforts to desacralize the divine, Ronsard suggests he might prefer leaving the Christian faith altogether, rather than be associated with such irreligious satirists. The acceptability of satire depends on its object; for a Catholic like Ronsard, who here and elsewhere uses satire and sarcastic jokes to ridicule his religious foes, a "risée" at the expense of his own faith is out of bounds and blasphemous. Less than fifty verses later, he uses the exact same satirical tactics as his Calvinist enemies. He describes Luther and Calvin, sacred men for people of the Protestant faith, in the following manner:

> Et toutesfois, Seigneur, par un mauvais destin,
> Je ne sçay quell croté apostat Augustin,[36]
> Un Picard usurier, un teneur de racquette
> Un mocqueur, un pipeur, un bon nieur de debte
> Qui vend un benefice et à deux et à trois,
> Un paillard, un causeur, un renyé françoys,[37]
> Nous presche le contraire, et tellement il ose
> Qu'à toy la verité, sa mensonge il oppose.

(Nevertheless, Lord, by a cruel fate,
I do not know what sort of shit-covered apostate Augustinian,
A Picardian money-lender, an empty boaster
A mocker, a deceiver, a good denier of debt
Who sells the same benefice to two or three different people,
A letch, a bigmouth, a Frenchman who has disowned his country,
Preaches the opposite to us, and is so audacious
That he contrasts his lies to Your truth.)[38]

These are scathing, sardonic portrayals of the founders of two key Protestant faiths. In the 1584 and 1587 editions of Ronsard's *Œuvres*, he removed the four verses attacking Calvin (vv. 103–6),[39] which he had plagiarized directly from the *Passevent parisien* of our other great Catholic polemicist, Artus Désiré (the only example of his doing so).[40] This description of Calvin is perhaps Désiré's most Rabelaisian, with its piling on of insults. (Is it Calvin or Panurge?) In this passage, Luther and Calvin are dishonest reprobates, who are filthy and corrupt and openly fight against God's truth. Ronsard appropriates the very language used in Calvinist polemics to describe the Catholic clergy and the pope and turns it back on them.

He provides some funny portrayals of Protestants in general, observing that in Geneva,

Il ne faut pas avoir beaucoup d'experience
Pour estre exactement docte en vostre science.
Les barbiers, les maçons en un jour y sont clercs,
Tant vos misteres saincts sont cachez et couvers!

(One does not need to have much experience
To be completely learned in your theology.
Barbers and masons in a day become clerics there,
Your faith's mysteries are so hidden and concealed!)[41]

Here Ronsard mocks what Protestants considered a primary advantage of their faith—its accessibility, with the translation of God's word into the vernacular and the dramatic reconfiguration of the priestly class. Ronsard turns this on its head and accuses Protestants of having a theological system so shallow that day laborers can quickly become experts.

He then offers a satirical, unflattering physical description of a typical Protestant. The performative quality of the pamphlet is striking. Ronsard sarcastically explains to his readers what one needs to do to be a good Calvinist:

> Il faut tant seulement avecques hardiesse
> Destester le Papat, parler contre la messe,
> Estre sobre en propos, barbe longue, et le front
> De rides labouré, l'œil farouche et profond,
> Les cheveux mal peignez, un soucy qui s'avalle,
> Le maintien renfrongné, le visage tout palle.
>
> (All one needs to do is to audaciously
> Hate the papacy, speak against Mass,
> Be sober in one's comments, have a long beard, and a forehead
> Furrowed with wrinkles, a fierce and profound gaze,
> Unkempt hair, consumed with worry,
> A sullen bearing, a completely pale face.)[42]

For Ronsard's Catholic audience, this would have proven extremely funny. It is a comic caricature, but it is also aggressively satirical, part of a larger assault on Protestant beliefs and customs.

One practice Ronsard mocks misogynistically and repeatedly in this pamphlet is that Calvinists allow women to actively participate in discussions of doctrine. At the conclusion of this anti-Protestant diatribe, he concludes:

> Aux femmes, aux enfans l'Evangile permettre,
> Les œuvres mespriser, et haut loüer la foy,
> Voylà tout le savoir de vostre belle loy.
>
> (To permit women and children to read the gospel,
> To despise good works, and loudly praise faith,
> Here is all the knowledge of your stately law.)[43]

Further developing his satirical point that this is a faith only for weak people (who could be weaker than a woman, after all?), he addresses Calvinist leadership:

> Vous ne pipés sinon le vulgaire innocent,
> Grosse masse de plomb qui ne voit ny ne sent,
> Ou le jeune marchant, le bragard gentilhomme,
> L'escollier debauché, la simple femme: et somme
> Ceux qui sçavent un peu, non les hommes qui sont
> D'un jugement rassis, et d'un sçavoir profond.
>
> (You deceive no one except innocent lowly people,

A big mass of lead that neither sees nor feels,
Perhaps the young merchant, the braggart nobleman,
The debauched schoolboy, the simple woman: in short,
Those who know a little, not men who are
Of sound judgment and profound knowledge.)[44]

This derisive description would of course appeal to Catholic readership, shown here to be people of sound judgment and deep understanding. It offers a satirical catalog of the types of people who would fall prey to the Calvinist faith, even if this comes a mere ten verses after Ronsard has explained that when he was younger, he was almost seduced by its "doux breuvage" (sweet drink).[45] He characterizes women as simple, and in the last half of the pamphlet, he lashes out at them:

> Je suis plain de despit quand les femmes fragilles
> Interpretent en vain le sens des Evangilles,
> Qui debvroient mesnager et garder leur maison.
>
> (I am filled with bitterness when fragile women
> Vainly interpret the meaning of the gospels,
> When they should be doing housework and maintaining their homes.)[46]

Ronsard inflames his Catholic audience by aggressively mocking Protestantism for the greater stature it ostensibly accords women, allowing them to leave the home and participate actively in matters of faith, including reading and interpreting God's word. This blend of sneering sarcasm and outraged vitriol is a highly pertinent illustration of the *risus sardonicus*.

Near the end of his *Remonstrance*, after pleading with the Crown to oppose these heretics, he tells his audience not to be afraid: "Ne craignés point aussi, vous bandes martialles, / Les corps effeminés des Ministres si palles" (Also do not fear, you warlike group, / The effeminate bodies of these Ministers who are so pale).[47] Here at the end of the pamphlet, he returns to the subject of Protestants' physical appearance, this time appropriating a gendered portrayal Protestants often used against Catholics. He contrasts the virility of his male Catholic audience with the feminine appearance of their Calvinist counterparts. The humor here degrades and insults his religious enemies by questioning their masculinity, a technique we have seen used many times by Protestants attacking the Catholic clergy.

To provide a better context for Ronsard's final pamphlet, his *Response aux injures et calomnies, de je ne sçay quells predicans et ministres de Genève*, it is helpful to examine the three-part *libelle* that provoked it. Titled *Response aux calomnies contenues au Discours et Suyte du Discours sur les Miseres de ce temps, Faits par Messire Pierre Ronsard, jadis Poëte, et maintenant Prebstre* (1563), it was the joint effort of two Calvinists, Antoine de la Roche-Chandieu and Bernard de Montméja,[48] and was a provocative and highly satirical response to Ronsard. La Roche-Chandieu had been a pastor of the Reformed Paris congregation from 1556 to 1562, while Bernard de Montméja, who arrived in Geneva from Toulouse in 1559, was named the pastor of Chauny (in Picardy) in 1561.[49] La Roche-Chandieu composed the first response, under the pseudonym "A. Zamariel," and Montméja produced the following two responses with the nom de plume "B. de Mont-Dieu." In a sense, one finds a satirical form of the "ghost of Rabelais" in this pamphlet. In the preface, using the satirical medical discourse of *le bon docteur Rabelais*, they describe their work as a medical intervention, the individual pamphlets presented as three "pillules" that Ronsard needs to take to cure his insanity. Since Ronsard has taken on their leader, Théodore de Bèze, they get right to the point, insisting, "Messire Pierre, Quand Theodore de Besze aura le vouloir et le loisir de te respondre, il t'apprendra à mieux parler, ou à te taire" (Messire Pierre, When Théodore de Bèze has the will and the time to respond to you, he will teach you how to speak better or shut up).[50] Thus the tone of the *libelle* is set from the first sentence, indeed from the title, with its dig at Ronsard, "jadis Poëte, et maintenant Prebstre" (formerly a Poet, and now a Priest).

A major rhetorical strategy in these three *libelles* is to argue that despite the poet's previous reputation, his poetic prowess is now lost, and his engagement in religious polemics is a sign of his faded glory. There are many instances of humor in these pamphlets, but frequently it is a pretext for violent verbal assault and is intended to provoke a strong response both from Ronsard and from the authors' Calvinist audience. This is the nature of the sardonic laugh, a laugh that is essentially counterfeit because of its disingenuous and aggressive nature.

The dedication to Ronsard is instructive; they let the poet know these three pills are to take while waiting for hellebore, the plant believed to cure insanity.[51] The dedication then ends with a quatrain that outlines all of the important themes of this *libelle*:

Ta Poésie, Ronsard, ta verolle, et ta Messe,
Par raige, surdité, et par des Benefices,

Font (rymant, paillardant, et faisant sacrifices)
Ton cœur fol, ton corps vain, et ta Muse Prebstresse.

(Your Poetry, Ronsard, your syphilis, and your Mass,
Through rage, deafness, and ecclesiastical Benefices,
Make (rhyming, debauching, and offering pagan sacrifices)
Your heart crazy, your body vain, and your Muse a priest's whore.)[52]

Keeping with the tripartite rhetorical device, Ronsard's defining trinity is his poetry (calling him a *rimeur* instead of a poet is of course derogatory), his debauchery (when not rhyming, he leads a dissolute life), and now his prostituting himself with his newfound muse. The mocking tone of the pamphlet is thus set, as are its three main lines of attack. The reference to Ronsard's deafness, which seems to be equated with, or a result of, his debauched lifestyle, will be repeated throughout the pamphlet, aggressively making fun of Ronsard's disability.[53]

The line of attack in this pamphlet is twofold; in addition to the assaults on Ronsard's character and person, even more space is dedicated to indignation at Ronsard's satirical attacks, which are portrayed as vicious and blasphemous. As La Roche-Chandieu laments in the opening verses of the first response, addressing past poets, "N'oyez vous pas gronder les vers pleins de blaspheme / Qu'un profane Sonneur parmi la France seme?" (Do you not hear the grinding out of verses filled with blasphemy / That a vulgar hack sows throughout France?)[54] Ronsard's satirical verses are characterized as profane and sacrilegious, not to mention poorly constructed. (A "sonneur" is hardly a poet.) In a move that by this time has been repeated dozens if not hundreds of times in this war of words, using a piece of rhetorical legerdemain La Roche-Chandieu explains he has no choice but to employ the same satirical register as his opponent, except that his verses are better: "Usez de mesme espée, en meilleure façon, / Opposans vers à vers, et chanson à chanson" (Use the same sword, in a better way, / Opposing verse against verse, song against song).[55]

As Bernd Renner and others have amply demonstrated, satire is intimately connected to the notion of *mélange*, going back to its Roman roots.[56] It is precisely this blending, or contaminating as La Roche-Chandieu sees it, that is excoriated in this first response to Ronsard. As he notes,

Car qui use du vers à chanter sainctement,
Il enrichit son or d'un riche diamant.

Mais le Poëte fol qui par le vers qu'il chante,
Verse dans nostre aureille une chose meschante,
Il corrompt la bonté du vin delicieux,
Y meslant du venin le mal pernicieux.

(For whoever uses lyrics to sing saintly music,
He enriches his gold with a rich diamond.
But the deranged Poet who, through the verses he sings,
Pours into our ear an evil thing,
He corrupts the goodness of delicious wine,
Mixing into it with this venom malicious evil.)[57]

A few verses later, he says of Ronsard, "Il a gasté son vin, et sa perle, et sa rose" (He spoiled his wine, and his pearl, and his rose).[58] The poet has gone from saintly songs to malicious satire filled with venom and perniciousness. He has sullied his former reputation, and the satire he has employed should have been beneath him. Ronsard's lowbrow polemical discourse is the ultimate proof of his fallen state. Also, in making fun of his deafness, La Roche-Chandieu suggests that Ronsard has become tone-deaf, incapable of hearing or recognizing the ugliness of his own verses.

Along with the accusation of poetic failure is the suggestion that neither Ronsard's satirical verses nor his newfound religious zeal is sincere: "Athée est, qui mentant maintient la Papauté, / De laquelle il se mocque et voit la faulseté" (He is an Atheist, and supports by lying the Papacy, / Which he mocks and sees as false).[59] Ronsard's mocking discourse is both irreligious and false; the poet writes his vitriolic verses to maintain his debauched lifestyle, which the pope subsidizes. La Roche-Chandieu contrasts the pious beauty of Marot and Bèze's translation of the Psalms with Ronsard's religious polemics:

Mais ce pendant Ronsard, estouppant de ses doigts,
Ses aureilles, à fin de n'ouir ceste voix,
Espand tout furieux l'aigreur de sa cholere.

(But instead Ronsard, stopping up with his fingers
His ears, in order not to hear this voice [the voice of the Psalms being
    sung],
Furiously spreads the sharpness of his wrath.)[60]

Continuing this line of attack, he lashes out at those who imitate Ronsard's style and creates a new verb, "Ronsardiser":

> Scaiches donc, ô Ronsard, et vous qui desprisez,
> Les serviteurs de Dieu, et qui Ronsardisez,
> Allaigres à mal dire, et tardifs à bien faire.
>
> (Know therefore, oh Ronsard, and all you who despise
> The servants of God, and who imitate Ronsard,
> Happy to speak evil, and are late to do good.)[61]

La Roche-Chandieu warns that if they attack the servants of God, they will receive in kind, with the "acier d'une langue tranchante" (steel of a cutting tongue).[62] This sharp tongue produces the kind of satire that elicits the *risus sardonicus*.

The last section of this first "pillule" focuses on the metamorphosis of Ronsard, who in changing "louange en opprobre" (praise to disgrace) (v. 334) and producing such intensely negative satire has gone from being France's Pindar to a tonsured monk. He has given up the laurel crown for the "mark of the great beast" (v. 346), and instead of singing, now brays horribly (v. 348), "estant transmué en estrange animal" (having metamorphosed into a strange animal) (v. 373). This metamorphosis is variously described: at times, Ronsard has transformed from a poet to a priest, at others, he is an animal, twisting his snout and grunting, wallowing in his filth. On the lighter side, the connection between monks and pigs recalls a host of comical and satirical precedents, such as Nouvelle 34 of the *Heptaméron*. On the much darker side, both Protestants and Catholics used animalistic descriptions of their adversaries with increasing frequency, a process of dehumanization that would lead to such atrocities as feeding to animals the victims of massacres, who were perceived as beastly. This is an extreme example of the potential connections between laughter and violence, the most virulent manifestation of tendentious humor.

The second pamphlet, which like the third was composed by Bernard de Montméja, is the shortest and addressed to Catherine de Medici, imploring her to cut ties with the pope and restore peace in the kingdom. In this second "response" we find a Juvenalian lament, with an allegorical description of how Virtue has been lost, chased away by Vice. The extended critique of the current state of affairs is blended with obsequious praise for the queen mother. At one point, the language becomes a bit aggressive:

> Il le [le roi] fault esloigner de l'avare Prestrise,
> Affublée du masque et vain tiltre d'Eglise,

> Ainsi qu'une putain, qui son mauvais renom
> Veult couvrir, en portant de Lucrece le nom.

> (You must keep him away from the avaricious Priesthood,
> Decked out with the mask and false title of the Church,
> Like a prostitute, who wants her bad reputation
> Hidden, by taking on the name of Lucretia.)[63]

This antagonistic attack on the Catholic Church and its leadership suggests that the priestly class is dominated by greed and compares it to a prostitute trying to hide her bad reputation by claiming she was raped. The reference to a mask is interesting, highlighting the theatrical aspects of the Catholic faith heavily satirized by other Protestant polemicists.

In the third "response," Montméja begins with a satirical epigram imitating Martial. The last line is both amusing and instructive: "Non tua Musa canit, sed tua Missa canit"; for Ronsard, it is no longer his Muse that is singing but rather his Mass, reinforcing the jab in the title of the pamphlet, "jadis Poëte, et maintenant Prebstre." However, this final salvo attacks Ronsard's satire much more than his religion. The opening section of this "pillule" associates Ronsard's satirical verse with the torture and death of Protestant martyrs. Montméja tells Ronsard:

> Haste toy de bonne heure, et devance la plume
> D'un tas de Lucians, dont la fureur s'allume,
> Pour faire que les bons, tous les jours mis à mort,
> Soyent chargez de la peine, et coulpables du tort.

> (Get going early, and be the first with your pen
> With a pile of Lucians, whose furor burns,
> To make it so that the righteous, every day put to death,
> Are charged with a crime, and made to look guilty of doing wrong.)[64]

Ronsard's formerly elevated poetic *furor* has been replaced with the blasphemous inspiration of Lucian, Ronsard's inspiration burning in the same way that martyrs are burned at the stake. This is the nature of the *risus sardonicus*; there is a reference to the comic writer Lucian, a pun on "s'allumer," and it all serves as a pretext for an impassioned description of the violence of martyrdom.

Later Montméja takes Ronsard to task for employing the exact rhetorical strategy he himself is using. Of Ronsard's attack on Théodore de Bèze, he says,

> Et toy-mesme, Ronsard, lors que pour *te mocquer*,
> Ou pour tes compaignons à cela *provoquer*,
> Tu l'as ouy preschant [Théodore de Bèze], tu sers de tesmoignage,
> Que jamais il ne tint qu'un paisible langage.
>
> (And you yourself, Ronsard, when in order to mock,
> Or in order to provoke your companions,
> You heard him [Théodore de Bèze] preach, you serve as a witness,
> That never did he offer anything but the language of peace.)[65]

Obviously for Montméja, Théodore de Bèze is a righteous man; seeing him vilified by Ronsard has led to a predictable result, namely Montméja's defensive rebuttal, confirming the effectiveness of Ronsard's polemical discourse. Montméja cannot countenance hostile mockery intended to provoke, though this is precisely the rhetorical strategy of his response. After drawing a sarcastic comparison between a typical papist and Ronsard (the former blindly follows false tradition, while Ronsard is motivated entirely by envy and greed), he then complains,

> Voila d'où te distille un vers plein de diffame,
> Et tout entremeslé de mensonge et de blasme.
> C'est le puant bourbier, d'où sortent ces esgouts,
> Qui tombent sur un seul de Besze, au nom de tous
> Quand tu es si maling, que d'imputer à vice,
> Le louable labeur d'un utile exercice
> Qu'il faisoit.
>
> (It is from here that you spread verses filled with slander,
> And all of it blended with lies and opprobrium.
> It is the stinking morass, from which is released this sewage
> That falls on a solitary de Bèze, in the name of all
> When you are so wicked, that you attribute to vice,
> The praiseworthy labor of a useful exercise
> That he was doing.)[66]

Again we see Ronsard's verses described as a blending, a mixture of vile lies and vicious attacks. Ronsard's work is a fetid bog, verbal sewage that spews forth and infects the populace. Citing Ronsard's famous attack against Bèze, Montméja urges his adversary to stop before it is too late:

> Tu conclus qu'il [Bèze] preschoit une Evangile armée,

> Un Christ empistollé tout noirci de fumée.
> Mais pour certain, Ronsard, tu conclus sottement:
> Eusses-tu dans Sorbonne aprins cest argument,
> Par lequel à bon droit un chacun peult cognoistre,
> Qu'un jour te rendit sot, et feit devenir Prebstre.
> Cesse donques, Ronsard, à tort et à travers,
> De vomir contre luy [Bèze] le venim de tes vers.
>
> (You conclude that he [Bèze] preached an armed gospel,
> A pistol-carrying Christ all darkened with smoke.
> But Ronsard, the truth is that is a stupid conclusion:
> Did you pick up that argument at the Sorbonne,
> By which anyone can legitimately know,
> That one day it made you stupid, and made you a Priest.
> Cease therefore, Ronsard, indiscriminately
> Vomiting on him [Bèze] the venom of your verses.)[67]

Montméja's outrage is centered on Ronsard's mocking caricature of someone he considers righteous and in a satirical portrayal embedded in a larger discourse of aggression and anger. Montméja's solution to this, unsurprisingly, is to produce a similar mocking caricature of the *prince des poètes*. Not long after this, he compares Ronsard's polemical language to the bagpipes (whose music was apparently appreciated in the sixteenth century about as much as it is today, and which are a striking contrast to the poet's lyre), noting that everyone who hears them gets angry.[68]

Later in the third "pillule," we find a reference to Artus Désiré, in yet another example of a satirist attacking his adversary for his satirical verses, underscoring the problematic nature of Christian zealots using rather unchristian means to attack their enemies:

> Ceux qui t'ont des François le Pindare appellé,
> T'appellent maintenant un prestre escervellé,
> Dont la Muse brehaigne, et du tout infertille,
> D'un Artus Desiré contrefaisant le stile,
> Et mettant en oubli de Pindare les sons,
> N'entonne desormais que des sottes chansons,
> Par lesquelles le blasme, et diffame il procure,
> De tout ce qui pourroit le bannir de sa Cure.
>
> (Those who called you the French Pindar,

> Now call you a hare-brained priest,
> Whose Muse is barren, completely infertile.
> Plagiarizing the style of Artus Désiré,
> And sending into oblivion the sounds of Pindar,
> Henceforth you only launch into stupid songs,
> That contain only opprobrium and slander
> About anything that could threaten his living.)[69]

The contrast between Ronsard, the French Pindar, and Ronsard, the deranged priest, whom he compares to Artus Désiré, is notable. The comparison of the massively erudite Ronsard to a populist, unsophisticated polemicist like Désiré must have stung.[70] For Protestant partisans, this passage would have likely evoked a sardonic laugh, laughter full of contempt and hostility.

The final pamphlet to examine in this chapter, the one by Ronsard richest in satire and sardonic laughter, is his response to the tripartite assault by La Roche-Chandieu and Montméja; while Ronsard claims their attack has had no effect on him, his defensiveness suggests otherwise. In his *Response aux injures et calomnies, de je ne sçay quells predicans et ministres de Genève* (1563), Ronsard builds on the medical metaphor and has his own amusing prescription to offer at the end in a short section titled "Aux bons et fidelles medecins predicans, sur la prise des trois pillules, qu'ils m'ont envoyée" (To the good and faithful preacher-doctors, on the taking of the three pills that they sent me). He lets them know that with "gayeté de cueur et sans froncer le sourcy j'ay gobbé et avallé les troys pillules que de vostre grace m'avez ordonnées" (a happy heart and without frowning, I gobbled up and swallowed the three pills that you prescribed to me).[71] After this sarcastic quip, he informs them that the pills had no effect, an assertion utterly undermined by the very existence of his own *Response*.

To begin, Ronsard addresses his religious enemies as a singular "miserable moqueur,"[72] thus setting the tone he will pursue in this pamphlet, criticizing the satire of his adversaries as vicious and impious, while at the same time using his own satirical barbs to evoke the *risus sardonicus* of his larger audience, the people of France. Ronsard does all sorts of things to make fun of his adversaries, displaying arrogant disdain. He repeatedly says that he wants to do battle with Bèze, who would be a worthy adversary, instead of these Calvinist hacks who are beneath him. Ronsard reveals the unsavory truth about Calvinists:

> Mais afin qu'on cognoisse au vray qu'en tes escolles
> Il n'y a que brocars, qu'injures, et parolles,
> Que nulle charité ta doctrine ne sent,
> Disciple de Satan tu blasmes l'innocent.
>
> (But so that people can know the truth that in your schools,
> There is nothing but barbs, insults, and words,
> That no charity can be felt in your doctrine,
> Disciple of Satan, you blame the innocent one.)[73]

Here Ronsard seeks to undermine the polemical war waged by Geneva. As we saw in chapter 4, it was during this period that the dissemination of satirical *libelles* from Geneva reached its apex. Ronsard capitalizes on that to suggest to his French audience that pamphleteering is the full substance of the Calvinist faith.[74] The ubiquity of these sardonic tracts is proof for Ronsard that the Genevan religion is uncharitable and godless. In the image he creates of their "schools" (in the sense of Sunday school), they spend their time not studying the gospel but coming up with new ways to insult the innocent faithful of France.

About two hundred lines into the pamphlet, Ronsard announces he is changing the topic and directly addresses the notion of cruel humor, castigating La Roche-Chandieu and Montméja for making fun of his deafness. He draws upon the tradition of Juvenalian *indignatio*, asking how they could possibly consider themselves Christian:

> Nouvel Evangeliste, incensé, plain d'oultrage!
> Vray enfant de Sathan, dy moy en quel passage
> Tu trouves qu'un Chrestien (s'il n'est bien enragé)
> Se doyve comme toy moquer d'un affligé?
> Ta langue monstre bien aux brocards qu'elle rue,
> Que tu portes au corps une ame bien tortue!
>
> (New Evangelist, foolish, filled with outrage!
> True child of Satan, tell me in what passage
> Do you find that a Christian (if he is not totally crazy)
> Is obliged like you to mock someone who is afflicted?
> Your speech shows well the barbs it spits out,
> That you have within you a tortured soul!)[75]

Ronsard then asks, "Moquer l'affligé sans t'avoir irrité / Est-ce pas estre athée et plain d'impiété?" (To mock someone afflicted who has not bothered you

/ Is this not being an atheist and full of impiousness?)⁷⁶ He then warns them about the ultimate consequence of their irreverent humor: "Dieu te punira, / Et comme tu te ris, de toy il se rira" (God will punish you, / And as you laugh, so will he laugh at you),⁷⁷ a satirical reworking of the biblical warning, "Do not be deceived: God is not mocked, for whatever one sows, that will he also reap" (Gal. 6:7). In a sort of mini-treatise on hostile laughter, Ronsard is trying to define the rules of the game—when it is appropriate to laugh and when it is not. He, like other polemicists, is trying to circumscribe and control laughter, to define limits and establish what is out-of-bounds. Much of his response is devoted to explaining why the humor in his adversaries' pamphlet is not actually funny but instead deeply offensive and unchristian.

Ronsard works his way through a point-by-point rebuttal of all the insults leveled at him, both defending himself and attacking his attackers for their deceitful and mean-spirited methods. Lest they accuse him of being dour and censorious, he explains how he spends his days:

> Je di le mot pour rire, et à la verité
> Je ne loge chés moy trop de severité.
> J'ayme à faire l'amour, j'ayme à parler aux femmes,
> A mettre par escrit mes amoureuses flames,
> J'ayme le bal, la dance, et les masques aussi,
> La musicque et le luth, ennemis du souci.
>
> (I jest in order to laugh, and in truth
> I do not keep in me too much severity.
> I like to make love, I like to speak to women,
> To put into writing my amorous flames,
> I like balls, dancing, and masquerades as well,
> Music and the lute, enemies of worry.)⁷⁸

This moment of levity, where Ronsard describes himself as free-spirited, fun-loving, and given to lighthearted laughter, is quickly supplanted by an extended sardonic attack on Protestants, which reveals him to be as vicious and vituperative as his adversaries.

Many of Ronsard's rebuttals begin with, "Tu dis" (You say). One such instance, though twenty lines long, is particularly useful and brings together many of the threads of Ronsard's response:

> Tu dis que j'ay blasmé cette teste Calvine,

Je ne le blasme pas, je blasme sa doctrine,
Quand à moy je le pense un trompeur, un menteur,
Tu le penses un ange, un apostre, un docteur,
L'apellant la lumiere et l'honneur des fidelles:
Si tu l'estimes tant, porte luy des chandelles:
Il n'aura rien de moy, par toute nation
On cognoist son orgueil et son ambition.
Tu dis que pour jazer et moquer à mon ayse,
Et non pour m'amander, j'allois ouyr de Baize:
Un jour estant faché me voulant défacher,
Passant pres le fossé, je l'allay voir prescher.
Et là, me servit bien la sourdesse benine,
Car rien en mon cerveau n'entra de sa doctrine,
Je m'en retourné franc j'estois venu,
Et ne vy seulement que son grand front cornu,
Et sa barbe fourchue, et ses mains renversées,
Qui promettoient le ciel aux tropes amassées:
Il donnoit Paradis au peuple d'alentour,
Et si [Et ainsi] pensoit que Dieu luy en deust de retour.

(You say that I criticized this leader Calvin,
I am not criticizing him, I am criticizing his doctrine,
As for me I think he is a deceiver, a liar,
You think that he is an angel, an apostle, a theologian,
Calling him the light and honor of the faithful:
If you esteem him so, take him some nice altar candles:
He will have nothing from me; throughout every nation
People know about his pride and his ambition.
You say that to gossip and to mock at my ease,
And not to improve myself, that I went to hear Bèze:
One day being annoyed and wanting to calm myself down,
Passing close to a ditch, I went to hear him preach.
And there, my benign deafness served me well,
For nothing into my brain entered of his doctrine,
I returned from it as free as when I had arrived,
And I only saw his big curved forehead,
His split beard, and his hands splayed,
Who promised heaven to the amassed troops:

He offered Paradise to the people gathered about,
And thus thought that God owed it to him in return.)[79]

Here Ronsard, while initially claiming he has no animosity against Bèze or Calvin, just their doctrine, produces a satirical character assassination. He mocks how Protestants revere Calvin, in spite of supposedly universal ("par toute nation") hatred of him. He follows this by sharing the story of hearing Bèze preach. Ronsard includes two notable details. First, he takes the mockery of his deafness and turns it on its head; thanks to his lack of hearing, he was not infected by Bèze's sermon. Then he focuses on the visual, providing a picture of Bèze with physical traits that mirror anti-Semitic representations of Jews, with his curved forehead and forked beard. The satire is aggressively mordant, and Ronsard ends by mocking the celestial promises of the Calvinist faith, suggesting that Bèze expects the Almighty to compensate him for his efforts. All of this would have been extremely effective in reaching his Catholic audience, even if his ostensible interlocutors are La Roche-Chandieu and Montméja. Bèze is portrayed as the ultimate Other, a Jew who sells a fraudulent form of salvation and expects to make a deal with God. There is humor here, but it is dark and menacing.

One issue Ronsard addresses is the relative quality of the poetry produced by each side. To counteract the accusation that he has traded in his former poetic prowess for the lowly versification of religious polemics, Ronsard has this to say:

> Ny tes vers ny les miens oracles ne sont pas,
> Je prends tant seulement les Muses pour ébas,
> En riant je compose, en riant je veux lire,
> Et voyla tout le fruit que je recoy d'escrire.
>
> (Neither your verses nor mine are oracles,
> I only take the Muses for recreation,
> While laughing I compose, and while laughing I want to read,
> And this is all the fruit I receive from writing.)[80]

He makes fun of their seriousness, insisting that he writes these verses while laughing. This is not a sardonic laugh but a light and playful one that undermines the gravity of theological debate. The equivalency he establishes between his adversaries' verses and his own ("Ny tes vers ny les miens oracles ne sont pas") downplays the importance of what they are doing.

He then takes La Roche-Chandieu and Montméja to task for their offensive language:

> Tu as en l'estomac un lexicon farcy
> De mots injurieux qui donnent à cognoistre
> Que mechant escolier tu as eu mechant maistre.
>
> (You have in your belly a lexicon stuffed
> With hurtful words that let it be known
> That as a wicked student you had a wicked master.)[81]

Ronsard suggests that his Calvinist adversaries have some sort of internal lexicon of abuse that they draw upon because it is the only discursive practice they have learned, like schoolchildren who never learned to express themselves in more dignified ways. His disdain is palpable in this section. He laments that his love poetry (he mentions his beloved Cassandra) has been appropriated through *contrafactum*, denigrating the former glory of his verses. At a certain point he lashes out:

> Tu ne le puis nyer! car de ma plenitude
> Vous estes tous remplis: je suis seul vostre estude,
> Vous estes tous yssus de la grandeur de moy,
> Vous estes mes sujets, et je suis vostre loy.
>
> (You cannot deny it! For from my fullness
> You are all filled: I am your only model,
> You are all descendants of my greatness,
> You are my subjects, and I am your law.)[82]

Here Ronsard portrays himself as an aggrieved father whose literary children have taken everything from him and turned it into something unworthy and undignified. This is an excellent example of the comic being castigated, as Ronsard treats the satirical verses of his adversaries as an assault on the dignified poetic tradition of which he is the founder. It further follows that anything good his adversaries have produced has come from him. These Protestant polemicists have taken the lyrical and erudite poetics of the Pléiade and reduced it to a lexicon of abuse and insults. Ronsard insists he must meet them at their level, while reminding them of the poetic heritage they have desecrated.

Ronsard calls Protestant theology "toute rance et puante et moisie" (totally rotten, stinking, and moldy)[83] and belittles Calvinist polemical efforts, comparing his rivals to street performers and hucksters, the same comparisons he had made previously and that we saw Viret making about Catholics in chapter 4. Throughout he maintains an air of dominance and superiority. He is a glorious poet; they are vulgar propagandists. He mocks their lowly language: "Ha que tu monstres bien que tu as du courage / Aussi sale et vilain qu'est vilain ton langage!" (You show so well that you have courage / As dirty and awful as your dreadful language).[84] He then insists: "car ce n'est moy qui sers / De bateleur au peuple et de farce au vulgaire" (for it is not I who serves / as a street performer for the lowly people or a *farceur* entertaining commoners).[85] Ronsard maintains that he will not indulge in the lower discursive and performative practices of his adversaries, yet this is precisely what his *Response* does. Like his Genevan counterparts, he uses insults, mockery, and satire in part to provoke the laughter of his coreligionists. He seeks simultaneously to constrain and to create laughter. The laughter this sort of vituperative discourse evokes is the sardonic laugh, laughter that is bitter and angry, menacing and potentially violent.

While Ronsard soon stopped writing polemics, Parisian Catholics' anger would only increase in the coming years. A decade after the outbreak of war, Paris would produce the bloodiest episode of the religious conflict in France, the St. Bartholomew's Day Massacre. Along with violent actions will come more aggressive words, and other writers will take up where Ronsard leaves off. Once war begins in the kingdom, pamphlets will include more political and economic arguments, comic plays and *moralités polémiques* all but disappear, and, after the St. Bartholomew's Day Massacre, Protestant invective will include calls for regicide. It is just one of the many ironies of France's religious conflicts and civil wars that it will be a Parisian Catholic who assassinates Henri III in 1589, allegedly inspired by the publication that same year of Jean Boucher's vituperative pamphlet, *La Vie et faits notables de Henry de Valois*. In the early chapters of this book, we found some ambiguities and subtleties in polemical discourse and performance; at this concluding point, the dividing lines are firmly entrenched. Both sides have drawn extensively on satire to attack sacred figures and practices, while at the same time decrying this practice as blasphemous. Lighthearted and unrestrained laughter is all but eclipsed by the menacing snicker of the *risus sardonicus*.

Conclusion

To return to Freud's phrasing, *hostile jokes* that produce sardonic laughter have been the primary focus of this book, as has a growing hostility toward this type of humor, both of which change in important ways during this critical period in sixteenth-century France. In the plays and *libelles* examined in this study, I have shown how this type of destructive humor can condone or incite violence. A Protestant playwright mocking the Eucharist is intentionally provocative in a way that could easily lead to violence. A Catholic writer who makes light of burning heretics is using humor to condone cruelty.

The vast majority of the pamphlets and plays examined in this book are not well known, if known at all, even among specialists. It is heartening to see increased attention being paid to these works, which played such a critical role in the conflict between Catholics and Protestants, but much remains to be done. Why have we tended to neglect these writers and playwrights, whose works were widely read and had such a significant impact in Reformation-era France? I think this is at least in part because they offend our modern sensibilities. Do we really want to read about Renaissance Frenchmen encouraging genocide? But to understand the mentalities of people from this time, we need to pay more attention to these polemical works. As Denis Crouzet has insisted, an awareness of their content and tone is critical to understanding how people felt during this turbulent time in France's history.

The kind of cruel humor and vicious satire presented here is, in certain respects, nothing new. The targets of these attacks, whether figures like the pope and Calvin, or practices such as Lent and monasticism, were almost exclusively religious, and long before the Reformation religious figures and practices had been frequently satirized, with *fabliaux* and farces mocking dissolute priests and scheming monks. However, the Reformation represents a monumental, fundamental shift in this type of satire and in the kinds of performances and publications that served as vehicles for these attacks. Long-established theatrical traditions, such as farces and *moralités*, become weaponized in Reformation-era France. Mockery of badly behaved monks is one thing; Protestant satire calling for the abolition of monasticism itself is of a different order of magnitude. Some of the most memorable scenes in Dante's *Divine Comedy* involve strongly satirical representations of corrupt popes, but satire that calls for the end of the papacy is an entirely different matter.

We have seen examples of propagandists exchanging barbs, which illustrates how these polemical works were read not just by fellow partisans but also by the opposing camp. It helps us to understand the reach and impact of a writer like Artus Désiré when he is referenced repeatedly by his Genevan adversaries. Nowhere in the period examined here is this sort of exchange more evident than in Ronsard's *Discours* and the many Protestant responses it provoked, including the three-part pamphlet discussed in chapter 6, leading Ronsard further into vitriolic exchange. With teeth bared, mocking, sardonic laughter dominates both sides' attacks. The previous hesitations and prevarications concerning the use of aggressive satire one finds in the plays of Marguerite de Navarre or the polemical works of Pierre Viret are gone. From this point forward, with the outbreak of full-blown war in France, the violent nature of the rhetoric in these *libelles* will only increase, and the anger over jokes considered blasphemous by their targets will continue to grow. The mordant satire used by both sides will continue to be viewed as proof of the satirists' ungodliness. Previously acceptable forms of humor will be condemned, due in no small part to their increasingly vicious nature. Over the course of the century, the works of Renaissance France's most celebrated humorist, Rabelais, once worthy of being read aloud to the king, become examples of ungodly, blasphemous humor. Religious polemics, with their harsh and destructive forms of humor and satire, contribute greatly to this shift, as militant stridency supplants ambiguous playfulness. This vicious strain of satire made all types of satire, even Rabelais's, disreputable.

Moving beyond the time period considered here, there are wider, important implications resulting in no small part from the new forms of satire used in this religious conflict. In the causes and events leading to the creation of modernity (an admittedly slippery term) and, more narrowly, the establishment of secular space in Europe, the religious polemical humor of the early decades of the sixteenth century plays a central role, much more so than has been previously recognized. As the violent quality of Reformation-era humor and satire intensified, it was used more and more to attack and undermine the sacred,[1] creating a slippery slope that would eventually lead to a libertine atheist like Cyrano de Bergerac in the seventeenth century and an anticlerical satirist like Voltaire in the eighteenth. That intensely devout and zealous believers largely made this possible is one of sixteenth-century France's greatest ironies. This is not to make the case for direct influence but rather to insist that these religious polemics represent a fundamental shift in the history of French satire. As Hoffmann observes, "The Reformation that emerges from French satires proves revolutionary less in any immediately political, instrumental way, however, than for how it established some of the attitudes from which later times would eventually conduct Europe's most daring political experiments."[2] As Hoffmann also notes, "It would prove a deep mistake, however, to surmise that . . . these men count as early 'rationalists' or skeptics of religion."[3]

These religious adversaries constantly called each other atheists, in the same way that today one can insult someone by accusing him of having sex with his mother; both serve as the ultimate insult precisely because of the absurdity of the slur and its taboo nature. And yet less than a century later, one could in fact be an avowed atheist. This is not to suggest that this was a popular position—far from it. Prison and even death were very real possibilities for *libertins*. Instead, I wish merely to observe that what was previously unthinkable became possible. Catholic and Protestant polemicists, because of their deep, mutual distrust of each other's beliefs and practices, repeatedly used humor and satire to denigrate and demean people and practices their adversaries considered sacred. Once they engaged in these tactics, Pandora's box was opened and there was no turning back. Paradoxically, Bergerac's and Voltaire's anti-religious satires find their roots in these sixteenth-century religious polemics. At times you can even glimpse the dread felt by these religious extremists, a tacit understanding that they were engaged in something so vicious and out-of-bounds that it would have larger, unintended results. One returns to Erasmus's foundational reference to the sardonic laugh: the warrior Ajax preparing for combat "with a laugh on his grim face." In this time of intense religious conflict, without precedent in France, deeply devout believers took up the pen or took to the stage to discredit, mock, and attack their religious adversaries. The jokes they made, always at their adversaries' expense, were done so with teeth laid bare, false laughter whose sardonicism underscored its violent intent. Efforts to curb such extreme satire were largely doomed, and religious debate in France would never again be the same.

NOTES

Introduction

1. Credit for this phrase goes to my colleague Paul Scott, who takes great pleasure in coming up with alliterative phrases such as this one. His current book project on zombies is titled "Cognitive Cadavers."

2. While I understand the argument George Hoffmann presents in his recent book, *Reforming French Culture: Satire, Spiritual Alienation, & Connection to Strangers* (Oxford: Oxford University Press, 2017) that a less anachronistic designation of the two sides would be reformed Christian and unreformed or Roman Christian, I am sticking with the traditional designations of Protestant/Calvinist/Huguenot on the one side and Catholic on the other. I agree with Hoffmann's conclusion, "No name is innocent" ("A Note on Naming").

3. See Antónia Szabari, *Less Rightly Said: Scandals and Readers in Sixteenth-Century France* (Stanford: Stanford University Press, 2010), 1–22.

4. Hoffmann, *Reforming French Culture*, 78.

5. See my discussion of this episode in *Rabelais's Radical Farce: Late Medieval Comic Theater and Its Function in Rabelais* (Aldershot, UK: Ashgate, 2010), 162–67.

6. References to Rabelais's work are taken from *Œuvres complètes*, ed. Mireille Huchon (Paris: Gallimard, 1994). Translations of Rabelais's work are taken from *The Complete Works of François Rabelais*, trans. Donald M. Frame (Berkeley: University of California Press, 1991).

7. See chapter 6 of R. J. Knecht, *The French Civil Wars, 1562–1598* (Harlow, UK: Longman, 2000).

8. *Remonstrance envoyée au roy par la noblesse de la religion reformée du païs et comté du Maine, sur les assassinats, pilleries, saccagements de maisons, seditions, violentens de femmes et autres exces horribles commis depuis la publication de l'Edit de pacification dedans ledit comté; et presentée à Sa Majesté à Rossillon le 10 jour d'aoust, 1564*, 56. Throughout, transcriptions have been lightly modernized—i replaced with j, u with v, & with et, and contractions silently resolved. Unless otherwise indicated, all translations are mine.

9. "Et certes il est impossible que ces monstres, qui sous la forme d'hommes outrepassent la fureur des Tigres, ne sautent de jour en jour, d'une cruauté en une autre." Ibid., 14.

10. Ibid., 22, emphasis mine.

11. Heliogabalus, or Elagabalus, was Roman emperor from 218 to 222 CE. He had a reputation for extreme decadence and fanaticism.

12. *Remonstrance envoyée au roy*, 31, emphasis mine.

13. See Sigmund Freud, *Jokes and Their Relation to the Unconscious*, ed. and trans. James Strachey (New York: Norton, 1960), 106–39.

14. Ibid., 114–15.

15. Ibid., 163.

16. See William Barker's helpful introduction to his selection of *Adages of Erasmus* (Toronto: University of Toronto Press, 2001).

17. *Opera omnia*, ed. Felix Heinimann and Emanuel Kienzle, vol. II.5 (Amsterdam: North-Holland Publishing, 1981), 289–97. For a useful discussion of the sardonic laugh, see Frank Lestringant, "Rire en Sardaigne et ailleurs: Le rire du voyageur à la Renaissance," in *Rire à la Renaissance*, ed. Marie Madeleine Fontaine (Geneva: Droz, 2010), 195–217. See also Marie Madeleine Fontaine's brief treatment of this form of laughter in her conclusion to the volume *Rire à la Renaissance*, 457–58.

18. *Opera omnia*, 289.

19. Book VII, emphasis mine. I am grateful to my colleague Anthony Corbeill for helping me here and elsewhere to do justice to the Latin.

20. According to his dedicatory letter to Marguerite de Valois, Joubert had first written the treatise in Latin in 1560. For a recent study on this treatise, see Rosanna Gorris-Camos, "Penser le rire et rire de cœur: Le *Traité du ris* de Laurent Joubert, médecin de l'âme et du cœur," in *Rire à la Renaissance*, ed. Marie Madeleine Fontaine (Geneva: Droz, 2010), 141–61.

21. Laurent Joubert, *Traité du ris*, vol. 1, ch. 26 (Paris: Nicolas Chesneau, 1579). Unless otherwise indicated, English translations are taken from Gregory de Rocher's *Treatise on Laughter* (Tuscaloosa: University of Alabama Press, 1980).

22. Joubert, *Traité du ris*, vol. 2, preface, 156. Rocher, *Treatise on Laughter*, 70.

23. Joubert, *Traité du ris*, vol. 3, ch. 13.

24. Joubert, *Traité du ris*, vol. 2, ch. 2, 173. Rocher, *Treatise on Laughter*, 75.

25. Joubert, *Traité du ris*, vol. 2, ch. 7, 214. Rocher, *Treatise on Laughter*, 88. Translation modified.

26. Joubert, *Traité du ris*, vol. 2, ch. 7, 214. Rocher, *Treatise on Laughter*, 88.

27. Attacks against the use of classical pagan models for satire, or for that matter writing deemed Rabelaisian, increase as the polemical battle accelerates. As we will see, polemicists such as Pierre Viret struggle in their works to explain how their Lucian-inspired attacks are justifiable while those of their adversaries are unworthy and even ungodly. By the end of the century, Jean Boucher, one of the Catholic League's most strident leaders, would rant about Protestants' irreligion in his *Sermons de la simulée conversion et nullité de la prétendue absolution de Henri de Bourbon* (Paris: Chaudière, 1594), comparing them to Rabelais and a host of other satirical miscreants: "Et qui tous [les hérétiques] ont cela, de l'heritage de leurs peres, d'estre rieurs et moqueurs. Telles ont esté les railleries d'un Diagoras [de Melos], d'un Theodorus [l'athée], d'un Epicure, d'un Lucian, et en nostre temps d'un Rabelais, et de ceux de sa confrairie." (And they all have this, the legacy of their fathers—they are laughers and

mockers. Such was the scoffing of Diagoras [of Melos], of Theodorus [the Atheist], of Epicurus, of Lucian, or in our time of Rabelais, and those of his ilk.) (Sermon III, 143). See my article, "Le *risus sardonicus* de Jean Boucher," *Œuvres et Critiques* 38, no. 2 (2013): 25–38.

28. M. A. Screech, *Laughter at the Foot of the Cross* (London: Allen Lane, Penguin Press, 1997). Screech's book is intended for an audience of non-specialists. A limitation of his work is that it portrays both sixteenth-century Christianity and humor as more homogeneous than they actually were. Similarities can certainly be found between Catholic and Protestant humor, but important differences exist as well, and there are multiple forms of humor to be found in the context of this conflict.

29. Ibid., 7.

30. Ibid., 239.

31. Ibid., 24.

32. Ibid., 33–38.

33. Hoffmann, *Reforming French Culture*, 167.

34. See a recounting of the Affaire in R. J. Knecht, *Renaissance Warrior and Patron: The Reign of Francis I* (Cambridge: Cambridge University Press, 1994), 313–21.

35. Gabrielle Berthoud's *Antoine Marcourt Réformateur et Pamphlétaire* (Geneva: Droz, 1973) remains the most complete study on Antoine Marcourt.

36. For scholarship on the evolution of satire in France during this period, see Pascal Debailly, *La Muse indignée* (Paris: Classiques Garnier, 2012) and his earlier article, "Le rire satirique," *Bibliothèque d'Humanisme et Renaissance* 56 (1994): 695–717. See also Bernd Renner's extensive scholarship on the topic, including *"Difficile est saturam non scribere": L'Herméneutique de la satire rabelaisienne* (Geneva: Droz, 2007), *La Satire dans tous ses états* (Geneva: Droz, 2009), and "From *Satura* to *Satyre*: François Rabelais and the Renaissance Appropriation of a Genre," *Renaissance Quarterly* 67, no. 2 (2014): 377–424.

37. Berthoud accurately describes Marcourt's placard as filled with "violence verbale." *Antoine Marcourt*, 218.

38. Hangest's *Contre les tenebrions Lumiere evangelicque* (Paris: [Jean Petit, 1534]) represents the first Catholic response to Marcourt's placard. See Claude Postel, *Traité des invectives au temps de la Réforme* (Paris: Les Belles Lettres, 2004), 57. Postel's work is invaluable to anyone attempting to navigate the pamphlets from this period.

39. As this book will show, while this initial response was rather weak, the eventual Catholic response would be more successful than has been previously suggested. In his important book *Hatred in Print: Catholic Propaganda and Protestant Identity during the French Wars of Religion* (Aldershot, UK: Ashgate, 2002), Luc Racaut demonstrates that, while "the Protestant representation of Catholicism is more familiar to the modern reader ... Catholic representations were nonetheless more successful in the short term in fostering distrust and hatred of the Protestants" (5). More recently, George Hoffmann supports Racaut's argument but also points out that he goes too far and levels some of the same arguments against Protestant satire that were previously used against Catholic polemicists (*Reforming French Culture*, 12).

40. Hoffmann explains that reformists were mostly humanist-trained lawyers and

made lousy theologians, which made satire a natural choice for them to "get out in front of their adversaries' objections and change the terms of this contest" (*Reforming French Culture*, 22).

41. There has been a good amount of scholarship devoted to Marie Dentière. Most notably is Mary McKinley, "The Absent Ellipsis: The Edition and Suppression of Marie Dentière in the Sixteenth and the Nineteenth Century," in *Women Writers in Pre-Revolutionary France: Strategies of Emancipation*, ed. Colette Winn and Donna Kuizenga (New York: Garland, 1997), 85–100, and her excellent critical edition and translation of Dentière's work, *Epistle to Marguerite de Navarre and Preface to a Sermon by John Calvin* (Chicago: University of Chicago Press, 2004). Other scholarship on Dentière includes Thomas Head, "Marie Dentière: A Propagandist for the Reform," in *Women Writers of the Renaissance and Reformation*, ed. Katharina M. Wilson (Athens: University of Georgia Press, 1987), 260–83; Gabrielle Berthoud's brief discussion in *Antoine Marcourt*; Irena Backus, "Marie Dentière: Un cas de feminisme théologique à l'époque de la Réforme?" *Bulletin de la Société de l'histoire du Protestantisme Français: Études historiques* 137 (1991): 177–95; Cynthia Skenazi, "Marie Dentière et la prédication des femmes," *Renaissance and Reformation/Renaissance et Réforme* 21 (1997): 5–18; William Kemp and Diane Desrosiers-Bonin, "Marie d'Ennetières et la petite grammaire hébraique de sa fille d'après la dédicace de l'Epistre à Marguerite de Navarre," *Bibliothèque d'humanisme et Renaissance* 50 (1998): 117–34; and, most recently, Kirsi Stjerna's chapter on Dentière in *Women and the Reformation* (Malden, MA: Blackwell, 2009), 133–47.

42. While there is not a lot of scholarship on Marguerite's plays, the two best sources are Geneviève Hasenohr and Olivier Millet's edition of the plays, vol. 4 in *Œuvres complètes* (Paris: Champion, 2002) and a special issue of *Renaissance and Reformation/Renaissance et Réforme* 26 (Fall 2002), edited by Olga Anna Duhl. More recently, see Scott Francis, "Guéris-toi toi-même: La réflexivité du jugement dans La Comédie de Mont-de-Marsan de Marguerite de Navarre," *Nottingham French Studies* 51, no. 2 (2012): 125–35.

43. The only full-length study on Désiré is Frank S. Giese, *Artus Désiré: Priest and Pamphleteer of the Sixteenth Century* (Chapel Hill: North Carolina Studies in the Romance Languages and Literatures, 1973), which is more of a critical bibliography than a monograph. More recent scholars to engage with Désiré's work include Denis Crouzet, the first to call for a reassessment of the importance of the pamphleteer in *Les Guerriers de Dieu: La violence au temps des troubles de religion, vers 1525–vers 1610*, 2 vols. (Seyssel: Champ Vallon, 1990); Szabari, *Less Rightly Said*; Chris Flood, "La France satirisée, satyrisée et fragmentée: L'autoreprésentaiton factionnelle au temps des guerres de religion," in *Littérature et politique: Factions et dissidences de la Ligue à la Fronde*, ed. Malina Stefanovska and Adrien Paschoud (Paris: Classiques Garnier, 2015), 75–96; and Hoffmann, *Reforming French Culture*.

44. Crouzet, *Les Guerriers de Dieu*, 1:191.

45. Hoffmann, *Reforming French Culture*, 17.

46. Some of the best scholarship on the Conards can be found in two articles by Dylan Reid, "Carnival in Rouen: A History of the Abbaye des Conards," *Six-*

teenth Century Journal 32, no. 4 (2001): 1027–55 and "The Triumph of the Abbey of the Conards: Spectacle and Sophistication in a Rouen Carnival," in *Medieval and Early Modern Ritual: Formalized Behavior in Europe, China and Japan*, ed. Joëlle Rollo-Koster (Leiden: Brill, 2002), 147–73. Other important studies that touch on the Conards include Philip Benedict, *Rouen during the Wars of Religion* (Cambridge: Cambridge University Press, 1981); Peter Burke, *Popular Culture in Early Modern Europe* (London: Temple Smith, 1978; reprint, Aldershot, UK: Ashgate, 1994); Natalie Zemon Davis, *Society and Culture in Early Modern France* (Stanford: Stanford University Press, 1965); and Henry Heller, *The Conquest of Poverty: The Calvinist Revolt in Sixteenth Century France* (Leiden: Brill, 1986).

47. A modern edition of the play is found in *Deux moralités de la fin du Moyen-Âge et du temps des guerres de Religion*, ed. Jean-Claude Aubailly and Bruno Roy (Geneva: Droz, 1990). The two most helpful scholarly works on the Basoche are Marie Bouhaïk-Gironès, *Les Clercs de la Basoche et le théâtre comique (Paris, 1420–1550)* (Paris: Champion, 2007) and Howard Graham Harvey, *The Theatre of the Basoche: The Contributions of the Law Societies to French Mediaeval Comedy* (Cambridge, MA: Harvard University Press, 1941). Bouhaïk-Gironès's study is much more detailed and draws heavily on archival resources. Another important study is Jody Enders's chapter on the Basoche in *Rhetoric and the Origins of Medieval Drama* (Ithaca: Cornell University Press, 1992), 129–61.

48. Two volumes on this topic are Véronique Ferrer, Frank Lestringant, and Alexandre Tarrête, eds., *Sur les Discours des misères de ce temps de Ronsard: "D'une plume de fer sur un papier d'acier"* (Orléans: Paradigme, 2009) and Emmanuel Buron and Julien Gœury, *Lectures de Ronsard: Discours des misères de ce temps* (Rennes: Presses Universitaires de Rennes, 2009).

49. For examples of this, see my *Rabelais's Radical Farce*.

50. As Hoffmann notes in his discussion of Conrad Badius's *Comedie du pape malade*, for example, "Laughter at the expense of Franciscans harked back to an age-old distrust of Cordeliers, popular villains in many late medieval tales. But Badius' relentless attacks strike a more strident tone, one befitting the higher pitch of Reformation satire" (*Reforming French Culture*, 80).

51. For an important consideration of the various types and uses of satire in the French Renaissance, see the essays in Renner, *La Satire dans tous ses états*. For a thoughtful study that explores the evolution of satire in farce, see Sara Beam, *Laughing Matters: Farce and the Making of Absolutism in France* (Ithaca: Cornell University Press, 2007).

52. Daniel Ménager, *La Renaissance et le rire* (Paris: Presses Universitaires de France, 1995), 135.

53. As he categorically observes, "None of her works is ironic. None is funny." Edwin M. Duval, "Erasmus and the 'First Renaissance' in France," in *A History of Modern French Literature*, ed. Christopher Prendergast (Princeton: Princeton University Press, 2017), 59.

54. Hoffmann, *Reforming French Culture*, 42.

55. See Max Engammare's article that refers specifically to the constraints Calvin

placed on laughter, "Gens qui rient, Jean qui pleure: Rires de Genevois surprise dans les Registres du Consistoire au temps de Calvin," in *Rire à la Renaissance*, ed. Marie Madeleine Fontaine (Geneva: Droz, 2010), 93–106.

56. Ménager, *La Renaissance et le rire*, 185. Another important study on this phenomenon is Beam, *Laughing Matters*. Most recently, Hoffmann's *Reforming French Culture*, which focuses on Protestant satire, should be required reading on the topic.

1. The Affaire des Placards and the Early Stages of Pamphlet Warfare

The translation for the epigraph is: "He who wants to pluck . . . is plucked."

1. Antoine Marcourt, *The Boke of Marchauntes, right necessarye unto all folks. Newly made by the lorde Pantapole, right expert in suche busynesse, nere neyghbour unto the lorde Pantagrul* (London: Thomas Godfraye, 1534). The pamphlet was the first work published by Pierre de Vingle, who would become one of the preeminent printers of Protestant propaganda. Vingle had fled Lyon the previous year, where he worked with his father-in-law, the famous printer Claude Nourry (best known for having published Rabelais's *Pantagruel*), eventually arriving in Neuchâtel. See Berthoud, *Antoine Marcourt*, 15, 111; see also Eugénie Droz, "Pierre de Vingle, l'imprimeur de Farel," in *Aspects de la propagande religieuse* (Geneva: Droz, 1957), 38–78. For a discussion of the English translations of the *Livre des marchans*, see Berthoud, *Antoine Marcourt*, 140–46.

2. Protestant polemicists, in particular Jean Calvin, would insist repeatedly on the *simplicity* and *accessibility* of their language, in contrast to the convoluted and deceptive rhetoric of their Catholic theologian adversaries. See Francis Higman's seminal work on the topic, *The Style of John Calvin in His French Polemical Treatises* (London: Oxford University Press, 1967). More recently, George Hoffmann does an excellent job connecting this simplicity with French Protestants' use of satire. See *Reforming French Culture*, 108–10.

3. The later edition with the poem moved to the front was published in Geneva in 1558 by François Jacquy, Antoine Davodeau, and Jacques Bourgeois.

4. My thanks to Jeff Persels for this translation.

5. In her monograph on Marcourt, Gabrielle Berthoud explains that Thierry Dufourt had proposed that this slightly odd ending was an anagram for "Anthoi Marcour prêcheur à la ville poli" (*Antoine Marcourt*, 120).

6. Hoffmann's *Reforming French Culture* offers the best discussion of this fundamental question about French reformist satire, which he also connects to French reformists' feelings of alienation. He argues this satire would not have been effective in converting wavering Catholics to the reformist cause.

7. See Gabrielle Berthoud, "*Le Livre des marchans* d'Antoine Marcourt et Rabelais," in *François Rabelais: Ouvrage publié pour le quatrième centenaire de sa mort, 1553–1953* (Geneva: Droz, 1953), 89. In the article, she takes to task French Rabelais specialists who insist that reformers like Marcourt were incapable of laughing.

8. Wes Williams defines Pantapole as "one who can sell anything." See *Pilgrimage*

and Narrative in the French Renaissance (New York: Clarendon Press, 1998), 280. My colleague Anthony Corbeill pointed out that the noun "pantapoles" does occur in a late Greek inscription from Syria, meaning "huckster."

9. See my article, "Le *risus sardonicus* de Jean Boucher." Most recently, see Hoffmann's insightful discussion of fundamental differences between Rabelais and Protestant polemicists (and I would include Catholic polemicists as well) in the section "Rabelais's Defection from the Reformation," in *Reforming French Culture*, 92–97.

10. See Ariane Bayle, "Six questions sur la notion d'obscénité dans la critique rabelaisienne," in *Obscénités renaissantes*, ed. Hugh Roberts, Guillaume Peureux, and Lise Wajeman (Geneva: Droz, 2011), 379–92. She presents a compelling history of reactions to Rabelais's obscenity, from the sixteenth to the twenty-first century, synthesizing modern critics' views, including Lefebvre, Bakhtin, Rigolot, Defaux, Jeanneret, Screech, and Duval. She makes the point that in the context of sixteenth-century religious controversy, it is as much (if not more) Rabelais's heterodoxy as his obscenity that was cause for concern among contemporaries, citing a 1553 letter from Calvin that mentions Rabelais's *Pantagruel* and the scandal it provoked (382).

11. Berthoud, *Antoine Marcourt*, 112.

12. As Berthoud concludes, "Le pseudo-cousin de Pantagruel goûte les romans rabelaisiens, mais ce n'est pas l'esprit des 'bons géants' qui l'anime. Les 'disciplines restaurées' ne sont pas pour lui le gage d'une renaissance intellectuelle ou scientifique; leur mission première, c'est d'assurer le triomphe de la vérité évangélique." (The pseudo-cousin of Pantagruel enjoys the Rabelaisian novels, but it is not the spirit of the "good giants" that is his focus. For Marcourt, the "restored disciplines" do not serve as a sign of an intellectual or scientific renaissance; their primary mission is to assure the triumph of the evangelical truth.) Ibid., 276.

13. See John Calvin, *Des Scandales qui empeschent aujourdhuy beaucoup de gens de venir a la pure doctrine de l'Evangile, et en desbauchet d'autres*, ed. Olivier Fatio (Geneva: Jean Crespin, 1550; Geneva: Droz, 1984), 138.

14. Berthoud, *Antoine Marcourt*, 115n14.

15. For a detailed analysis of the changing content of later editions of the pamphlet, see ibid., 119–39.

16. Berthoud seems to suggest as much toward the end of her article on the *Livre des marchans* and Rabelais: "Le sérieux est désormais de mise; le temps de la plaisanterie et des amusements profanes est passé" (Henceforth seriousness is called for; the time for pleasantries and vulgar amusements has passed) ("*Le Livre des marchans* d'Antoine Marcourt et Rabelais"), 90.

17. Hoffmann uses this broadside as an example of a wider phenomenon in the production of polemical pamphlets, namely their frequent modifications, as they were expanded, redacted, renamed, and rebranded. Referring to the *Articles veritables* as "the most famous polemical piece of reformed satire ever distributed in France," he notes that "Marcourt expanded the work into his *Petit Traicté de la saincte Eucharistie* the month following, and, only a month or so later, the still longer *Déclaration de la messe*." *Reforming French Culture*, 176.

18. Berthoud accurately describes both broadsides by Marcourt as filled with "violence verbale" (*Antoine Marcourt*, 218).

19. Rabelais, *Œuvres complètes*, 655; *Complete Works of François Rabelais*, 545.

20. Rabelais, *Œuvres complètes*, 655n2.

21. Rabelais, *Œuvres complètes*, 655. *Complete Works of François Rabelais*, 545.

22. Michael J. Heath, *Rabelais* (Tempe, AZ: Medieval & Renaissance Texts & Studies, 1996), 111.

23. M. A. Screech, among others, has suggested the Béda-Bragmardo connection. See *Rabelais* (Ithaca: Cornell University Press, 1979), 161–62. If Rabelais's inspiration for Janotus comes from Hangest, this further strengthens the argument for a 1535 publication of *Gargantua*.

24. Postel, *Traité des invectives au temps de la Réforme*, 57.

25. Ibid.

26. Racaut, *Hatred in Print*, 5.

27. I concur with Hoffmann's assertion in *Reforming French Culture* that Racaut has done so "at the expense of devaluing reformed [efforts] with some of the same arguments traditionally leveled against unreformed [Catholic] writers" (12n33).

28. Natalie Zemon Davis, "City Women and Religious Change," in *Society and Culture in Early Modern France* (Stanford: Stanford University Press, 1965), 86.

29. See the introduction's notes for scholarship on Dentière.

30. Skenazi, "Marie Dentière et la prédication des femmes," 6. While Dentière's Catholic nemesis, Jeanne de Jussie, claimed that Dentière had been an abbess, McKinley doubts this. *Epistle*, 9n18.

31. Unless otherwise noted, all biographical details are taken from Head, "Marie Dentière." The greatest amount of detail I have been able to find about her children comes from Isabelle Graesslé, *Vie et légendes de Marie Dentière* (Geneva: Bulletin du Centre protestant d'études, 2003), but she only gives details about three of her daughters.

32. See the introduction to her translation of Dentière's *Epistle*, 6–9.

33. Ibid., 7.

34. See Head, "Marie Dentière," 280–81nn11, 12.

35. Mary McKinley, "Marie Dentière's *Epistle to Marguerite de Navarre* and the *Heptameron*," in *Teaching French Women Writers of the Renaissance and Reformation*, ed. Colette H. Winn (New York: MLA, 2011), 273.

36. McKinley, introduction to her translation of the *Epistle*, 2.

37. Ibid., 12.

38. Ibid., 13.

39. Ibid., 14.

40. In an insightful essay that highlights Dentière's radicalism, McKinley points out that this section of the pamphlet was left out in the edition produced in the nineteenth century by the Swiss scholar Aimé-Louis Herminjard. See McKinley, "The Absent Ellipsis."

41. Zemon Davis, "City Women and Religious Change," 85.

42. Translation slightly modified. Translations of this work are taken from McKinley's edition of the *Epistle*, 61.

43. Marie Dentière, *Epistre tres utile faicte et composée par une femme chrestienne de Tornay, envoyée à la Royne de Navarre seur du Roy de France: Contre les Turcz, Juifz, Infideles, Faulx chrestiens, Anabaptistes, et Lutheriens* ([Geneva] "Antwerp": [Jean Girard] "Martin Lempereur," 1539), 74. For Saint Cosme, Antoine Oudin offers a definition for "Heurter à la boutique de S. Cosme": *"prendre la verole, & avoir besoin de Chirurgien"* (To knock on the door of Saint Cosmos's office: to be afflicted with syphilis and need a surgeon). *Curiositez françoises* (Paris: Antoine de Sommaville, 1640), 271. Thus the patron saint of surgeons is associated with eunuchs because men are castrated as a final cure for syphilis. Saint Damien is the patron saint of lepers. It is hard to say if "Saint Roct" is a deformation of "Saint Roche" (Rocco/Roch/Rock in English), the patron saint of dogs and frequently invoked against the plague, or it may be a homonymic pun on "rotter," which Cotgrave defines as "To belch, or breake wind upwards." Connecting this (pseudo) saint to vomiting suggests the latter.

44. As he observes, "Too immoderate to speak meaningfully to those holding mixed views, reformed satire would seem aimed less at converting the recalcitrant than at drawing starker devotional boundaries. There lingers over much religious writing of the period the suspicion not only of preaching to the choir, but of warning readers that the congregation's singing was meant for some ears and not others" (Hoffmann, *Reforming French Culture*, 170).

45. See McKinley, "The Absent Ellipsis."

46. McKinley provides an account of this encounter between Calvin and Dentière in the introduction of her translation of the *Epistle*, 19.

47. All citations are taken from McKinley's improved translation of the *Letters of John Calvin*, ed. Jules Bonnet (Edinburgh: Thomas Constable, 1855–57), 2:57, along with further modifications provided by Anthony Corbeill. For example, the Jules Bonnet translation makes it sound like Dentière was apologizing to Calvin and asking him not to take her censorious remarks seriously, since she smiled while making them. The original letter is taken from John Calvin, *Opera omnia*, ed. Edouard Cunitz, Johann-Wilhelm Baum, and Eduard Wilhelm Eugen Reuss (Braunschweig: C. A. Schwetschke, 1863–1900), vol. 12, no. 824, 377–78.

48. See Freud, *Jokes and Their Relation to the Unconscious*, 114–15.

2. Early Evangelical and Reformist Comic Theater

The translation for the epigraph is: "I cannot control my laughter" (v. 338).

1. See Jeff Persels's article on this subject, which remains the most important examination of this topic: "The Sorbonnic Trots: Staging the Intestinal Distress of the Roman Catholic Church in French Reform Theater," *Renaissance Quarterly* 56, no. 4 (2003): 1089–1111.

2. Glenn Ehrstine, *Theater, Culture, and Community in Reformation Bern, 1523–*

1555 (Leiden: Brill, 2002), 28. Ehrstine's study highlights an important contrast in Switzerland, as there are many more examples of German-language theater.

3. Francis M. Higman, "La Littérature polémique calviniste au XVIe siècle," in *Lire et découvrir: La circulation des idées au temps de la Réforme* (Geneva: Droz, 1998), 444. This is part of a larger argument Higman makes in comparing French and German pamphlets. For starters, the French ones are much longer, going into the hundreds of pages and containing few, if any, illustrations. The German pamphlets, in contrast, are very short and published in larger format with many illustrations.

4. Both of these plays can be found in the *Recueil des sotties françaises*, vol. 1, ed. Marie Bouhaïk-Gironès, Jelle Koopmans, and Katell Lavéant (Paris: Classiques Garnier, 2014). A "béguin" is a type of hat that symbolizes mourning. See the volume's introduction for a definition (or perhaps more accurately, the impossibility of a precise definition) of a *sottie*. Although genres (even the term "genre" is admittedly anachronistic) such as *sottie*, *moralité*, and farce are extremely fluid (in the introduction, the editors refer to them collectively as "poly-systems" [11]), and it is impossible to distinguish categorically among them, typically a *sottie* contains the presence of fools ("sots") and their leader, such as Mère Folie in these plays. *Sotties* do not tend to contain much action but instead typically comprise a series of monologues and dialogues. For further reading, see Heather Arden, *Fools' Plays: A Study of Satire in the Sottie* (New York: Cambridge University Press, 1976) and Olga Anna Duhl, *Folie et rhétorique dans la sottie* (Geneva: Droz, 1994).

5. See *Recueil des sotties françaises*, 312. While various theories have been proposed regarding the origin of the epithet "Huguenot," Sutherland and others posit this as a plausible theory. See N. M. Sutherland, *The Huguenot Struggle for Recognition* (New Haven: Yale University Press, 1980), 101.

6. *Sottie des béguins*, in *Recueil des sotties françaises*, 321, v. 99. According to the footnote about "predicants," this could be the first usage in French of the term. Citing Rey's *Dictionnaire historique de la langue française*, the editors explain that the term first appears in 1523, possibly in this play, meaning "preacher" with a pejorative connotation; beginning in 1529 it designates Protestant ministers.

7. Strengthening the connection between devotion and celebration, Sundays during Lent traditionally included forms of entertainment such as plays.

8. *Sottie du monde*, in *Recueil des sotties françaises*, 342. This prefatory explanation is taken from the edition of the play printed in Lyon by Pierre Rigaud, without a date, but before 1631. This explains the use of "Huguenot," a term that did not come into usage until around 1560, according to Sutherland, "forged in the conspiracy of Amboise" (*The Huguenot Struggle for Recognition*, 101). This preface gives further credence to the theory that "Huguenot" is derived from *Eidgenosse*, the confederates aligned against the Duke of Savoy.

9. As the editors of the *Recueil* note in their introduction to the play, "le sens précis de cette scène finale, qui doit cacher la clef de l'interprétation, reste assez obscure" (the exact meaning of this final scene, which must hide the key to the play's interpretation, remains rather obscure) (341).

10. There were likely earlier performances of the play, for which there are no re-

cords. See the introduction of Werner Helmich, *Moralités françaises*, vol. 3 (Geneva: Slatkine, 1980), xi. In *Les Moralités polémiques ou la controverse religieuse dans l'ancien théâtre français* (Geneva: Slatkine Reprints, 1970), Émile Picot speculates about the probability that a play performed in Geneva in 1546, listed as *La Chrestienté malade*, was Malingre's. While Malingre's name does not explicitly appear in the published version, the title page contains an anagram (*Y me vint mal a gré*) and the play ends with an acrostic that spells out his name. For Picot's discussion on Malingre and this play, see 48–60.

11. Jean-Pierre Bordier, "Satire traditionnelle et polémique moderne dans les moralités et les sotties françaises tardives," in *Satira e beffa nelle commedie europpee del Rinascimento*, ed. Maria Chiabò and Federico Doglio (Rome: Torre d'Orfeo, 2002), 111.

12. A good example of this comes during Pantagruel's educational tour of France, when he is in Bourges studying law (*Pantagruel*, ch. 5). This is how the legal glosses (the *Pandectes*) are described: "les livres luy sembloyent une belle robbe d'or triumphante et precieuse à merveilles, qui feust brodée de merde" (*Œuvres complètes*, 231) (the law books seemed to him a beautiful golden gown that was bordered with shit) (*Complete Works*, 149).

13. C2r.

14. D2r.

15. As Jeff Persels rightly notes, "where there is scatological detail, the modern reader normally expects invective.... Malingre accordingly obliges, stooping to characterize the teachings and practices of the Roman Catholic Church as 'ordure' (filth) (line 290) and even 'crapulation' (drunken excess) (line 1304)." "The Sorbonnic Trots," 1100. For the most important, comprehensive study on uroscopy, see Michael Stolberg, *Uroscopy in Early Modern Europe*, trans. Logan Kennedy and Leonhard Unglaub (Aldershot, UK: Ashgate, 2015).

16. [D6]r.

17. As Crouzet notes in *Les Guerriers de Dieu*, 1:46, referring to Catholic and Protestant polemical works, "Ils ont été envisagés moins comme instruments de propagande politique et de défense confessionnelle que comme expressions des systèmes de représentations dont le propre est de structurer les gestuelles violentes.... un combat dont le sens premier fut de produire la violence tout en la dénonçant chez l'ennemi" (They had been considered less political propaganda tools and defenses of the faith than expressions of representative systems whose particularity was to structure violent gestures.... a combat whose greatest meaning is to produce violence while at the same time denouncing that of the enemy).

18. [D7]v.

19. E1v–E2r.

20. See the excellent edition of this play by Claude Longeon, *La Farce des theologastres* (Geneva: Droz, 1989).

21. See Patricia F. Cholakian and Rouben C. Cholakian, *Marguerite de Navarre: Mother of the Renaissance* (New York: Columbia University Press, 2006), 82, 136, 148–49.

22. See Antónia Szabari's discussion of this play in chapter 2 of *Less Rightly Said*, 44–64.

23. This character is admittedly ambiguous and seems at first to represent Luther (his character is even called "Mercury from Germany"), but he introduces himself by saying, "Je suis Berquin" (v. 487).

24. For examples of this trope, see farces such as *La Farce des femmes qui se font passer maîtresses*, in *Recueil de Florence: 53 farces imprimées à Paris vers 1515*, ed. Jelle Koopmans (Orléans: Paradigme, 2011), 233–50 and *La Farce des femmes qui apprennent à parler latin*, 251–72 or Mimin, the hapless protagonist of *La Farce de Maître Mimin étudiant*, in *Recueil de farces, 1450–1550*, ed. André Tissier (Geneva: Droz, 1986–98), 3:213–72.

25. The linguistic humor of this scene anticipates Rabelais's satirical scenes of the Limousin student's speech in *Pantagruel* (ch. 6) and Janotus de Bragmardo's performance in *Gargantua* (chs. 18–20). For a discussion of those episodes, see my *Rabelais's Radical Farce*, 101–10, 118–20.

26. See Longeon's edition of *La Farce des theologastres*, 91n for vv. 292–96.

27. See Natalie Zemon Davis's classic essay, "Women on Top," in *Society and Culture in Early Modern France* (Stanford: Stanford University Press, 1965), 124–51.

28. Of the many accounts of these events, three that I have drawn upon are James K. Farge's seminal work, *Orthodoxy and Reform in Early Reformation France: The Faculty of Theology of Paris, 1500–1543* (Leiden: Brill, 1985), 200–206; Pierre Jourda's biography, *Marguerite d'Angoulême: Duchesse d'Alençon, Reine de Navarre* (Paris: Champion, 1930), 1:173–78; and Cholakian and Cholakian, *Marguerite de Navarre*, 168–70.

29. Cholakian and Cholakian, *Marguerite de Navarre*, 169–70. They cite Martha Walker Freer's 1895 biography of the queen. She indicates that Marguerite's response to the arrests was to pardon the offenders and "to be content, as she was, with the reparation obtained by their arrest."

30. Farge cites two letters, one from Johann Sturm to Martin Bucer and the other a letter from Jean Calvin to François Daniel. *Orthodoxy and Reform in Early Reformation France*, 204n234.

31. See the introduction for examples of this newfound scholarly interest.

32. See Hasenohr and Millet's introduction to *Théâtre*, 12–13. They describe this group of plays as containing some of the structures of morality plays coupled with a farcical register.

33. Bernd Renner deals extensively with this development with regard to Rabelais, which he outlines in the introduction of his book *"Difficile est saturam non scribere,"* appropriately titled "Rabelais: Du farceur au satiriste," 9–24.

34. This is also the argument Lucien Febvre made in his seminal work on Marguerite's *Heptaméron, Amour sacré, amour profane* (Paris: Gallimard, 1944).

35. See Hasenohr and Millet, introduction to *Théâtre*, 7–18.

36. Charles Mazouer, "Marguerite de Navarre et le mystère médiéval," *Renaissance and Reformation/Renaissance et Réforme* 26 (2002): 62.

37. Put simply, negative theology, or the *via negativa*, is a form of mysticism which holds that an understanding of God is beyond human reason and cannot be approached through immanent perception.

38. Jelle Koopmans, "L'allégorie théâtrale au début du XVIᵉ siècle: Le cas des pièces 'profanes' de Marguerite de Navarre," *Renaissance and Reformation/Renaissance et Réforme* 26 (2002): 82.

39. Adding further to this humor was the fact that female characters were primarily played by male actors, although in Marguerite's case, Brantôme remarked that her plays were performed by the ladies of her court ("les filles de sa Court"). Pierre de Bourdeille Brantôme, *Œuvres complètes de Pierre de Bourdeille, seigneur de Branthôme*, ed. Prosper Mérimée and Louis Lacour (Paris: Pierre Jannet, 1858–95), 8:15.

40. As Michel Rousse has observed, while farce does provide the occasional "rire utopique et libérateur" (utopian and liberating laughter), "l'ordre établi reste tout-puissant" (established order remains all-powerful). See his "Mystères et farces à la fin du Moyen Âge," in *La Scène et les tréteaux: Le théâtre de la farce au Moyen Âge* (Orléans: Paradigme, 2004), 255. Many scholars of popular culture have debated the potentially subversive nature of so-called popular culture (Mikhail Bakhtin, Robert Muchembled, Peter Burke, Natalie Zemon Davis, Sara Beam, among others); as far as theatrical farce is concerned, Michel Rousse has offered a compelling summation: "[La farce] ne colporte pas une conscience politique des problèmes sociaux en cause. La farce ne se veut qu'exceptionnellement critique à l'égard des institutions, et l'expression d'une opposition claire au système social en vigueur est pratiquement absente." (Farce does not promote a cause or political awareness of social problems. Farce is almost never interested in a critique of institutions and there is a nearly complete absence of any expression of strong opposition to the social system in place.) (260).

41. See Hasenohr and Millet's introduction to *Théâtre*, 232. Another possible inspiration for this play is Mathieu Malingre, *Moralité de la maladie de Chrestienté* (Neuchâtel: Pierre de Vingle, 1533), ed. Werner Helmich, vol. 3 of *Moralités françaises* (Geneva: Slatkine, 1980).

42. All translations, unless otherwise noted, are taken from Régine Reynolds-Cornell's translation of the plays, *Théâtre profane* (Ottawa: Dovehouse Editions, 1992).

43. Marguerite de Navarre, *Heptaméron*, ed. Nicole Cazauran (Paris: Folio, 2000), 308.

44. The fact that the manuscript of this play contains marginal notes giving stage directions suggests that the play was performed.

45. See Ménager, *La Renaissance et le rire*, 135ff. Pascal Debailly provides a helpful explanation of the nature of the laughter in this play. The maid's laugh resembles the "rire noble" of Renaissance satirical laughter defined by Debailly. The three main components of satirical laughter are "une visée explicitement morale"; "une subjectivité qui s'engage dans le jugement critique"; and "une forme noble." See "Le rire satirique," 716–17. Concerning the final requirement, it is useful to consider that Marguerite's aristocratic farces contain little of the vulgar and scatological humor of traditional farce, and the dialogue is much more sententious.

46. While Hasenohr and Millet discuss many of the problems associated with dating the composition of the plays, they tentatively offer possible dates as 1535 for *Le Mallade* (*Théâtre*, 233) and 1535 or 1536 for *L'Inquisiteur* (264). This makes their

assertion that the Inquisitor represents Mattieu Ory, France's royal inquisitor, somewhat problematic, since at the start of the play, the Inquisitor states that he has been in this position for four years (v. 19).

47. For Saulnier's hypothesis, see his Notice in *Théâtre profane* (Paris: Droz, 1946), 35ff. For Hasenohr and Millet's theory, see their edition of *Théâtre*, 264–65.

48. The work was published in Lyon by Jean de Tournes, who is most notable for publishing female authors such as Pernette du Guillet and Louise Labé.

49. Clément Marot, *Œuvres poétiques*, ed. Gérard Defaux (Paris: Classiques Garnier, 1990), 1:109–10. See also Hasenohr and Millet, *Théâtre*, 573n38.

50. See Alan Hindley's and Cynthia J. Brown's respective introductions to their editions of Pierre Gringore's *Jeu du prince des sotz et de mère sotte*: *Le Jeu du Prince des Sotz et de Mère Sotte*, ed. Alan Hindley (Paris: Champion, 2000) and *Œuvres polémiques rédigées sous le règne de Louis XII*, ed. Cynthia J. Brown (Geneva: Droz, 2003).

51. See Saulnier, *Théâtre profane*, 36.

52. See Robert D. Cottrell, "Lefèvre d'Étaples and the Limits of Biblical Interpretation," *Œuvres et Critiques* 20 (1995): 83–86. Building on Saulnier's suggestions concerning various evangelicals represented by the children (Clérot represents Clément Marot, Janot represents Jean Calvin, etc.), Régine Reynolds-Cornell suggests in the notes of her English translation of Marguerite de Navarre's plays that the child Jacot could represent Jacques Lefèvre d'Étaples (*Théâtre profane*, 80n18).

53. Ménager, *La Renaissance et le rire*, 135.

54. See Debailly, "Le rire satirique," 716–17.

55. It was published in the *Suyte des marguerites de la Marguerite* (Lyon: Jean de Tournes, 1547).

56. The best article that touches on this play is Koopmans, "L'allégorie théâtrale au début du XVIe siècle." See also Hasenohr and Millet's helpful introduction to *Théâtre*.

57. Moses' horns are a result of St. Jerome's translation of the Hebrew word for "shining," which could also mean "horned." Jerome used "cornuta" in Latin, meaning "horned." The key passage is Exodus 34:29–35. Because of the difficulty of the Hebrew phrasing, this misunderstanding persisted throughout the Renaissance. The most famous representation of a horned Moses is Michelangelo's statue, commissioned by Pope Julius II.

58. While Reynolds-Cornell translates this as "lips," I am opting for the more literal translation of "teeth."

59. Translation mine.

60. After the tempest, during which Panurge showed himself a total coward, in the tradition of the *soldat fanfaron*, he declares, "Et ne crains rien que les dangiers" (I fear nothing except danger) (*Quart livre*, ch. 23), a direct reference to the fifteenth-century *Monologue du Franc Archier de Bagnolet*. See Rabelais, *Œuvres complètes*, 595n7.

61. As François Rigolot explains, "Il s'agit de substituer aux appâts trompeurs des plaisirs sensuels une adhésion aux valeurs spirituelles d'un christianisme renouvelé." *Poésie et Renaissance* (Paris: Seuil, 2002), 209.

62. Chris Baldick, "Satire," *Oxford Concise Dictionary of Literary Terms* (Oxford: Oxford University Press, 2001), 228.

63. Ibid.

3. Artus Désiré, Renaissance France's Most Successful, Forgotten Catholic Polemicist

The translations of the epigraphs are as follows: "And he [Calvin] will create such a verbal skirmish / By means of mockery, / That in the end there will be trouble"; "Therefore laugh your fill, with this sober and holy laugh."

1. Crouzet, *Les Guerriers de Dieu*, 1:191.

2. More recently, Antónia Szabari discussed Artus Désiré in her monograph *Less Rightly Said*; see 126–39. See also Flood, "La France satirisée, satyrisée et fragmentée." There remains much work to be done on this controversial, largely unknown figure.

3. Crouzet, *Les Guerriers de Dieu*, 1:191. As mentioned in the introduction, Giese's work *Artus Désiré* represents the only book-length work on Désiré, and is really only a critical bibliography.

4. For a more complete recounting of these events, see Giese, *Artus Désiré*, 21–31.

5. Ibid., 10.

6. Ibid.

7. See my article, "Le *risus sardonicus* de Jean Boucher."

8. Giese, *Artus Désiré*, 75.

9. Cotgrave defines "Franctopin" as "A clowne, carle, churle, chuffe, clusterfist, hind, boore." The *Francs taupins* were originally soldiers taken from the lower ranks of society who developed a very negative reputation. With "taupins," there is also a play on "taupe" or mole. This epithet is used by both sides. While Désiré will claim it as his own invention, as we saw in the last chapter, it appears more than a decade earlier in *Moralité de la maladie de Chrestienté*. The image of the mole emphasizes the destructive nature of the other side, burrowing through the garden of Christianity.

10. Giese, *Artus Désiré*, 82.

11. B2v. I am using the 1547 Rouen edition found in the bibliography. *French Vernacular Books*, ed. Andrew Pettegree, Malcolm Walsby, and Alexander Wilkinson (Leiden: Brill, 2007) does not list this edition (Giese does) but does list a total of fifteen different printings of the *Deffensoire*.

12. C3r.

13. "Scandale" has a much more negative sense here than it does today. While I translated it as "sin," it is even stronger than that. Cotgrave offers the definition for "scandale" as "occasion or cause of another man's sinning." The "scandale" is the new heresy that takes people away from the true faith and leads them to damnation. From a Catholic perspective, there is nothing more perilous than this particular "scandale." See Scott Francis's study on the meaning of "scandale" in "Scandalous Women or Scandalous Judgment? The Social Perception of Women and the Theology of Scandal in the *Heptaméron*," *L'Esprit Créateur* 57, no. 3 (2017): 33–45.

14. C3v.

15. C2v. Here and elsewhere, Désiré creates a metonymic association with heresy by describing the audacious behavior of women carrying around tracts such as French translations of Luther, which is the image suggested here.

16. As Giese notes in his bibliography of Désiré's works (*Artus Désiré*), there are editions of *Le Deffensoire* published in 1547, 1548, 1549, 1550, and 1552 (there are later editions as well; one can access on Gallica a 1567 Paris edition of the work: http://gallica.bnf.fr/ark:/12148/bpt6k109329p.r=desire%2C+artus.langFR). I have consulted the 1549 and 1550 editions, both published in Rouen, but am using the 1552 edition published in Lyon because it contains many typographical corrections. The advantage of the earlier editions, however, is that they contain several engravings that are missing in the 1552 Lyon edition.

17. My thanks to Jeff Persels for pointing this out. The latter title is much stronger and emphatic, however; Randle Cotgrave defines "Defensoire" as "Defensorie, which defendeth, gardeth, or preserveth" (*A Dictionarie of the French and English Tongues* [London: Adam Islip, 1611]).

18. A4r.

19. In the 1549 edition, this will become "Du temps qui court," and by 1567, this final chapter will have disappeared altogether, with "Des femmes theologiennes" as the last chapter of the *libelle*.

20. C1r.

21. C3v.

22. D3v.

23. [D7]v.

24. E1r.

25. [D7]v–[D8]r.

26. [I6]r.

27. K2r.

28. K2v. This passage unintentionally recalls Rabelais's satires against the Sorbonne, such as the narrator's assertion about the veracity of Gargantua's "strange" birth (*Gargantua*, ch. 6), a critical part Rabelais later removed, telling the reader that one must believe because, as the Sorbonne argues, it is written and one must have faith. Unlike Rabelais's highly ironic assertion, here I read Désiré's assertion as utterly sincere, a rather weak attempt to counter Erasmus's argument.

29. *Pantagruel*, chs. 21–22.

30. This line is missing from the 1552 edition but is found in the 1550 edition. It is difficult to say whether this represents some sort of (self) censorship; perhaps this attack on the Franciscans was deemed excessive.

31. This recalls Rabelais's classic phrase from the prologue of *Pantagruel* (which he added in the 1542 edition), "je le maintiens jusques au feu, exclusive" (214) (I maintain this up to the stake *exclusive* [but no further]) (134).

32. K3r–K3v, emphasis mine.

33. See Zemon Davis, "Women on Top."

34. Louise Labé, *Œuvres complètes*, ed. François Rigolot (Paris: GF-Flammarion,

1986), 42. Translation taken from Louise Labé, *Complete Poetry and Prose: A Bilingual Edition*, ed. Deborah Lesko Baker, trans. Annie Finch (Chicago: University of Chicago Press, 2006), 43.

35. K3v.

36. K6v.

37. There are at least two different printings of this in 1553, one in Rouen, listed in the bibliography, and another printed in Paris by Magdaleine Boursette. A third edition, which does not reveal the place or date of its publication, is listed in WorldCat as being published in 1553. Giese (*Artus Désiré*) does not offer a date in his bibliography of Désiré's works.

38. Artus Désiré, *Les Batailles et victoires du Chevalier Celeste contre le Chevalier Terrestre* (Rouen: Louis du Mesnil, [1553]), 10.

39. 3v.

40. 4v.

41. 5r.

42. 7r. In the edition published without a date, this passage is slightly modified and "les bourréez de Paris" is replaced by "le rost des bourreaux de France."

43. See *Gargantua*, ch. 17.

44. 17r.

45. 19r.

46. This is not to suggest that such a juxtaposition is necessarily intentional. It is far more likely that the choice was random. Still, the coincidence is striking.

47. 18v. This neologism conflates "diabolic" with "theologian."

48. 140r.

49. Reading a passage like this one, it is hard not to think about Homenaz and his rants against heretics in Rabelais's *Quart livre* (chs. 50–53), especially in chapter 53 when he goes on a tirade: "Encores ces diables Hæeticques ne les [Decretales] voulent aprendre et scavoir. Bruslez, tenaillez, cizaillez, noyez, pendez, empallez, espaultrez, demembrez, extenterez, decouppez, fricassez, grislez, transonnez, crucifies, bouillez, escarbouillez, escartelez, debezillez, dehinguandez, carbonnadez ces meschans Hæreticques" (663). (Besides, these heretic devils will not learn and know them. Burn them, tear them with pincers, cut with shears, drown, hang, impale, break their shoulders, disembowel, chop to bits, fricassee, grill, slice up, crucify, boil, crush, quarter, smash to bits, unhinge, charcoal-broil these wicked heretics) (553). Could Désiré's Papist have served at least in part as a model for Homenaz? It is certainly tempting to think so.

50. 20r.

51. 140v.

52. Giese, *Artus Désiré*, 102. See George Hoffmann's insightful exploration of Bèze's *libelle* in *Reforming French Culture*, 166–68.

53. As Giese notes (*Artus Désiré*), *Passevent parisien* attracted a lot of attention, going through at least seven separate editions in 1556. The pamphlet was published anonymously, and Giese lays out the evidence for and against authorship by Désiré. Some have proposed that the pamphlet's author was Antoine Cathelan, a view shared

with some reservations by Giese. However, Désiré himself claimed authorship in subsequent writings, Geneva thought he was the author and referred to him and the *Passavent* in the *Comedie du pape malade* (1561), and the opening lines of the tract include references to "désiré," a common auto-referential wordplay found in many of our Norman priest's writings. The arguments against his authorship are principally stylistic and are not convincing.

54. This is a clear reference to Rabelais's "moutons de Panurge." *Quart livre*, ch. 8.

55. [3]v.

56. On this topic, see Natalie Zemon Davis, "The Rites of Violence," in *Society and Culture in Early Modern France* (Stanford: Stanford University Press, 1965), 152–87.

57. Hoffmann discusses this extensively in *Reforming French Culture* and makes a convincing argument that reformist attacks on sacred rituals like the Eucharist would have turned away any wavering Catholic and served instead to further alienate Geneva reformists from their French Catholic compatriots.

58. 10v.

59. 22r.

60. 26v.

61. 29r, where he refers to him as "un monstre et un Badin en chaire."

62. See my *Rabelais's Radical Farce*, 34n23.

63. 41r.

64. 45v.

65. My thanks to Jeff Persels for this insight.

66. Cotgrave defines "passe-par-tout" as "a resolute fellow" (*Dictionarie*).

67. In his edition of Désiré's *Contrepoison* (Geneva: Droz, 1977), Jacques Pineaux suggests that Pierre du Quignet is most likely a reference to the celebrated fourteenth-century jurist Pierre de Cognières, who is also mentioned by Rabelais and Du Bellay. See his introduction to the *Contrepoison*, 2.

68. Bienvenu piles on the epithets against Désiré. His main target, however, is Désiré's style. Bienvenu addresses the author, saying, "Aussi ton livre est sot / Et aussi bien rithmé que poix en pot" (Also your book is stupid / And as well rhymed as pitch in a pot) (18). He refers to Désiré's writing as "sottes farces, singeries, et badinage" (stupid farces, monkey business, banter) (3).

69. "Guillot" is a stock name, like "Bob" or "Bill" for us.

70. Artus Désiré, *Grandes chroniques et annalles de passe par tout, chroniqueur de Geneve, avec l'origine de Jean Covin, faucement surnommé Calvin* (Lyon: Benoist Rigaud and Jean Saugrain, 1558), 3.

71. Huguet defines "Christaudin" as a "surnom donné aux réformés." Edmond Huguet, *Dictionnaire de la langue française du seizième siècle*, 7 vols. (Paris: Champion, 1925–67).

72. Désiré, *Grandes chroniques*, 3.

73. At a certain point, Passepartout explains that if the king really understands the gravity of the situation, "[il] exterminera la race" (he will exterminate the race) (ibid., 43), essentially a call for genocide.

74. Ibid., 6–7.

75. Ibid., 8.

76. Cotgrave defines "chasseur de mouches" as "A kill-flye; a Braggadochio; also, a vaine or idle fellow" (*Dictionarie*).

77. Désiré, *Grandes chroniques*, 25.

78. Ibid., 54.

79. The edition I am referencing contains an error. It has Maistre Pierre telling the story, but at the end, it is Maistre Pierre who asks the follow-up question.

80. *Pantagruel*, chs. 21–22. See my discussion of this episode, in particular the competing performances, in *Rabelais's Radical Farce*, 129–38.

81. Désiré, *Grandes chroniques*, 81.

82. Ibid., 98.

83. Ibid., 116–17.

84. See Elizabeth Eisenstein's seminal work, *The Printing Press as Agent of Change: Communications and Cultural Transformations in Early Modern Europe*, 2 vols. (Cambridge: Cambridge University Press, 1979). Her thesis has been challenged by Adrian Johns in *The Nature of the Book: Print and Knowledge in the Making* (Chicago: University of Chicago Press, 1998) and, most recently, within the specific context of the dissemination of French reformist satire, by George Hoffmann in *Reforming French Culture*, 171–72.

85. Chapter 4 will focus on this phenomenon.

86. It was true, however, for his son, Henri Estienne the younger, who died bitter and alone. See Hoffmann's chapter on Henri Estienne (*Reforming French Culture*, 73–101).

87. This stock name is often used in a derogatory way. Cotgrave defines "Guillot le Songeur" as "A dreaming fellow, a dull sleepy logger-head" (*Dictionarie*).

88. Désiré, *Les Disputes*, 2r.

89. Furetière offers the following definition: "gras, se dit aussi des saletez et obscenitez. Il faut estre bien mal appris pour dire des mots *gras* dans une compagnie; on fuit cet homme-là à cause qu'il a la langue *grasse*." (bawdy, also meaning filthy and obscene. One must be poorly educated to say *filthy* words in good company; one avoids that man because he has a *foul* mouth.) Antoine Furetière, *Le Dictionnaire universel*, 3 vols. (Paris, 1690). In modern French, this becomes *gros mot*, meaning a swear word.

90. 7v.

91. 8v–9r.

92. 41r.

93. It is interesting to note that François Sagon was also a Norman priest. For a description of the Marot-Sagon dispute, see Robert J. Hudson, "Marot vs. Sagon: Heresy and the Gallic School, 1537," in *Representations of Heresy in French Art and Literature*, ed. Gabriella Scarlatta and Lidia Radi (Toronto: University of Toronto Press, 2017), 159–87.

94. Artus Désiré, *Plaisans et Armonieux cantiques de devotion, composez sur le chant des hymnes de nostre mere saincte Eglise à la louange de Dieu et de ses saincts: Qui est un second Contrepoison aux Cinquante deux chansons de Clement Marot* (Paris: Pierre Gaultier, 1561).

95. There is also a pun on "marotte," the mock scepter held by the fool.

96. Désiré, *Combatz du fidelle papiste*, 14v. See Pineaux's introduction to Désiré, *Contrepoison*, 17.

97. Pineaux, introduction to Désiré, *Contrepoison*, 18–24.

98. Ibid., 25.

99. [5]v.

100. This points again to Désiré's religious allegiance trumping his fealty to the French king (the duke was aligned with Spain and fought against France), as would be made more strikingly clear two years later when he was caught trying to entice the king of Spain to intervene in France's affairs.

101. 9v–10r.

102. 23r.

103. 29v.

104. 39v.

105. As Crouzet asserts in his discussion of Catholic humor, "La violence abolit dans le rire les frontières reconnues, entre la mort et la vie, entre le dominant et le dominé, entre le maître et les disciples, entre le bourreau et le condamné, parce que, précisément, elle relève d'un pouvoir absolu, immense, illimité qui ne peut être que le pouvoir de Dieu s'exerçant aussi bien dans les gestes que les paroles des fidèles de l'ancienne religion." (Violence in laughter abolishes recognized borders, between life and death, between the dominant and the dominated, between master and servant, between the executioner and the condemned, precisely because it comes from an absolute power that is immense, limitless and can only be the power of God that is practiced by both the gestures and words of the faithful of the ancient religion.) *Les Guerriers de Dieu*, 1:339.

106. Ibid., 1:191.

107. While the estimated number of copies most likely serves as proof of their popularity, it is also possible that it indicates instead that Désiré's works received major funding in order to flood the market. While we know that an enormous number of his pamphlets were printed, we do not know what percentage of them were actually read.

108. On Gallica and Google Books, one can find scanned copies of several of Désiré's *libelles*, but many more still remain unavailable. There are no modern critical editions of any of his works, an unfortunate lacuna in Reformation-era religious polemics. Given his contemporary importance, underscored by Crouzet, producing editions of his works would be beneficial to scholars. It is perhaps because Désiré's views are so at odds with our modern sensibilities that this work has not yet been undertaken.

109. See *La Comédie à l'époque d'Henri II et de Charles IX*, vol. 7, ed. Enea Balmas and Monica Barsi (Florence and Paris: Leo S. Olschki and Presses Universitaires de France, 1995), 181–87.

110. According to Enea Balmas, Artus Désiré is represented as L'Affamé; Villegagnon is likely Outrecuidé; the moderate Sébastien Castellion is represented as L'Ambitieux; and Antoine de Mouchy is depicted as Le Zélateur. See his introduc-

tion to the play in *La Comédie à l'époque d'Henri II et de Charles IX*, esp. 205–9. See also the notes in this edition that provide sources and evidence for these connections.

111. Hoffmann's *Reforming French Culture* begins with a description of the performance of this play, with Conrad Badius playing the lead role.

112. *La Comédie à l'époque d'Henri II et de Charles IX*, 215.

113. Ibid., 215–16.

114. Ibid., 216.

115. As George Hoffmann aptly puts it, "In short, satire let some indulge the more uncharitable traits they worked so hard to suppress in the rest of their lives" (*Reforming French Culture*, 4).

116. Ibid., 42.

117. While the pope's register vacillates between octosyllabic and decasyllabic verse, the supporting characters speak almost exclusively in octosyllabic verse.

118. Persels, "The Sorbonnic Trots," 1105. Persels's exploration of this play is the finest and most insightful I have read. For a compelling historical discussion of the play, see Sara Beam, "Calvinist 'Comedie' and Conversion during the French Reformation: *La Comedie du Pape malade* (1561) and *La Comedie du Monde malade et mal pensé* (1568)," in *French Renaissance and Baroque Drama: Text, Performance, and Theory*, ed. Michael Meere (Newark: University of Delaware Press, 2015), 63–82.

4. Geneva's Polemical Machine

The translation for the epigraph is: For example, there are some who have cold laughs, which seem almost torn from their throats.

1. Andrew Pettegree, "Genevan Print and the Coming of the Wars of Religion," in *Revisiting Geneva: Robert Kingdon and the Coming of the French Wars of Religion*, ed. S. K. Barker, St. Andrews Studies in French History and Culture, no. 4 (St. Andrews: Centre for French History and Culture of the University of St. Andrews, 2012), 53.

2. Robert M. Kingdon, *Geneva and the Coming of the Wars of Religion in France* (Geneva: Droz, 1956), 103. I do, however, agree with George Hoffmann's point in *Reforming French Culture* that reformist efforts were ultimately a failure. As he notes in his concluding chapter, "this study has entertained a starkly different possibility, namely that reformers, themselves, provoked many French into discovering an unsuspected allegiance to their old Church. The story told in these pages has proven less a tale of Catholic victory than one of—there is hardly a more polite way to put it—Reformation failure" (191).

3. The most obvious omission in this chapter is Calvin himself, who produced a number of satirical tracts. As stated elsewhere, however, I have chosen to focus on vernacular works aimed at a larger audience, and so many of Calvin's works were either written in Latin or translations of Latin works. I do discuss Calvin's revealing preface to Viret's *Disputations chrestiennes*, which offers insights into the religious leader's views on humor and satire. It is also true that Calvin was much more wary of satire than were other reformist writers.

4. Francis M. Higman, "Le Domaine français," in *La Réforme et le livre*, ed. Jean-François Gilmont (Paris: Éditions du Cerf, 1990), 133–34.

5. As M. A. Screech has observed, highlighting a difference between Calvin and Viret, Calvin said that laughter at the expense of one's enemies should be moderate: "Calvin's moderation and relative pity [were] not always respected even within the Reformed Church. When . . . Pierre Viret . . . planned to publish his *Disputations chrestiennes* in which laughter plays a large part, Calvin hesitated." *Laughter at the Foot of the Cross*, 45.

6. As Robert Dean Linder noted, "Viret wrote nearly all of his books and pamphlets for popular consumption rather than for the more limited reading public to whom most of the other Calvinist authors addressed themselves, namely, the intellectual class and ecclesiastical divines." *The Political Ideas of Pierre Viret* (Geneva: Droz, 1964), 11.

7. For scholarship on the evolving reception of Lucian in France during the sixteenth century, see Christopher Robinson, "The Reputation of Lucian in Sixteenth-Century France," *French Studies* 29 (1975): 385–97; Claude-Albert Mayer, *Lucien de Samosate et la Renaissance française* (Geneva: Slatkine, 1984); and Christiane Lauvergnat-Gagnière, *Lucien de Samosate et le lucianisme en France au XVIe siècle* (Geneva: Droz, 1988). As for Lucian's importance in Rabelais's work, see part 2 of Romain Menini's massively erudite *Rabelais altérateur: "Græciser en françois"* (Paris: Classiques Gallimard, 2014), "Nasier, le nez de Lucian," where he takes issue with Lauvergnat-Gagnière's assertion that Lucian's work is not central to Rabelais's project.

8. Francis M. Higman, *Piety and the People: Religious Printing in French 1511–1551*, St. Andrews Studies in Reformation History (Aldershot, UK: Ashgate, 1996), 385. Viret's first published work, which appeared a year earlier, the *Epistre consolatoire envoyée aux fideles qui souffrent persecution pour le Nom de Jesus et Verité evangelique*, is much less polemical. The printer Jean Girard was involved with the dissemination of many of Viret's works.

9. A5r.

10. One of the best examples of this is when Gargantua refers to monks as the "mache-merdes" (shit-eaters) of society, as they listen to people's confessions, an auricular form of ingesting sin. *Gargantua*, ch. 40. In his conversation with Panurge about the relationship between food and monastic hours in chapter 15 of the *Tiers livre*, Frère Jean lays out the connections between monastic life and gluttony, describing monks lighting the "la marmite claustrale" (398) (claustral cooking pot) (302).

11. [A7]v–[A8]r. It should be noted that the pun here, conflating saintliness ("saincture") with a girdle or a belt ("ceincture"), is only noticeable when *reading* the text.

12. [A8]r. My thanks to Jeff Persels for helping me parse this passage.

13. To be clear, by "masses" I mean everyone. There is not at this time a strict distinction between high and low culture. So-called lowbrow or popular entertainment was enjoyed by everyone, from commoners to royalty. See Burke, *Popular Culture in Early Modern Europe*, esp. xvi.

14. F3r.
15. Matthew 16:18.
16. P4r–v.
17. K1r–v.
18. See 1 Kings 18:22–40, as discussed in the introduction.
19. Michel de Montaigne, *Essais* I.50, "Sur Démocrite et Héraclite," ed. Pierre Villey and V.-L. Saulnier (Paris: Presses Universitaires de France, 1965).
20. Proverbs 26:5.
21. [DD8]v.
22. Few have written more about the Horatian principles of *dulci et utile* in the context of Renaissance satire than Bernd Renner. See his *"Difficile est saturam non scribere," La Satire dans tous ses états* (Geneva: Droz, 2009), and "From Satura to Satyre: François Rabelais and the Renaissance Appropriation of a Genre," *Renaissance Quarterly* 67, no. 2 (2014): 377–424.
23. 4v, emphasis mine. Cotgrave offers helpful definitions for some of the key words Calvin uses. He defines "jaserie" as "[a] prating, pratting, babbling, jangling; tittle tattle, garrulity, idle chat." He defines "plaisanterie" as "feasting, merriment, flowting, scoffing, scurrilitie, wittie (but knavish) conceits" (*Dictionarie*). For an interesting exploration of the *scurra*, the Roman figure from which is derived "scurrilité," see Philip Corbett, *The Scurra* (Edinburgh: Scottish Academic Press, 1986). Corbett offers a double definition of the *scurra*: "On the one hand we find the professional mime player, endowed with a variety of skills but best known for his malicious tongue; on the other the amateur man about town, city wit and scandal-monger whose chief characteristic also is malicious intent" (4). He also notes that the *scurra* is replaced by the *ioculator*, enters into French as the *jongleur*, while the *scurra* character is lost.
24. He mentioned it in a letter to Antoine Fumée in 1542. As Hoffmann observes, "Within scant years, Calvin was backpedaling from satiric horseplay and enacting laws to curtail laughter during services" (*Reforming French Culture*, 167).
25. 5v.
26. 6v–7r.
27. 7v.
28. 8r–8v.
29. 8v.
30. 8l.
31. *Pantagruel*, ch. 6.
32. 22.
33. See Higman, *The Style of John Calvin in His French Polemical Treatises*.
34. 29–31.
35. 41–42.
36. 35.
37. Both had a much more favorable reception in the first half of the century, with early humanists such as More and Erasmus translating Lucian, many revering Diogenes, and Rabelais's work being replete with references to both.

38. 40. Although neither Viret nor Calvin makes it explicit, this passage and others cause one to think that they are referring to Rabelais, known as the French Lucian.

39. 41.

40. 64.

41. 47.

42. 48.

43. 57–58.

44. "Car la verité mesme n'a pas ce privilege d'estre employee à toute heure et en toute sorte: son usage, tout noble qu'il est, a ses circonscriptions et limites" (1078) (For the truth itself does not have the privilege to be employed at any time and in any way; its use, noble as it is, has its circumscriptions and limits). Michel de Montaigne, *The Complete Essays of Montaigne*, trans. Donald M. Frame (Stanford: Stanford University Press, 1958), 864.

45. 79–80, emphasis mine.

46. 1:212.

47. 1:104.

48. 1:116.

49. 1:356.

50. 3:291.

51. 3:293–94.

52. See Charles-Antoine Chamay's introduction to his edition of the *Satyres chrestiennes de la cuisine papale* (Geneva: Droz, 2005).

53. Pierre Viret, *La Physique papale faite par maniere de devis et par dialogues* (Geneva: Jean Girard, 1552), 82.

54. As Jelle Koopmans has pointed out, the performance of devilish characters feasting on victims in the kitchen finds its roots in the medieval *mystère* tradition and was to be taken up later by Protestant polemicists like Viret. See *Le Théâtre des exclus au Moyen Âge* (Paris: Imago, 1997), 162.

55. Viret, *La Physique papale*, 281.

56. For "mouerie," Huguet offers the following: "faire la moue—Faire la grimace; faire la moue à—Tourner en ridicule."

57. 320–21 (although page 321 is incorrectly printed as page 322).

58. A further pun can be found in the double meaning of the near homonym "farce/farci," the latter being a culinary term meaning "stuffed."

59. 322.

60. *Satyres chrestiennes de la cuisine papale*, lvii.

61. See Kingdon, *Geneva and the Coming of the Wars of Religion in France*, 98–99 and Pettegree, "Genevan Print and the Coming of the Wars of Religion," 54.

62. For the best discussion of Montaigne's "Des Cannibales" within the context of reformist satire, see chapter 7 of Hoffmann, *Reforming French Culture*. Frank Lestringant has published extensively on this topic. See his seminal work, *Une Sainte horreur ou le voyage en Eucharistie XVIe–XVIIIe siècles* (Paris: Presses Universitaires de France, 1996).

63. See his introduction, especially xxxvi–li. He makes a convincing case that the pamphlet's author was Théodore de Bèze and not, among other previous suggestions, Pierre Viret.

64. See his dedicatory letter to Odet de Châtillon in the *Quart livre*, 520.

65. Bernd Renner, "Rire et satire à l'aube des guerres civiles: L'exemple des *Satyres chrestiennes de la cuisine papale*," *Romanic Review* 101, no. 4 (2010): 664.

66. As Hoffmann notes, "if ever there were a classical form marked as intrinsically pagan, it might be satire" (*Reforming French Culture*, 22).

67. Chamay sees this as a reference to Bèze's youthful past and a justification for previous facetious actions and writings during his carefree time as a student in Paris. See *Satyres chrestiennes de la cuisine papale*, lxi–lxii.

68. Hoffmann makes the same point I am making here when he notes, "But de Bèze also sensed the tension between playful derision and deeper pious purposes" (*Reforming French Culture*, 167).

69. Chamay makes this observation in a footnote, *Satyres chrestiennes de la cuisine papale*, 6n9.

70. Ibid., xii.

71. III vv. 43, 239–40, 504.

72. See Alan Hindley's and Cynthia J. Brown's respective introductions in their editions of the play.

73. Koopmans, esp. chapter 3 in *Le Théâtre des exclus au Moyen Âge*.

74. For descriptions of these practices, see Jacques Heers, *Fêtes des fous et Carnavals* (Paris: Fayard, 1983); Mikhail Bakhtin, *Rabelais and His World*, trans. Helene Iswolsky (Cambridge, MA: MIT Press, 1968); Ingvild Salid Gilhus, "Carnival in Religion: The Feast of Fools in France," *Numen* 37 (1990): 24–52; Jelle Koopmans's introduction to his *Quatre sermons joyeux* (Geneva: Droz, 1984).

75. Tissier, ed., *Recueil de farces*, 10:323–88.

76. *La Farce de Maître Pathelin*, written around 1485, had been through sixteen editions by 1550. See Jean-Claude Aubailly, *Le Théâtre médiéval profane et comique* (Paris: Larousse, 1975), 151.

77. *Satyres chrestiennes*, Satire V, v. 464.

78. See Aquinas, *Summa Theologiae*, Part III, Questions 75–78. *Summa Theologiae* (Madrid: Editorial Catolica, 1951), 4:625–74; *Summa Theologica*, ed. and trans. the Fathers of the English Dominican Province (Westminster, MD: Christian Classics, 1981), 5:2439–73.

79. A likely reference to Duns Scotus, whose nickname was "Doctor subtilis" ("Docteur subtil" in French).

80. This work and others like it have more in common with Rabelais's *Quart livre*, which is much more biting and sardonic than his earlier works.

5. Abbeys of Misrule on the Stage

The translation of the epigraph is: "None of us is unaware. / What they have done in our country / Which is why it is appropriate that they be hated: / That is the point of our lessons."

1. As for the word *Conard*, it is an alternate spelling of "cornard," a cuckold. Natalie

Zemon Davis offers the following explanation: "To sixteenth-century observers, the words suggested the various uses of folly, sexuality, power, and noise. A *conard* was defined as a *sot*, or fool. The word also had associations with *con*, as in sixteenth-century pictures purporting that the female genitalia made fools out of men and were the source of male energy." See *Society and Culture in Early Modern France*, 99.

2. According to Henry Heller, "At the beginning of the sixteenth century the archbishop of Rouen had the highest income of any ecclesiastic in the Kingdom" (*The Conquest of Poverty*, 11).

3. For an important study on Rouen during this period, see Benedict, *Rouen during the Wars of Religion*. Although Luther's writings appeared relatively early in Rouen, the city did not have the extensive printing industry found in Paris and Lyon.

4. Ibid., 41.

5. Ibid., 51–52.

6. Heller, *The Conquest of Poverty*, 22.

7. Ibid., 60–61.

8. Reid, "Carnival in Rouen," 1028. He references Ilaria Taddei, *Fête, jeunesse et pouvoirs: L'Abbaye des Nobles Enfants de Lausanne* (Lausanne: Université de Lausanne, 1991), Benedict, Burke, Zemon Davis, and Heller.

9. Heller, *The Conquest of Poverty*, 2–3. Dylan Reid disputes the elite status of the Conards, arguing instead that they were primarily drawn from the "middling class." Reid, "The Triumph of the Abbey of the Conards," 151.

10. Reid, "The Triumph of the Abbey of the Conards," 147.

11. Ibid., 162.

12. See Mikhail Bakhtin's seminal work on this topic, *Rabelais and His World*, especially chapter 3, "Popular-Festive Forms and Images in Rabelais."

13. Reid, "The Triumph of the Abbey of the Conards," 158.

14. Ever since Bakhtin made the argument that the carnivalesque seeks to undermine the establishment in *Rabelais and His World*, critics have offered a wide variety of opinions on the matter. See my discussion of this in the introduction to my *Rabelais's Radical Farce*. In the context of Reformation-era religious polemics, the stakes are much higher and the dangers associated with the carnivalesque more acute.

15. Among the various theories about the Conards, Reid's ("The Triumph of the Abbey of the Conards") is the most convincing.

16. Reid, "The Triumph of the Abbey of the Conards," 171.

17. Heller, *The Conquest of Poverty*, 4, 6.

18. Reid, "The Triumph of the Abbey of the Conards," 173.

19. Benedict, *Rouen during the Wars of Religion*, 85.

20. *Théâtre et propagande aux débuts de la Réforme: Six pièces polémiques du Recueil La Vallière*, ed. Jonathan Beck (Geneva: Slatkine, 1986), 51.

21. Ibid., 27–28.

22. Ibid., 28. Beck points out that these *moralités polémiques* find their roots in the Middle Ages, after events such as the Western Schism and the Hundred Years' War. See Picot, *Les Moralités polémiques*.

23. Ibid., 49.
24. Ibid., 47–48.
25. Beck argues for the former view (see *Théâtre et propagande*, 51–62) while Reid, asserting that Beck misread a source, argues for a single group. See Reid, "Carnival in Rouen," 1037n28.
26. See Beck, *Théâtre et propagande*, 109 and Reid, "Carnival in Rouen," 1044.
27. As Reid notes, there are no records of female members of the Conards, and typically this role would have been played by a cross-dressed male actor. See "Carnival in Rouen," 1037.
28. 113r, vv. 212–13.
29. 113v, v. 250.
30. 116r, vv. 189–94.
31. 116v, vv. 146–50.
32. 117r, vv. 190–91.
33. See 2 Corinthians 1:3–6.
34. 117r, v. 176.
35. 329r, vv. 208–9.
36. See, for example, *Le Gentilhomme et son page* in vol. 10 of *Recueil de farces*, ed. Tissier, 183–223.
37. 331r, v. 320.
38. Beck, *Théâtre et propagande*, 210.
39. 382r, vv. 24–25, 382v, vv. 35–36.
40. 383v, vv. 100–103.
41. 384v, vv. 174–75. The sense here is that they need to burn the actual people; another common practice was to burn an effigy of someone who had been found guilty of heresy but not captured.
42. Among the many critics who have referred to this 1548 edict from Parlement, Charles Mazouer calls it "hautement symbolique." *Le Théâtre français de la Renaissance* (Paris: Champion, 2002), 11.
43. Joachim Du Bellay, *La Deffence, et illustration de la langue françoyse*, part II, ch. 4, ed. Jean-Charles Monferran (Paris: Arnoul l'Angelier, 1549; Geneva: Droz, 2001), 138.
44. Stephanie Lysyk, "Love of the Censor: Legendre, Censorship, and the Theater of the Basoche," *Cardozo Studies in Law and Literature* 11 (1999): 118.
45. Bouhaïk-Gironès, *Les Clercs de la Basoche et le théâtre comique*, 67.
46. Lysyk, "Love of the Censor," 119. For a more extensive analysis of the *cause grasse* tradition, see Bouhaïk-Gironès, *Les Clercs de la Basoche*, ch. 3.
47. See Lysyk, "Love of the Censor," 121.
48. See Bouhaïk-Gironès, *Les Clercs de la Basoche*, 139–41.
49. *Deux moralités*, 73. All references to the play are taken from Aubailly and Roy's edition of the play.
50. v. 40.
51. vv. 489–90.
52. vv. 509–10. See also the notes regarding these verses for an explanation of the insult, which rimes "veaux" with the "Beau" in "Beauvais."

53. This occurs beginning in v. 509.

54. 76.

55. vv. 809–10.

56. Commenting on this paradox, Enders has observed, "To a large degree, the history of the Basoche is the history of the relaxation and reinstatement of censorship" (*Rhetoric and the Origins of Medieval Drama*, 152).

6. Ronsard the Pamphleteer

The epigraph translation is: "They live without punishment, and to hear them say it, / It is God who leads them, and they do nothing but laugh."

1. In the 1567 edition of Ronsard's *Œuvres* (Paris: Gabriel Buon), he included a volume also titled *Discours des miseres de ce temps* that brought together all of the pamphlets discussed in this chapter.

2. Pierre de Ronsard, *Institution pour l'Adolescence du Roy* (Paris: Gabriel Buon, 1562). See vv. 69–82.

3. Barbara B. Diefendorf, *Beneath the Cross: Catholics and Huguenots in Sixteenth-Century Paris* (New York: Oxford University Press, 1991), 8.

4. See ibid., 50–51.

5. Ibid., 60.

6. Ibid., 62.

7. Ibid., 63.

8. Pierre de Ronsard, *Discours des misères de ce temps*, ed. Malcolm Smith (Geneva: Droz, 1979), 7. Beyond France, Spain's ambassador wrote to Philip II about it, Mary Stuart's library contained a copy of the *Discours*, and Pope Pius V was aware of Ronsard's polemic. Ibid., 23–24.

9. Ibid., 21.

10. Ibid., 26.

11. Such works include Ferrer, Lestringant, and Tarrête, *Sur les Discours des misères de ce temps de Ronsard* and Buron and Gœury, *Lectures de Ronsard*. Recent articles on the *Discours* are too numerous to list here but several can be found in the bibliography.

12. All citations to Ronsard are taken from Paul Laumonier's twenty-volume edition of Ronsard's work, *Œuvres complètes* (Paris: Hachette, 1914–75). The *Second livre des meslanges* is found in 10:1–164.

13. Laumonier, *Œuvres complètes*, vol. 10, vv. 153–54.

14. In all of these polemical exchanges, it would be hard to find one more personal and filled with antipathy than the one between Ronsard and Bèze. See Malcolm Smith, *Ronsard & Du Bellay versus Bèze: Allusiveness in Renaissance Literary Texts* (Geneva: Droz, 1995). As he observes, "Two episodes in this long-running confrontation are fairly well known: Bèze's attack on Ronsard in 1550 in the preface of... *Abraham sacrifiant*, and Ronsard's attack on Bèze in 1562 for preaching a 'gospel of arms' in the first civil war. But what is not known is that these were simply two episodes in an enduring dispute" (7).

15. See Smith, *Ronsard & Du Bellay versus Bèze*, 11–12.
16. Laumonier, *Œuvres complètes*, 10:350, vv. 15–24. See S. K. Barker's discussion of this poem in *Protestantism, Poetry and Protest: The Vernacular Writings of Antoine de Chandieu (c. 1534–1591)* (Aldershot, UK: Ashgate, 2009).
17. See Francis Higman's introduction to the *Discours des misères de ce temps* (Paris: Le Livre de poche classique, 1993), 17.
18. *Continuation du Discours.* Laumonier, *Œuvres complètes*, 11:35, v. 6.
19. Laumonier, *Œuvres complètes*, 10:357–58, vv. 157–62, 171–74.
20. Ibid., 365, vv. 51–54.
21. Gustave Cohen, *Ronsard: Sa vie et son œuvre* (Paris: Gallimard, 1956), 205.
22. Laumonier, *Œuvres complètes*, 11:21, vv. 51–54.
23. Laumonier, *Œuvres complètes*, 11:35, vv. 1–8.
24. Ibid., 36, vv. 17–18.
25. The second hemistich becomes "se sourit de ses coups" (dropping the "il") to maintain the alexandrine versification.
26. Laumonier, *Œuvres complètes*, 11:36, vv. 27–28.
27. Ibid., 37, vv. 41–48, v. 48 cited.
28. Ibid., 42, vv. 119–22.
29. See Smith, *Ronsard & Du Bellay versus Bèze*, 20.
30. Laumonier, *Œuvres complètes*, 11:45, vv. 169–72.
31. Ibid., 47–48, vv. 204–8. Anne-Pascale Pouey-Mounou has highlighted the theatricality and performative quality of Ronsard's *Continuation* in "Des prêches, des armes et des livres: La figure de Théodore de Bèze dans la polémique des *Discours des miseres de ce temps* (1562–1563)," in *Writers in Conflict in Sixteenth-Century France: Essays in Honour of Malcolm Quainton*, ed. Elizabeth Vinestock, David Foster, and Neil Kenny (Durham: University of Durham Press, 2008), 153–72.
32. For an engaging exploration of these associations, see Frank Lestringant, "Ronsard, Prométhée et le Protestants," in *Sur les Discours des misères de ce temps de Ronsard*, 81–96. See also George Hoffmann's intriguing discussion of connections between New World cannibals and Reformists in *Reforming French Culture*, 189–214.
33. Laumonier, *Œuvres complètes*, 11:51, vv. 259–64.
34. See his *Response*, ibid., 171, v. 1082.
35. Ibid., 66, vv. 57–62.
36. Reference to Luther.
37. Reference to Calvin (vv. 103–9).
38. Ibid., 68, vv. 101–8.
39. See Laumonier's note, *Œuvres complètes*, 11:68.
40. See Pineaux's introduction to Désiré, *Contrepoison*, 8–9.
41. Laumonier, *Œuvres complètes*, 11:73, vv. 191–94.
42. Ibid., 73–74, vv. 195–200.
43. Ibid., 74–75, vv. 208–10.
44. Ibid., 76, vv. 221–26.
45. Ibid., 75, v. 212.
46. Ibid., 93, vv. 567–69.

47. Ibid., 104, vv. 801–2.

48. The use of "Messire" with a person's first name was customary for both secular priests and bishops.

49. The most exhaustive, useful study on Antoine de Chandieu is Barker, *Protestantism, Poetry and Protest*. I am only discussing one Protestant response to Ronsard, in part because it is the one the poet is most explicitly responding to in his next *libelle*. Barker has assembled a list of over twenty Protestant compositions (127–29).

50. All citations are taken from Jacques Pineaux's critical edition of the *Response*, found in *La Polémique protestante contre Ronsard* (Paris: Librairie Marcel Didier, 1973), 1:32.

51. This was the same treatment used by Ponocrates to cure Gargantua. See *Gargantua*, ch. 23.

52. *La Polémique protestante contre Ronsard*, 1:32, vv. 12–15.

53. In the growing field of disability studies, the various treatments of Ronsard's partial deafness would make for an interesting study.

54. *La Polémique protestante contre Ronsard*, 1:32, vv. 9–10.

55. Ibid., 34, vv. 23–24.

56. See the introduction to his monograph *"Difficile est saturam non scribere"* and the introduction to his edited volume, *La Satire dans tous ses états*, among examples previously cited.

57. *La Polémique protestante contre Ronsard*, 1:34, vv. 39–44.

58. Ibid., 35, v. 54.

59. Ibid., 41, vv. 183–84.

60. Ibid., 45, vv. 263–65.

61. Ibid., 45, vv. 273–75.

62. Ibid., 45, v. 280.

63. Ibid., 58, vv. 157–60.

64. Ibid., 68, vv. 25–28.

65. Ibid., 76, vv. 215–18, emphasis mine.

66. Ibid., 78, vv. 257–63.

67. Ibid., 80, vv. 311–18.

68. Ibid., 83, v. 372. For an interesting study on the uses of unpleasant and cacophonous noises and chatter in this polemical exchange between Ronsard and Montméja and La Roche-Chandieu, see Emily Butterworth, *The Unbridled Tongue: Babble and Gossip in Renaissance France* (Oxford: Oxford University Press, 2016), 101–26.

69. *La Polémique protestante contre Ronsard*, 1:85, vv. 413–20.

70. Being called out and humiliated by his Genevan adversaries provides a good explanation for why Ronsard removed the four verses about Calvin in his *Remonstrance* that he had taken from Désiré. As an astute external reader who made this observation noted, Ronsard likely wanted to have that comic, satirical portrait of Calvin as his own; it is a great example of *imitatio* gone awry. My thanks to the external reader for providing this insight.

71. Laumonier, *Œuvres complètes*, 11:176.

72. Ibid., 116, v. 1.

73. Ibid., 123, vv. 115–18.

74. There is something to Ronsard's complaint. George Hoffmann has written incisively about this in *Reforming French Culture*. In chapter 6, "From Communion to Communication," he makes the case that the satirical output from Geneva gave isolated reformist communities throughout France a sense of belonging. I share Hoffmann's view that reformist satire was much better at doing this than in making converts. I would argue that the same is true of the Catholic side. Désiré's and Ronsard's pamphlets, while directly addressing their Calvinist adversaries, are primarily intended to strengthen bonds among Catholics through their use of tendentious humor, which according to Freud serves "to turn the hearer, who was indifferent to begin with, into a co-hater or co-despiser." Freud, *Jokes and Their Relation to the Unconscious*, 163.

75. Laumonier, *Œuvres complètes*, 11:128, vv. 215–20.

76. Ibid., 128, vv. 225–26.

77. Ibid., 129, vv. 229–30.

78. Ibid., 145, vv. 549–54.

79. Ibid., 153–54, vv. 711–30.

80. Ibid., 163, vv. 921–24.

81. Ibid., 166, vv. 998–1000.

82. Ibid., 168, vv. 1035–38.

83. Ibid., 171, v. 1092.

84. Ibid., 173, vv. 1131–32.

85. Ibid., 175, vv. 1158–59.

Conclusion

1. There are limits to this, of course. No one was denying the Trinity or the veracity of Scripture.

2. Hoffmann, *Reforming French Culture*, 2.

3. Ibid., 82. He is referring specifically to Henri Estienne and Conrad Badius, although his comment applies to all of the polemicists discussed in this book.

BIBLIOGRAPHY

Primary Works

Alessandri, Alessandro. *Dies geniales*. Paris: Jean Roigny, 1539.
Aquinas, Thomas. *Summa Theologiae*. 5 vols. Madrid: Editorial Catolica, 1951.
———. *Summa Theologica*. Edited and translated by the Fathers of the English Dominican Province. 5 vols. Reprint. Westminster, MD: Christian Classics, 1981.
[Badius, Conrad]. *Comedie du pape malade et tirant à la fin*. [Geneva: Conrad Badius], 1561. *La Comédie à l'époque d'Henri II et de Charles IX*. Edited by Enea Balmas, Michel Dassonville, and Luigia Zilli. Florence and Paris: Leo S. Olschki and Presses Universitaires de France, 1986–97. *Comedie du pape malade*. Edited by Enea Balmas and Monica Barsi. Vol. 7 (1995), 179–273.
[Berquin, Louis de]. *La Farce des theologastres*. Edited by Claude Longeon. Geneva: Droz, 1989.
[Bèze, Théodore de]. *Satyres chrestiennes de la cuisine papale*. Geneva: Conrad Badius, 1560. Edited by Charles-Antoine Chamay. Geneva: Droz, 2005.
Bienvenu, Jacques. *Response au livre d'Artus Desiré, intitulé: Les grandes chroniques et Annales de Passe-partout*. Geneva: Jacques Berthet, 1558.
Boucher, Jean. *Sermons de la simulée conversion et nullité de la prétendue absolution de Henri de Bourbon*. Paris: Chaudière, 1594.
Brantôme, Pierre de Bourdeille, seigneur de. *Œuvres complètes de Pierre de Bourdeille, seigneur de Branthôme*. Edited by Prosper Mérimée and Louis Lacour. 13 vols. Paris: Pierre Jannet, 1858–95.
Calvin, John. *Letters of John Calvin*. Edited by Jules Bonnet. 2 vols. Edinburgh: Thomas Constable, 1855–57.
———. *Opera omnia*. Edited by Edouard Cunitz, Johann-Wilhelm Baum, and Eduard Wilhelm Eugen Reuss. 58 vols. Braunschweig: C. A. Schwetschke, 1863–1900.
———. *Des Scandales qui empeschent aujourdhuy beaucoup de gens de venir a la pure doctrine de l'Evangile, et en desbauchet d'autres*. Geneva: Jean Crespin, 1550. Edited by Olivier Fatio. Geneva: Droz, 1984.
———. *De scandalis quibus hodie plerique absterrentur, nonnullietiam alienantur à pura Evangelii doctrina*. Geneva: Jean Crespin, 1550.
Cotgrave, Randle. *A Dictionarie of the French and English Tongues*. London: Adam Islip, 1611.
Crespin, Jean. *Livre des martyrs*. [Geneva]: [Jean Crespin], 1554.

[De la Roche-Chandieu, Antoine, and Bernard de Montméja]. *Response aux calomnies contenues au Discours et Suyte du Discours sur les Miseres de ce temps, Faits par Messire Pierre Ronsard, jadis Poëte, et maintenant Prebstre.* [Orléans: Éloi Gibier], 1563.

Dentière, Marie. *Epistle to Marguerite de Navarre* and *Preface to a Sermon by John Calvin.* Edited and translated by Mary McKinley. Chicago: University of Chicago Press, 2004.

———. *Epistre tres utile faicte et composée par une femme chrestienne de Tornay, envoyée à la Royne de Navarre seur du Roy de France: Contre les Turcz, Juifz, Infideles, Faulx chrestiens, Anabaptistes, et Lutheriens.* [Geneva] "Antwerp": [Jean Girard] "Martin Lempereur," 1539.

[Dentière, Marie]. *La Guerre et deslivrance de la ville de Genesve.* Geneva, 1536. Edited by Albert Rilliet. Geneva: Charles Schuchardt, 1881.

Désiré, Artus. *Les Batailles et victoires du Chevalier Celeste contre le Chevalier Terrestre.* Rouen: Louis du Mesnil, [1553].

———. *Les Combatz du fidelle Papiste pelerin Romain, contre l'apostat Antipapiste, tirant à la synagogue de Geneve, maison babilonicque des Lutheriens.* Rouen: Robert and Jean du Gort, 1550.

———. *Le Contrepoison des cinquante deux chansons de Clement Marot, faulsement intitulees par luy Psalmes de David.* Paris: Pierre Gaultier, 1560. Edited by Jacques Pineaux. Facsimile reproduction. Geneva: Droz, 1977.

———. *Le Deffensoire de la Foy Chrestienne, contenant en soy le Miroër des Errantz, autrement dit Lutheriens.* Lyon: Thibaud Payen, 1552.

———. *Description De la Cité De Dieu.* Rouen: Robert and Jean du Gort, 1550.

———. *Les Disputes de Guillot le Porcher et de la Bergere de Sainct Denys en France contre Jehan Calvin.* Paris: Pierre Gaultier, 1559.

———. *Grandes chroniques et annalles de passe par tout, chroniqueur de Geneve, avec l'origine de Jean Covin, faucement surnommé Calvin.* Lyon: Benoist Rigaud and Jean Saugrain, 1558.

———. *Le Miroir des francs taupins, autrement dictz Antechrists: Auquel est contenu le deffensoire de la foy chrestienne.* Rouen: Jean du Gort, [1547].

———. *Plaisans et Armonieux cantiques de devotion, composez sur le chant des hymnes de nostre mere saincte Eglise à la louange de Dieu et de ses saincts: Qui est un second Contrepoison aux Cinquante deux chansons de Clement Marot.* Paris: Pierre Gaultier, 1561.

———. *Les Regretz, complainctes, et lamentations, d'une damoiselle, laquelle s'estoit retiree à Genesve pour vivre en liberté, avec la convertion d'icelle estant à l'article de la mort: Consolation pour les bons chrestiens, et exemple pour les mauvais.* Paris: Pierre Gaultier, 1558.

[Désiré, Artus]. *Passevent parisien respondant à pasquin Rommain.* Lyon, 1556.

Deux moralités de la fin du Moyen-Âge et du temps des guerres de Religion. Edited by Jean-Claude Aubailly and Bruno Roy. Geneva: Droz, 1990.

Du Bellay, Joachim. *La Deffence, et illustration de la langue françoyse.* Paris: Arnoul l'Angelier, 1549. Edited by Jean-Charles Monferran. Geneva: Droz, 2001.

Du Peron, Jacques Davy. *Oraison funebre sur la mort de Monsieur de Ronsard*. Paris: Frédéric Morel, 1586. Edited by Michel Simonin. Geneva: Droz, 1985.

Erasmus, Desiderius. *The Adages of Erasmus*. Translated with an introduction by William Barker. Toronto: University of Toronto Press, 2001.

———. "Risus sardonicus." Vol. II.5 in *Opera omnia*. Edited by Felix Heinimann and Emanuel Kienzle, 289–97. Amsterdam: North-Holland Publishing, 1981.

La Farce de Maître Pathelin. Edited by Michel Rousse. Paris: Folio classique, 1999.

French Vernacular Books. Books published in the French Language before 1601. Livres vernaculaires français. Livres imprimés en français avant 1601. Edited by Andrew Pettegree, Malcolm Walsby, and Alexander Wilkinson. 2 vols. Leiden: Brill, 2007.

Furetière, Antoine. *Le Dictionnaire universel*. 3 vols. Paris, 1690.

Gringore, Pierre. *Le Jeu du Prince des Sotz et de Mère Sotte*. Edited by Alan Hindley. Paris: Champion, 2000.

———. *Œuvres polémiques rédigées sous le règne de Louis XII*. Edited by Cynthia J. Brown. Geneva: Droz, 2003.

Hangest, Jérôme de. *De Christifera Eucharistia adversus nugiferos symbolistas*. Paris: Jean Petit, 1534.

———. *Contre les tenebrions Lumiere evangelicque*. Paris: [Jean Petit, 1534.]

———. *En controversie voye seure*. Paris: Jean Petit, 1536.

Huguet, Edmond. *Dictionnaire de la langue française du seizième siècle*. 7 vols. Paris: Champion, 1925–67.

Joubert, Laurent. *Traité du ris*. 3 vols. Paris: Nicolas Chesneau, 1579.

———. *Treatise on Laughter*. Translated by Gregory David de Rocher. Tuscaloosa: University of Alabama Press, 1980.

Labé, Louise. *Complete Poetry and Prose: A Bilingual Edition*. Edited by Deborah Lesko Baker, translated by Annie Finch. Chicago: University of Chicago Press, 2006.

———. *Œuvres complètes*. Edited by François Rigolot. Paris: GF-Flammarion, 1986.

Lucian. "Lucius or the Ass." Translated by M. D. MacLeod. Vol. 8 of *Lucian*, 47–145. Cambridge, MA: Harvard University Press, 1993.

[Malingre, Matthieu]. *Moralité de la maladie de chrestienté*. Neuchâtel: Pierre de Vingle, 1533. Edited by Werner Helmich. Vol. 3 of *Moralités françaises*. Geneva: Slatkine, 1980.

[Marcourt, Antoine]. *Articles veritables sur les horribles, grandz et importables abuz de la Messe papale*. N.p., n.d.

———. *The Boke of Marchauntes, right necessarye unto all folks: Newly made by the lorde Pantapole, right expert in suche busynesse, nere neyghbour unto the lorde Pantagrul*. London: Thomas Godfraye, 1534.

———. *Livre des marchans, fort utile à toutes gens pour cognoistre de quelles marchandises on se doit donner garde d'estre deceu*. Neuchâtel: Pierre de Vingle, 1533.

Marot, Clément. *Œuvres poétiques*. Edited by Gérard Defaux. 2 vols. Paris: Classiques Garnier, 1990, 1993.

Montaigne, Michel de. *The Complete Essays of Montaigne*. Translated by Donald M. Frame. Stanford: Stanford University Press, 1958.

———. *Les Essais*. Edited by Pierre Villey and V.-L. Saulnier. 3 vols. Paris: Presses Universitaires de France, 1965.
Navarre, Marguerite de. *Heptaméron*. Edited by Nicole Cazauran. Paris: Folio, 2000.
———. *Marguerites de la Marguerite des princesses tres illustres royne de Nauarre*. Lyon: Jean de Tournes, 1547.
———. *Théâtre*. Edited by Geneviève Hasenohr and Olivier Millet. Vol. 4 in *Œuvres complètes*. Paris: Champion, 2002.
———. *Théâtre profane*. Translated with an introduction by Régine Reynolds-Cornell. Ottawa: Dovehouse Editions, 1992.
———. *Théâtre profane*. Edited by V.-L. Saulnier. Paris: Droz, 1946.
Oudin, Antoine. *Curiositez françoises*. Paris: Antoine de Sommaville, 1640.
La Polémique protestante contre Ronsard. Edited by Jacques Pineaux. 2 vols. Paris: Librairie Marcel Didier, 1973.
Rabelais, François. *The Complete Works of François Rabelais*. Translated with an introduction by Donald M. Frame. Berkeley: University of California Press, 1991.
———. *Œuvres complètes*. Edited by Mireille Huchon. Paris: Gallimard, 1994.
Recueil de farces, 1450–1550. Edited by André Tissier. 12 vols. Geneva: Droz, 1986–98.
Recueil de Florence: 53 farces imprimées à Paris vers 1515. Edited by Jelle Koopmans. Orléans: Paradigme, 2011.
Recueil des sotties françaises. Vol. 1. Edited by Marie Bouhaïk-Gironès, Jelle Koopmans, and Katell Lavéant. Paris: Classiques Garnier, 2014.
Remonstrance envoyee au roy par la noblesse de la religion reformee du païs et comté du Maine, sur les assassinats, pilleries, saccagements de maisons, seditions, violements de femmes & autres exces horribles commis depuis la publication de l'Edit de pacification dedans ledit comté; et presentee à Sa Maiesté à Rossillon le x. jour d'aoust. 1564. N.p., [1564].
Ronsard, Pierre de. *Discours des misères de ce temps*. Edited by Francis Higman. Paris: Le Livre de poche classique, 1993.
———. *Discours des misères de ce temps*. Edited by Malcolm Smith. Geneva: Droz, 1979.
———. *Discours des miseres de ce temps*. Vol. 6 of *Œuvres de Pierre de Ronsard*. Paris: Gabriel Buon, 1567.
———. *Œuvres complètes*. Edited by Jean Céard, Daniel Ménager, and Michel Simonin. 2 vols. Paris: Gallimard, 1993.
———. *Œuvres complètes*. Edited by Paul Laumonier. 20 vols. Paris: Hachette, 1914–75.
Sottie à dix personnages, jouée à Genève en la place du Molard, le dimanche des Bordes, l'an 1523. Lyon: Pierre Rigaud, n.d.
Théâtre et propagande aux débuts de la Réforme: Six pièces polémiques du Recueil La Vallière. Edited by Jonathan Beck. Geneva: Slatkine, 1986.
Tory, Geoffroy. *Champfleury*. Paris: Geoffroy de Tory and Gilles de Gourmont, 1529.
Les Triomphes de l'Abbaye des Conards. Rouen: Nicolas Dugord, 1587.
Les Triomphes de l'Abbaye des Conards. Edited by Marc de Montifaud. Paris: Librairie des bibliophiles, 1874.

Viret, Pierre. *De la difference qui est entre les superstitions des anciens gentilz et payens, et les erreurs et abuz qui sont entre ceux qui s'appellent chrestiens: Et de la vraye manière d'honnorer Dieu, la Vierge Marie, et les Sainctz.* [Geneva]: [Jean Girard], 1542.

———. *Disputations chrestiennes, en manière de deviz, divisées par dialogues.* 3 vols. Geneva: Jean Girard, 1544.

———. *La Physique papale faite par maniere de devis et par dialogues.* Geneva: Jean Girard, 1552.

Secondary Works

Angenot, Marc. *La Parole pamphlétaire: Typologie des discours modernes.* Paris: Payot, 1982.

Arden, Heather. *Fools' Plays: A Study of Satire in the Sottie.* New York: Cambridge University Press, 1976.

Aubailly, Jean-Claude. *Le Théâtre médiéval profane et comique.* Paris: Larousse, 1975.

Backus, Irena. "Marie Dentière: Un cas de feminisme théologique à l'époque de la Réforme?" *Bulletin de la Société de l'histoire du Protestantisme Français: Études historiques* 137 (1991): 177–95.

Bakhtin, Mikhail. *Rabelais and His World.* Translated by Helene Iswolsky. Cambridge, MA: MIT Press, 1968. Reprint, Bloomington: Indiana University Press, 1984.

Baldick, Chris. "Satire." *Oxford Concise Dictionary of Literary Terms.* Oxford: Oxford University Press, 2001.

Barbier, Jean-Paul. *Bibliographie des Discours politiques de Ronsard.* Geneva: Droz, 1984.

Barker, S. K. *Protestantism, Poetry and Protest: The Vernacular Writings of Antoine de Chandieu (c. 1534–1591).* Aldershot, UK: Ashgate, 2009.

———, ed. *Revisiting Geneva: Robert Kingdon and the Coming of the French Wars of Religion.* St. Andrews Studies in French History and Culture, no. 4. St. Andrews: Centre for French History and Culture of the University of St. Andrews, 2012.

Barnaud, Jean. *Pierre Viret: Sa vie et son œuvre.* Saint-Amans: Carayol, 1911.

Bayle, Ariane. "Six questions sur la notion d'obscénité dans la critique rabelaisienne." In *Obscénités renaissantes*, edited by Hugh Roberts, Guillaume Peureux, and Lise Wajeman, 379–92. Geneva: Droz, 2011.

Beam, Sara. "Calvinist 'Comedie' and Conversion during the French Reformation: *La Comedie du Pape malade* (1561) and *La Comedie du Monde malade et mal pensé* (1568)." In *French Renaissance and Baroque Drama: Text, Performance, and Theory*, edited by Michael Meere, 63–82. Newark: University of Delaware Press, 2015.

———. *Laughing Matters: Farce and the Making of Absolutism in France.* Ithaca: Cornell University Press, 2007.

Benedict, Philip. *Rouen during the Wars of Religion.* Cambridge: Cambridge University Press, 1981.

Berthoud, Gabrielle. *Antoine Marcourt: Réformateur et Pamphlétaire.* Geneva: Droz, 1973.

———. "*Le Livre des marchans* d'Antoine Marcourt et Rabelais." In *François Rabelais: Ouvrage publié pour le quatrième centenaire de sa mort, 1553–1953*, 86–92. Geneva: Droz, 1953.

Berthoud, Gabrielle, et al. *Aspects de la propagande religieuse*. Geneva: Droz, 1957.

Bertrand, Dominique. *Dire le rire à l'Âge Classique: Représenter pour mieux contrôler*. Aix-en-Provence: Publications de l'Université de Provence, 1995.

Bogel, Fredric V. *The Difference Satire Makes: Rhetoric and Reading from Jonson to Byron*. Ithaca: Cornell University Press, 2001.

Bordier, Jean-Pierre. "Satire traditionnelle et polémique moderne dans les moralités et les sotties françaises tardives." In *Satira e beffa nelle commedie europpee del Rinascimento*, edited by Maria Chiabò and Federico Doglio, 109–33. Rome: Torre d'Orfeo, 2002.

Bouhaïk-Gironès, Marie. *Les Clercs de la Basoche et le théâtre comique (Paris, 1420–1550)*. Paris: Champion, 2007.

Bouwsma, William J. *John Calvin: A Sixteenth-Century Portrait*. Oxford: Oxford University Press, 1988.

Burke, Peter. *Popular Culture in Early Modern Europe*. London: Temple Smith, 1978. Reprint, Aldershot, UK: Ashgate, 1994.

Buron, Emmanuel, and Julien Gœury. *Lectures de Ronsard: Discours des miseres de ce temps*. Rennes: Presses Universitaires de Rennes, 2009.

Butterworth, Emily. *The Unbridled Tongue: Babble and Gossip in Renaissance France*. Oxford: Oxford University Press, 2016.

Champion, Pierre. *Ronsard et son temps*. Paris: Champion, 1925.

Cholakian, Patricia F., and Rouben C. Cholakian. *Marguerite de Navarre: Mother of the Renaissance*. New York: Columbia University Press, 2006.

Classen, Albrecht. *Laughter in the Middle Ages and Early Modern Times: Epistemology of a Fundamental Human Behavior, Its Meaning, and Consequences*. Berlin: De Gruyter, 2010.

Cohen, Gustave. *Ronsard: Sa vie et son œuvre*. Paris: Gallimard, 1956.

Corbett, Philip. *The Scurra*. Edinburgh: Scottish Academic Press, 1986.

Cottrell, Robert D. "Lefèvre d'Étaples and the Limits of Biblical Interpretation." *Œuvres et Critiques* 20 (1995): 79–95.

Crousaz, Karine, and Daniela Solfaroli Camillocci. *Pierre Viret et la diffusion de la Réforme*. Lausanne: Éditions Antipodes, 2014.

Crouzet, Denis. *Les Guerriers de Dieu: La violence au temps des troubles de religion, vers 1525–vers 1610*. 2 vols. Seyssel: Champ Vallon, 1990.

Cummings, Brian. *The Literary Culture of the Reformation: Grammar and Grace*. Oxford: Oxford University Press, 2002.

Debailly, Pascal. *La Muse indignée*. Vol. 1. Paris: Classiques Garnier, 2012.

———. "Le rire satirique." *Bibliothèque d'Humanisme et Renaissance* 56 (1994): 695–717.

Debbagi Baranova, Tatiana. *A Coup de libelles: Une culture politique au temps des guerres de religion (1562–1598)*. Geneva: Droz, 2012.

Demerson, Guy. "Mythologie antique et satire politique: Les *Discours* de Ronsard."

In *Influence de la Grèce et de Rome sur l'occident moderne*, edited by René Chevallier, 101–7. Paris: Société d'édition "Les Belles Lettres," 1977.

Diefendorf, Barbara B. *Beneath the Cross: Catholics and Huguenots in Sixteenth-Century Paris*. New York: Oxford University Press, 1991.

Droz, Eugénie. "Pierre de Vingle, l'imprimeur de Farel." In *Aspects de la propagande religieuse*, 38–78. Geneva: Droz, 1957.

Duhl, Olga Anna. *Folie et rhétorique dans la sottie*. Geneva: Droz, 1994.

Duval, Edwin M. "Erasmus and the 'First Renaissance' in France." In *A History of Modern French Literature*, edited by Christopher Prendergast, 47–70. Princeton: Princeton University Press, 2017.

———. "The Place of the Present: Ronsard, Aubigné, and the 'Misères de ce Temps.'" *Yale French Studies* 80 (1991): 13–29.

Ehrstine, Glenn. *Theater, Culture, and Community in Reformation Bern, 1523–1555*. Leiden: Brill, 2002.

Eisenstein, Elizabeth. *The Printing Press as Agent of Change: Communications and Cultural Transformations in Early Modern Europe*. 2 vols. Cambridge: Cambridge University Press, 1979.

Enders, Jody. "Of Protestantism, Performativity, and the Threat of Theater." *Mediaevalia* 22 (1999): 55–74.

———. "Rhetoric and Comedy." In *The Oxford Handbook of Rhetorical Studies*, edited by Michael J. MacDonald. New York: Oxford University Press, 2017.

———. *Rhetoric and the Origins of Medieval Drama*. Ithaca: Cornell University Press, 1992.

———. "Violence, théâtralité, et subjectivité dans la rhétorique médiévale." In *Èthos et Pathos: Le statut du sujet rhétorique*, edited by François Cornilliat and Richard Lockwood, 267–78. Paris: Champion, 2000.

Engammare, Max. "Gens qui rient, Jean qui pleure: Rires de Genevois surprise dans les Registres du Consistoire au temps de Calvin." In *Rire à la Renaissance*, edited by Marie Madeleine Fontaine, 93–106. Geneva: Droz, 2010.

Farge, James K. *Orthodoxy and Reform in Early Reformation France: The Faculty of Theology of Paris, 1500–1543*. Leiden: Brill, 1985.

Febvre, Lucien. *Amour sacré, amour profane*. Paris: Gallimard, 1944.

Ferrer, Véronique, Frank Lestringant, and Alexandre Tarrête, eds. *Sur les Discours des misères de ce temps de Ronsard: "D'une plume de fer sur un papier d'acier."* Orléans: Paradigme, 2009.

Flood, Chris. "La France satirisée, satyrisée et fragmentée: L'autoreprésentation factionnelle au temps des guerres de religion." In *Littérature et politique: Factions et dissidences de la Ligue à la Fronde*, edited by Malina Stefanovska and Adrien Paschoud, 75–96. Paris: Classiques Garnier, 2015.

Fontaine, Marie Madeleine, ed. *Rire à la Renaissance*. Geneva: Droz, 2010.

Francis, Scott. "Guéris-toi toi-même: La réflexivité du jugement dans La Comédie de Mont-de-Marsan de Marguerite de Navarre." *Nottingham French Studies* 51, no. 2 (2012): 125–35.

———. "Scandalous Women or Scandalous Judgment? The Social Perception of

Women and the Theology of Scandal in the Heptaméron." *L'Esprit Créateur* 57, no. 3 (2017): 33–45.

Freud, Sigmund. *Jokes and Their Relation to the Unconscious*. Edited and translated by James Strachey. New York: Norton, 1960.

Frisch, Andrea. "Les *Discours* de Pierre de Ronsard: Une Poétique de l'oubli?" *Tangence* 87 (2008): 47–61.

Giese, Frank S. *Artus Désiré: Priest and Pamphleteer of the Sixteenth Century*. Chapel Hill: North Carolina Studies in the Romance Languages and Literatures, 1973.

Gilhus, Ingvild Salid. "Carnival in Religion: The Feast of Fools in France." *Numen* 37 (1990): 24–52.

Gilmont, Jean-François, ed. *La Réforme et le livre: L'Europe de l'imprimé (1517–1570)*. Paris: Éditions du Cerf, 1990.

Gorris-Camos, Rosanna. "Penser le rire et rire de cœur: Le *Traité du ris* de Laurent Joubert, médecin de l'âme et du cœur." In *Rire à la Renaissance*, edited by Marie Madeleine Fontaine, 141–61. Geneva: Droz, 2010.

Graesslé, Isabelle. *Vie et légendes de Marie Dentière*. Geneva: Bulletin du Centre protestant d'études, 2003.

Griffin, Dustin. *Satire: A Critical Reintroduction*. Lexington: University of Kentucky Press, 1994.

Gruner, Charles R. *The Game of Humor: A Comprehensive Theory of Why We Laugh*. New Brunswick, NJ: Transaction Publishers, 1997.

Guynn, Noah D. "A Justice to Come: The Role of Ethics in *La Farce de Maistre Pierre Pathelin*." *Theatre Survey* 47 (2006): 13–31.

Harvey, Howard Graham. *The Theatre of the Basoche: The Contributions of the Law Societies to French Mediaeval Comedy*. Cambridge, MA: Harvard University Press, 1941.

Hayes, Bruce. "The *Affaire des placards*, Polemical Humour, and the Sardonic Laugh." *French Studies* 70, no. 3 (2016): 332–47.

———. "'De rire ne me puys tenir': Marguerite de Navarre's Satirical Theater." In *La Satire dans tous ses états*, edited by Bernd Renner, 183–200. Geneva: Droz, 2009.

———. *Rabelais's Radical Farce: Late Medieval Comic Theater and Its Function in Rabelais*. Aldershot, UK: Ashgate, 2010.

———. "Le *risus sardonicus* de Jean Boucher." *Œuvres et Critiques* 38, no. 2 (2013): 25–38.

Head, Thomas. "Marie Dentière: A Propagandist for the Reform." In *Women Writers of the Renaissance and Reformation*, edited by Katharina M. Wilson, 260–83. Athens: University of Georgia Press, 1987.

Heath, Michael J. *Rabelais*. Tempe, AZ: Medieval & Renaissance Texts & Studies, 1996.

Heers, Jacques. *Fêtes des fous et Carnavals*. Paris: Fayard, 1983.

Heller, Henry. *The Conquest of Poverty: The Calvinist Revolt in Sixteenth Century France*. Leiden: Brill, 1986.

Helmich, Werner. *Moralités françaises*. Vol. 3. Geneva: Slatkine, 1980.

Higman, Francis M. *Lire et découvrir: La circulation des idées au temps de la Réforme*. Geneva: Droz, 1998.

———. *Piety and the People: Religious Printing in French, 1511–1551*. St. Andrews Studies in Reformation History. Aldershot, UK: Ashgate, 1996.

———. "Ronsard's Political and Polemical Poetry." In *Ronsard the Poet*, edited by Terence Cave, 241–85. London: Methuen, 1973.

———. *The Style of John Calvin in His French Polemical Treatises*. London: Oxford University Press, 1967.

Hoffmann, George. *Reforming French Culture: Satire, Spiritual Alienation, & Connection to Strangers*. Oxford: Oxford University Press, 2017.

Hudson, Robert J. "Marot vs. Sagon: Heresy and the Gallic School, 1537." In *Representations of Heresy in French Art and Literature*, edited by Gabriella Scarlatta and Lidia Radi, 159–87. Toronto: University of Toronto Press, 2017.

Johns, Adrian. *The Nature of the Book: Print and Knowledge in the Making*. Chicago: University of Chicago Press, 1998.

Jourda, Pierre. *Marguerite d'Angoulême: Duchesse d'Alençon, Reine de Navarre*. 2 vols. Paris: Champion, 1930.

Keller, Marcus. "The Struggle for Cultural Memory in Ronsard's *Discours des misères de ce temps*." In *Memory and Community in Sixteenth-Century France*, edited by David LaGuardia and Cathy Yandell, 205–41. Aldershot, UK: Ashgate, 2015.

Kemp, William, and Diane Desrosiers-Bonin. "Marie d'Ennetières et la petite grammaire hébraïque de sa fille d'après la dédicace de l'Epistre à Marguerite de Navarre." *Bibliothèque d'humanisme et Renaissance* 50 (1998): 117–34.

Kingdon, Robert M. *Geneva and the Coming of the Wars of Religion in France*. Geneva: Droz, 1956.

Kirby, Torrance. "Emerging Publics of Religious Reform in the 1530s: The Affair of the Placards and the Publication of Antoine de Marcourt's *Livre des marchans*." In *Making Publics in Early Modern Europe: People, Things, Forms of Knowledge*, edited by Bronwen Wilson and Paul Yachnin. New York: Routledge, 2010.

Knecht, R. J. *The French Civil Wars, 1562–1598*. Harlow, UK: Longman, 2000.

———. *Renaissance Warrior and Patron: The Reign of Francis I*. Cambridge: Cambridge University Press, 1994.

Koopmans, Jelle. "L'allégorie théâtrale au début du XVIe siècle: Le cas des pièces 'profanes' de Marguerite de Navarre." *Renaissance and Reformation/Renaissance et Réforme* 26 (2002): 65–89.

———, ed. *Quatre sermons joyeux*. Geneva: Droz, 1984.

———. *Le Théâtre des exclus au Moyen Âge*. Paris: Imago, 1997.

Langer, Ullrich. "La Response de P. de Ronsard gentilhomme vandomois: L'agonie de la subjectivité éthique?" In *Èthos et Pathos: Le statut du sujet rhétorique*, edited by François Cornilliat and Richard Lockwood, 237–48. Paris: Champion, 2000.

Lauvergnat-Gagnière, Christiane. *Lucien de Samosate et le lucianisme en France au XVIe siècle*. Geneva: Droz, 1988.

Lebègue, Raymond. "La Pléiade et le théâtre." In *Lumières de la Pléiade*, edited by Roland Antonioli, 87–96. Paris: Librairie J. Vrin, 1966.

———. *La Tragédie religieuse en France: Les Débuts (1514–1573)*. Paris: Champion, 1929.

Lenient, Charles. *La Satire en France ou la littérature militante au XVIe siècle*. 2 vols. Paris: Hachette, 1877.

Lestringant, Frank. "Rire en Sardaigne et ailleurs: Le rire du voyageur à la Renaissance." In *Rire à la Renaissance*, edited by Marie Madeleine Fontaine, 195–217. Geneva: Droz, 2010.

———. *Une Sainte horreur ou le voyage en Eucharistie XVIe–XVIIIe siècles*. Paris: Presses Universitaires de France, 1996.

Linder, Robert Dean. *The Political Ideas of Pierre Viret*. Geneva: Droz, 1964.

Lysyk, Stephanie. "Love of the Censor: Legendre, Censorship, and the Theater of the Basoche." *Cardozo Studies in Law and Literature* 11 (1999): 113–33.

Matheson, Peter. *The Rhetoric of the Reformation*. Edinburgh: T&T Clark, 1998.

Mayer, Claude-Albert. *Lucien de Samosate et la Renaissance française*. Geneva: Slatkine, 1984.

Mazouer, Charles. "Marguerite de Navarre et le mystère médiéval." *Renaissance and Reformation/Renaissance et Réforme* 26 (2002): 51–64.

———. *Le Théâtre français de la Renaissance*. Paris: Champion, 2002.

McKinley, Mary. "The Absent Ellipsis: The Edition and Suppression of Marie Dentière in the Sixteenth and the Nineteenth Century." In *Women Writers in Pre-Revolutionary France: Strategies of Emancipation*, edited by Colette Winn and Donna Kuizenga, 85–100. New York: Garland, 1997.

———, ed. and trans. *Epistle to Marguerite de Navarre* and *Preface to a Sermon by John Calvin*. Chicago: University of Chicago Press, 2004.

———. "Marie Dentière's *Epistle to Marguerite de Navarre* and the *Heptameron*." In *Teaching French Women Writers of the Renaissance and Reformation*, edited by Colette H. Winn, 273–84. New York: MLA, 2011.

Ménager, Daniel. *La Renaissance et le rire*. Paris: Presses Universitaires de France, 1995.

———. *Ronsard: Le Roi, le poète et les hommes*. Geneva: Droz, 1979.

Menini, Romain. *Rabelais altérateur: "Græciser en françois."* Paris: Classiques Gallimard, 2014.

Millet, Olivier. "Calvin pamphlétaire." In *Le Pamphlet en France au XVIe siècle*, 9–22. Collection de l'École Normale Supérieure de Jeunes Filles no. 25. Cahiers V.-L. Saulnier no. 1. Paris: École normale supérieure de jeunes filles, 1983.

Monro, David Hector. *Argument of Laughter*. Victoria: Melbourne University Press, 1951.

Morreall, John. *Comic Relief: A Comprehensive Philosophy of Humor*. Malden, MA: Wiley-Blackwell, 2009.

Muchembled, Robert. *Culture populaire et culture des élites dans la France moderne (XVe–XVIIIe siècles)*. Paris: Flammarion, 1978.

Niceron, Jean-Pierre. *Mémoires pour servir à l'histoire des hommes illustres, de la république des lettres, avec un catalogue raisonné de leurs ouvrages*. 43 vols. Paris: Briasson, 1727–45.

Perdrizet, Pierre. *Ronsard et la Réforme*. Paris, 1902. Reprint, Geneva: Slatkine Reprints, 1970.

Persels, Jeff. "The Sorbonnic Trots: Staging the Intestinal Distress of the Roman Catholic Church in French Reform Theater." *Renaissance Quarterly* 56, no. 4 (2003): 1089–1111.

Persels, Jeff, and Russell Ganim, eds. *Fecal Matters in Early Modern Literature and Art*. Aldershot, UK: Ashgate, 2004.

Petit de Julleville, Louis. *La Comédie et les moeurs en France au Moyen Âge*. Paris: Léopold Cerf, 1896.

Pettegree, Andrew. *Reformation and the Culture of Persuasion*. Cambridge: Cambridge University Press, 2005.

Picot, Émile. *Les Moralités polémiques ou la controverse religieuse dans l'ancien théâtre français*. Geneva: Slatkine Reprints, 1970.

Pineaux, Jacques. "Poésie et prophétisme: Ronsard et Théodore de Bèze dans la querelle des *Discours*." *Revue d'Histoire littéraire de la France* 78 (1978): 531–40.

Postel, Claude. *Traité des invectives au temps de la Réforme*. Paris: Les Belles Lettres, 2004.

Pouey-Mounou, Anne-Pascale. "L'Absolu et le libre plaisir dans l'*Elégie à Loïs des Masures* du 'talentueux' Ronsard." *Littératures Classiques* 37 (1999): 45–56.

———. "Des prêches, des armes et des livres: La figure de Théodore de Bèze dans la polémique des *Discours des miseres de ce temps* (1562–1563)." In *Writers in Conflict in Sixteenth-Century France: Essays in Honour of Malcolm Quainton*, edited by Elizabeth Vinestock, David Foster, and Neil Kenny, 153–72. Durham: University of Durham Press, 2008.

Racaut, Luc. *Hatred in Print: Catholic Propaganda and Protestant Identity during the French Wars of Religion*. Aldershot, UK: Ashgate, 2002.

Reid, Dylan. "Carnival in Rouen: A History of the Abbaye des Conards." *Sixteenth Century Journal* 32, no. 4 (2001): 1027–55.

———. "The Triumph of the Abbey of the Conards: Spectacle and Sophistication in a Rouen Carnival." In *Medieval and Early Modern Ritual: Formalized Behavior in Europe, China and Japan*, edited by Joëlle Rollo-Koster, 147–73. Leiden: Brill, 2002.

Reid, Jonathan A. *King's Sister—Queen of Dissent: Marguerite de Navarre (1492–1549) and Her Evangelical Network*. 2 vols. Leiden: Brill, 2009.

Renner, Bernd. *"Difficile est saturam non scribere": L'Herméneutique de la satire rabelaisienne*. Geneva: Droz, 2007.

———. "Rire et satire à l'aube des guerres civiles: L'exemple des *Satyres chrestiennes de la cuisine papale*." *Romanic Review* 101, no. 4 (2010): 655–71.

———, ed. *La Satire dans tous ses états*. Geneva: Droz, 2009.

———. "From *Satura* to *Satyre*: François Rabelais and the Renaissance Appropriation of a Genre." *Renaissance Quarterly* 67, no. 2 (2014): 377–424.

Rigolot, François. *Poésie et Renaissance*. Paris: Seuil, 2002.

———. "Poétique et politique: Ronsard et Montaigne devant les troubles de leur temps." In *Ronsard et Montaigne: Ecrivains engagés?* edited by Michel Dassonville, 57–69. Lexington, KY: French Forum, 1989.

Robinson, Christopher. "The Reputation of Lucian in Sixteenth-Century France." *French Studies* 29 (1975): 385–97.

Rousse, Michel. *La Scène et les tréteaux: Le théâtre de la farce au Moyen Âge*. Orléans: Paradigme, 2004.

Screech, M. A. *Laughter at the Foot of the Cross*. London: Allen Lane, Penguin Press, 1997.

———. *Rabelais*. Ithaca: Cornell University Press, 1979.

Seidel, Michael. *Satiric Inheritance: Rabelais to Sterne*. Princeton: Princeton University Press, 1979.

Shaw, Helen A. "Conrad Badius and the *Comedie du pape malade*." PhD diss., University of Pennsylvania, 1934.

Skenazi, Cynthia. "Marie Dentière et la prédication des femmes." *Renaissance and Reformation/Renaissance et Réforme* 21 (1997): 5–18.

Smith, Malcolm. *Ronsard & Du Bellay versus Bèze: Allusiveness in Renaissance Literary Texts*. Geneva: Droz, 1995.

Spacks, Patricia Meyer. "Reflections on Satire." *Genre* 1 (1968): 13–30.

Stjerna, Kirsi. *Women and the Reformation*. Malden, MA: Blackwell, 2009.

Stolberg, Michael. *Uroscopy in Early Modern Europe*. Translated by Logan Kennedy and Leonhard Unglaub. Aldershot, UK: Ashgate, 2015.

Suerbaum, Almut, George Southcombe, and Benjamin Thompson, eds. *Polemic: Language as Violence in Medieval and Early Modern Discourse*. Aldershot, UK: Ashgate, 2015.

Sutherland, N. M. *The Huguenot Struggle for Recognition*. New Haven: Yale University Press, 1980.

Szabari, Antónia. *Less Rightly Said: Scandals and Readers in Sixteenth-Century France*. Stanford: Stanford University Press, 2010.

Taddei, Ilaria. *Fête, jeunesse et pouvoirs: L'Abbaye des Nobles Enfants de Lausanne*. Lausanne: Université de Lausanne, 1991.

Weitz, Eric. *The Cambridge Introduction to Comedy*. Cambridge: Cambridge University Press, 2009.

Williams, Wes. *Pilgrimage and Narrative in the French Renaissance*. New York: Clarendon Press, 1998.

Zemon Davis, Natalie. *Society and Culture in Early Modern France*. Stanford: Stanford University Press, 1965.

INDEX

Adages (Erasmus), 5
Aeneid, 100, 107, 109
Affaire des placards, 8–9, 13, 15–29, 56, 133
Aggressiveness, 1–3, 5, 13, 15, 18, 28, 33, 35, 39, 54, 65, 68, 81, 83, 85, 88, 91, 99, 118, 149, 152, 155, 162, 164
Ajax (character), 5, 166
d'Albret, Jeanne, 33, 93
Alessandri, Alessandro, 6
Allusion, 17, 19, 51, 93, 99, 126
Amours de Cassandre, 136, 138
Anger, 2–3, 6, 11, 73, 80, 97, 124, 139, 153, 155, 162, 164
Anti-Catholicism, 9, 15–16, 111, 121, 124
Antiquitez de Rome, 95
Aquinas, Thomas, Saint, 118
Articles veritables sur les horribles, grandz et importables abuz de la Messe papale, 8, 16, 19–22, 29
Atheism / Atheists, 7, 18, 73, 93, 102, 151, 158, 165
Aubailly, Jean-Claude, 130–32
Audience, 3–4, 9, 17–18, 22, 24, 27, 31, 36–37, 46, 48, 51–52, 56–60, 62, 65–66, 70, 72, 77, 80, 86–91, 94–95, 111, 122, 124, 126–27, 129, 131, 136, 140–41, 144, 147–48, 156–57, 160
Augustine, Saint, 103, 145
Authority, 19, 36, 38, 42, 45, 47–48, 62, 67, 95–96, 118, 127, 135, 141
Avarice. *See* Greed

Badius, Conrad, 10, 12, 55, 67, 86–91, 93, 112, 140, 171, 187, 197
Basoche, 11, 48, 120–32
Beckett, Samuel, 53
Béda, Noël, 9, 22, 39, 47, 57
Bellay, Joachim du, 95, 129
Berquin, Louis de, 30, 36–38, 42
Bèze, Théodore de, 10, 70, 72, 92, 108, 112–15, 117, 119, 134–35, 138, 141, 143, 149, 151, 153–54, 156, 159–60
Bible / Biblical reference, 7, 8, 19, 27, 29, 34, 38–39, 44, 48, 53, 59, 61, 62–63, 66, 68, 79, 86, 93–94, 96–97, 100, 104, 106–7, 111, 126, 140, 143, 147–48, 155, 158. *See also* New Testament; Old Testament
Bienvenu, Jacques, 73
Blasphemy, 1, 8–9, 22, 75, 77, 83, 85, 89, 101–3, 111, 114–15, 145, 150, 153, 162, 164
Bordier, Jean-Pierre, 33
Boucher, Jean, 57, 162
Bouchet, Jean, 37
Briçonnet, Guillaume, 39
Burning at the stake, 9, 11, 21, 36, 48, 57–61, 65, 68–69, 71, 74–75, 77–80, 84, 121, 123, 129, 131, 153, 163

Calvin, Jean, 9, 18, 25, 27–30, 37, 55, 63, 67, 70–71, 73, 75–76, 79–83, 89, 92–93, 98–102, 104, 113–14, 119, 141–42, 146, 160, 164
Calvinism / Calvinists, 3, 9–10, 18, 24, 59, 68, 70–73, 75–76, 81–86, 88, 93, 100, 121, 123, 131, 133–37, 140, 142, 144–49, 156–57, 160–61

Candle imagery, 20–21, 24, 34, 122, 159
Catholic Church, 15, 17, 19, 21, 27, 32–34, 36, 37, 61, 67, 95–96, 108–9, 115, 153
The Carnivalesque / carnivals, 4, 60, 67, 116, 119, 121–22, 126
Catherine de' Medici, 56, 133–34, 140–41, 152
Catholicism / Catholics, 2–4, 10–11, 15, 22–23, 28, 39, 56, 66, 94–96, 104, 107, 109–11, 114–15, 118, 134–37, 140, 148, 152, 162
Catholic-Protestant relations, 2, 9, 15, 71, 84, 86, 92, 94, 133, 163. *See also* Catholics; Protestants
Castigation, 1, 4, 10, 75, 85, 145, 157, 161
Chamay, Charles-Antoine, 111, 114
Champfleury, 101
Chansons spirituelles, 54
Charles IX, 3, 56, 134, 141
Children, 4, 8, 24–25, 32, 48–52, 54, 64, 69, 110, 122, 134, 139, 142, 147, 157, 161
Cholakian, Patricia, 39
Cholakian, Rouben, 39
Christ, 7–8, 10, 19–20, 27, 29, 33, 48, 52, 79, 82–83, 85, 90, 96, 104, 106, 109–11, 118, 143, 155
Christianity, 30, 96, 100, 103–4, 106, 112, 116, 119, 145
De Christifera Eucharistia adversus nugiferos symbolistas, 22
Cicero, 5, 101, 109
Circle of Meaux, 38
Circulation of literature, 2, 10, 15, 22, 29–30, 49, 56, 64, 78, 85–86, 92, 100, 112, 138, 143, 157
Clergy, 12, 18–19, 21, 35, 62, 68, 72, 91, 108–9, 111, 126, 146, 148
Cohen, Gustave, 140
Les Combatz du fidelle Papiste pelerin Romain, contre l'apostat Antipapiste, tirant à la synagogue de Geneve, maison babilonicque des Lutheriens, 66–69
Comedie du pape malade et tirant à la fin, 10, 12, 36, 55, 67, 86–89, 91, 140

Comedy, 1, 12, 38, 73, 91, 119, 125, 129. *See also* Comic conventions
Comic conventions, 37–38, 41, 49, 52, 54, 65, 72–73, 94, 96, 106, 113, 115, 140–41, 143–44, 147, 152, 161
Conards de Rouen, 11, 48–49, 120–32
Contempt, 4, 8, 45, 76, 100, 104, 107, 156
Continuation des amours de Cassandre, 136
Continuation du Discours des miseres de ce temps, 136, 141–44
Contrafactum, 54, 81, 161
Contre les tenebrions Lumiere evangelicque, 16, 23–24
Le Contrepoison des cinquante deux chansons de Clement Marot, faulsement intitulees par luy Psalmes de David, 81–84
Conversion, 17–18, 43, 48–49, 51, 73, 76–77, 87, 89, 91, 111, 134, 137
Costume / Clothing, 19, 52, 67, 94, 107, 116–17, 122, 125
Cotgrave, Randle, 18, 36, 94–95
Cotton, Noël, 123
Crespin, Jean, 71
Cross-dressing, 4, 19, 67, 116–17
Crouzet, Denis, 10, 55–56, 85, 163
Cruel humor, 5, 157, 163,
Cruelty, 3, 5, 7–8, 49, 51–52, 125, 129, 139, 142, 157, 163
Cyrano de Bergerac, 106, 165

Dante, 164
Davis, Natalie Zemon, 24, 27, 41, 65, 120
Debate, 13, 22, 24–25, 29, 46, 52, 112, 122, 133, 160, 166. *See also* Polemics
Debauchery, 19, 73, 109, 150
Le Deffensoire de la Foy Chrestienne, 57, 60–66
De la difference qui est entre les superstitions des anciens gentilz et payens, et les erreurs et abuz qui sont entre ceux qui s'appellent chrestiens, 93–98

La Deffence, et illustration de la langue françoyse, 129
Democritus, 96–97, 105
Dentière, Marie, 10, 15–16, 18, 25, 27–29
Depravity, 20, 74
Description, 3–4, 6–7, 18, 21, 26, 28–29, 73, 76, 86, 101, 110, 114, 122, 142, 144, 146, 148, 152–53
Description de la Cité de Dieu, 66
Désiré, Artus, 10, 55–91, 92, 137, 140, 146, 155–56, 164
Dialogue, 36, 41, 53, 66–67, 73, 79–81, 98–108, 124–25, 137
Diatribe, 2, 16, 23–24, 32, 35, 37, 62, 64, 66, 147
Diefendorf, Barbara, 133–36
Dies geniales, 6
Diogenes, 102
Discours des misères de ce temps, 8–9, 11, 133, 136, 140–41, 144
Disguise, 19–20, 52, 94–95, 116–17
Disputations chrestiennes, en manière de deviz, divisées par dialogues, 92–108, 113
Les Disputes de Guillot le Porcher et de la Bergere de Sainct Denys en France contre Jehan Calvin, 78–81
Dogs / Dog metaphor, 4–5, 73, 82, 105, 142
Drag. *See* Cross-dressing
Drama. *See* Plays
Drunkenness, 71, 90, 110–11, 115, 140
Duke of Savoy, 25–26, 31–32, 82
Duval, Edwin, 12

Edict of Ambroise, 3
Editions, 16–17, 19, 56, 86, 93, 146
Effeminacy, 19, 28, 106–7, 148
L'Église, Noblesse et Pauvreté qui font la lessive, 123–25
Elegie à Guillaume des Autels, 138–39
Elegie à Des Masures, 138, 140
Elegie à Guillaume des Autels, 138–40
Elijah, 8, 97, 99, 104
Elisha, 8

En controversie voye seure, 24–25
Endings, 10–11, 16, 20, 32, 44, 51, 87, 89, 91, 105–6, 125–29, 132, 141, 147–49, 160
Enfants sans souci, 48–49, 53, 131
Epicureanism, 24, 60, 73, 100, 136
Epistola Magistri Benedicti Passavanti, 70
Epistre tres utile faicte et composée par une femme chrestienne de Tornay, envoyée à la Royne de Navarre seur du Roy de France: Contre les Turcz, Juifz, Infideles, Faulx chrestiens, Anabaptistes, et Lutheriens, 26–28
Epithet, 6, 59, 72
Erasmus, 5–7, 53, 62, 105, 142, 165
Essais, 97, 104, 112
Estienne, Robert, 78
Eucharist, 13, 20, 22–23, 51, 71, 118, 163
Evangelicalism / Evangelicals, 39–44, 48–50, 54, 89–90, 124
Eve, 27, 33
Excess, 2, 12, 22, 24, 37–38, 41, 60, 67, 90–91, 98, 111, 127
Excremental imagery, 6, 112, 115, 146

Fabliaux, 12, 18, 164
Fanaticism, 3, 20, 57, 70
Farce, 10–12, 18, 26, 30–31, 36–44, 47–49, 52, 54, 60, 76–77, 94, 96, 109–12, 116–17, 122, 125, 127–29, 132, 162
Farce de la cornette, 117
La Farce des theologastres, 30, 36–38, 42
Farce des veaulx, 122
Female voice, 10, 24–26, 29
Farel, Guillaume, 25, 27–29, 70–71
Les Femmes qui apprennent à parler latin, 37
Les Femmes qui se font passer maîtresses, 37
Femininity, 19, 28, 66, 107, 117, 148
Feminism, 27, 111
Flood, Chris, 85
Food / Eating, 18–19, 28, 51, 108–10, 112, 114, 118
Fool, 31–33, 45, 52, 54, 72, 74, 87, 94, 97, 104, 116–18

Framing, 16, 52, 87
François I, 8, 39, 112, 137
François II, 133–34, 138
Freud, Sigmund, 4–5, 19, 25, 137, 163
Froment, Antoine, 25, 27
Furor. *See* Anger

Gargantua (character)/*Gargantua*, 6, 22, 38, 40, 68, 88, 94, 112, 119, 122
Gender, 19, 24–28, 37, 46, 61–62, 67, 111, 148
Geneva / Genevans, 9–12, 16, 25–32, 33, 37, 59, 68, 70–74, 78–80, 82–84, 86–87, 92–119, 121, 133, 137, 143–44, 146, 149, 157, 162, 164
Gesture, 4, 6, 31, 41, 67
Giese, Frank S., 56–57, 69
Girard, Jean, 27
Gluttony, 18–19, 35, 60, 90, 94–95, 109, 117, 119. *See also* Excess
God / gods, 8, 21, 28, 42, 44, 51, 58, 62, 66, 71–72, 79–83, 88–89, 94, 96, 100–5, 109, 111, 115, 118, 130, 134, 139, 142, 145
Gospel. *See* Bible
Grandes chroniques et annalles de passe par tout, 66; *chroniqueur de Geneve, avec l'origine de Jean Covin, faucement surnommé Calvin*, 55, 73–74, 76–78
Greed, 18, 35, 43, 72–73, 87, 109, 131, 153–54
Grimace/frown, 5, 107, 117, 156
Gringore, Pierre, 37, 49, 116
La Guerre et deslivrance de la ville de Genesve, 15, 25

Hangest, Jérôme de, 9–10, 15, 22–25, 56–57
Hasenohr, Geneviève, 47
Heath, Michael J., 22
Heller, Henry, 121, 123
Hatred, 8, 23–24, 76, 104, 129, 133, 135, 160
Henry II, 137
Henri III, 5, 121, 162
Heptaméron, 44, 152

Heraclitus, 96–97
Hérésie, frère Simonie, Force, Scandale, Procès et l'Église, 127–28
Heresy / Heretics, 9, 11, 22, 23, 25, 29, 33, 36–37, 48, 55–64, 66, 69, 71, 74–75, 78, 82–85, 121, 123, 127–28, 131, 140–41, 148, 163
Heterodoxy, 18, 65–66, 78, 124, 129
Heterogeneity, 11–12, 124
Higman, Francis, 30, 93
Hoffmann, George, 2, 8, 11–12, 28, 91, 165
Homer, 5
Homonym, 17, 26
Horace, 54, 99, 105, 112–13
Huchon, Mireille, 21
Huguenots, 3, 23, 31–32, 90, 118, 123, 134–35
Humanism / Humanists, 7, 9, 22, 33–34, 48, 80–81, 90, 93, 95, 98, 100, 103, 129, 134, 138
Hypocrisy, 28, 33–34, 48–49, 51, 54, 64, 102, 109–10, 115, 117, 124, 137, 143

The Iliad, 5
Indulgences, 12, 19, 59, 109
Infidelity, 11, 60, 72, 132
L'Inquisiteur, 40, 43, 47–54
Insincerity, 2, 5, 29, 79, 110–11, 131, 149
Institution pour l'Adolescence du Roy, 134
Insults, 8, 35, 46, 59, 67, 76, 79, 89, 91, 121, 140, 146, 148, 157–58, 161–62, 165
Intolerance, 18, 57, 99
Invective, 2, 7, 35, 60, 69–70, 74, 91, 118, 137, 140, 145, 162
Irony, 13, 19–20, 87, 102, 104, 106, 114, 162, 165

Jeu du prince des sotz et de mère sotte, 49, 116
Jews, 68, 160
Jokes, 2, 4–5, 13, 19, 21–22, 26, 28, 31, 38, 43, 60, 64, 68, 80, 91, 94–95, 98–99, 102, 104, 111, 113–15, 124, 127, 131, 145, 163–64, 166

Joubert, Laurent, 5–7, 53
Juvenal / Juvenalian tradition, 25, 54, 99, 112, 141, 152
Juxtaposition, 5, 44, 69, 77, 95, 110, 152

Kingdon, Robert, 92
Koopmans, Jelle, 41, 116

Labé, Louise, 65
Language, 10, 15, 24, 45, 47, 51–52, 57, 62, 66, 79, 87–88, 98, 99, 146, 152, 161–62; aggressive language, 15, 34–35, 104, 127, 152; figurative language, 50; offensive language, 100–102, 161; polemical language, 155–56; sacred language, 49
Lasciviousness, 12, 24, 47, 59–60, 67, 95. *See also* Lust
Latin language, 7, 9–10, 16, 22–24, 37, 43, 62, 70, 95–96, 98, 100–101, 108, 116–17, 128
Laughter: aggressive laughter, 2–13; in Dentière, Marie, 29; in Désiré, Artus, 59–91; in farce, 33–38; in Hangest, Jérôme de, 23–25; in Marcourt, Antoine, 16–21; in Marguerite de Navarre, 39–54; in morality plays, 125–32; in Rabelais, François, 2, 22; in Ronsard, Pierre de, 137–62; Sardonic laughter, 4–13, 15, 19, 21–22, 29, 33, 35–36, 38, 45–47, 52–53, 57, 68, 73, 80–81, 89–91, 94, 97, 99, 105, 107, 118–19, 125, 128–29, 137, 142, 144, 148–49, 152–53, 156, 162–64, 166; in *Satyres chrestiennes de la cuisine* papale, 112–19; in Viret, Pierre, 95–112
Law/lawlessness, 4, 35, 67, 71, 74–75, 82–83, 127, 130, 147, 161
Lawyers, 31, 33, 43, 121
Lefèvre d'Étaples, Jacques, 50
Lent, 31, 39, 68, 80, 96, 109–10, 117, 122, 128, 164
Literary style. *See* Style
Liturgy, 24, 72, 101, 108, 111, 117
Livre des marchans, fort utile à toutes gens pour cognoistre de quelles marchandises on se doit donner garde d'estre deceu, 9, 16–21, 33, 93, 131
Lizet, Pierre, 70
Longeon, Claude, 37
Louis XII, 116
Lucian, 5, 93, 100, 102–3, 105, 153
Lust, 18, 59–60, 95
Luther, Martin, 18, 23, 32, 36–37, 58, 59, 63, 67, 121, 124, 140–41, 145–46
Lutheranism / Lutherans, 26, 33, 37, 66, 69, 121, 124, 127

Le Maistre d'escolle, la mere et les troys escolliers, 128–29
Maître Mimin étudiant, 128
Malingre, Matthieu, 30, 33–35
Le Mallade, 40–48, 52, 80
Marcourt, Antoine, 9, 15–16, 18–20, 22, 29, 33, 93, 131
Marguerites de la Marguerite des princesses tres illustres royne de Nauarre, 48
Marguerite de Navarre, 8, 10, 12, 13, 27, 30, 33, 36, 38–44, 47, 54, 77, 80, 89, 91, 93, 164
Marot, Clément, 9, 12, 48–49, 53, 63–64, 81–82, 112, 130, 139, 151
Mars et Justice, 11, 129–32
Mass, 9, 109–11, 118, 147, 150, 153
Massacre of Vassy, 135
Mazouer, Charles, 40–41
McKinley, Mary, 25–27
Ménager, Daniel, 12–13, 45, 51–52
Merchants, 16–18, 21, 47, 68, 120, 122, 131, 148
Metamorphoses, 109
Metaphor, 16, 51, 105, 107, 141, 156
Metonymy, 7, 45, 76, 117
Millet, Olivier, 40, 47
Le Ministre de L'Église, Noblesse, le Laboureur et le Commun, 125–27
Le Miroir des francs taupins, 57–59
Misogyny, 19, 27–28, 37, 41, 47, 60, 64–66, 105, 111, 147

Mockery, 4, 7–8, 13, 19, 36–37, 43, 46, 53–54, 58, 67–69, 71–72, 75–76, 83, 96–97, 100, 110, 113, 115, 141, 154, 160, 162, 164
Monks, 12, 18–19, 21–22, 33–35, 44, 47, 59–60, 80, 88–89, 94–95, 107–8, 114, 117, 124, 152, 164
Montaigne, Michel de, 97, 104, 112,
Montméja, Bernard de, 11, 149, 152–57, 160–61
Montmorency, Anne de, 23
Moralité de la maladie de chrestienté, 30, 33–36
Moralité de Mars et Justice, 129–32
Muret, Marc-Antoine, 138–39
Music, 24, 31, 137, 151, 155, 158
Mutilation, 3, 126

Nakedness, 3, 26
New Testament, 7, 25, 64, 96, 143,
Noblemen / Nobility, 3, 72, 124–25, 134–35, 148

Old Testament, 8, 97, 99
Ovid, 109

Paganism / Pagans, 79, 87, 93–96, 103, 107, 109, 112, 115, 125, 136, 145, 150
Pamphlets / Pamphleteers, 2–4, 8–13, 15–29, 30, 39, 57, 63, 70, 73–74, 76, 86, 91, 93–94, 111–12, 114, 116–19, 123, 129, 131, 133–62
Pantagruel (character) / Pantagruel, 6, 17–18, 21–22, 33, 40, 101, 112, 119, 122
Papists / Antipapists, 35, 66–69, 79, 81, 89, 106, 154
Parades, 4, 122
Paradox, 9, 25, 49, 90–91, 95, 165
Parlement de Paris, 39, 56, 70, 129–31
Partisanship, 3, 12, 32, 36, 87, 91, 119, 124, 126, 129, 131–32, 156
Passepartout (character), 73–78
Passevent parisien respondant à pasquin Romain, 70–74, 84, 87, 146
Pathelin (character), 117

Patriarchy, 19, 37, 117
Peace of Ambroise, 11
Performance / Performativity, 8, 12, 19, 28, 30, 36, 39, 44, 46, 49, 76–77, 83, 95, 106, 108–10, 112, 115, 117, 122–23, 129–30, 132, 144, 146, 162, 164
Persels, Jeff, 85, 91
Philip II of Spain, 56
La Physique papale faite par maniere de devis et par dialogues, 108
Pineaux, Jacques, 81–82
Plato / Platonism, 5, 106
Plays, 2, 15, 76, 117, 162–64; comic plays, 11–12, 37, 41, 44, 72, 76, 109, 116–17, 126–27, 129, 162; morality plays, 11, 33–38, 41, 86–91, 121–32, 140; *sotties*, 30–33, 41, 117, 123
Pléiade, 11, 129, 136, 161
Piety, 12, 19, 37, 43, 52, 76, 81, 85, 89, 91, 93, 98, 102–3, 109, 113, 140, 151, 156, 158
Plutarch, 109
Poetry, 16–17, 19, 39, 65, 107, 134, 136, 139, 149–50, 160–62
Polemics, 2–3, 12, 15, 18, 30, 33, 38, 48, 72, 88, 92, 106, 112, 114, 124, 128, 129, 131, 137, 146, 149, 151, 160, 162, 164–65
Pope, 10, 21, 34, 49, 72, 86–89, 91, 96, 116–17, 146, 151–52, 164
Pope Julius II, 49, 116
Populism, 10–11, 16–17, 52, 57, 80, 86, 100, 124–25, 156
Postel, Claude, 23
Power, 10, 19, 25, 27, 48, 54, 70, 96, 124, 126, 129–30, 133, 135
Priests, 8, 12, 18–19, 25, 34, 42, 51, 55–56, 59–60, 76, 78, 88, 97, 100–101, 104, 107–8, 110–11, 114–15, 117, 119, 124, 127, 134, 146, 149–50, 152–53, 155–56, 164
Printers, 27, 78, 86, 112
Printing, 9, 17, 27, 29, 30, 32, 55, 66, 78, 92, 142
Printing press, 2, 15, 78
Prologue, 16–17, 66, 86–89

Propaganda, 2, 15, 23–24, 40, 55–57, 76, 81, 86–87, 92, 136, 162, 164
Prostitutes, 34, 67, 72, 80, 96, 108, 150, 153
Protestants / Protestantism, 15, 18, 22, 23–25, 28, 57–59, 61–62, 68–69, 71, 77, 84–86, 94, 111, 116, 121–24, 128–31, 133–35, 137–38, 140–48, 152, 158, 160, 163
Protestant Reformation. See Reformation
Proverb, 5, 26, 87
Psalms (Bible) / Psalms (hymns) 24, 49, 52, 63–64, 81–82, 85, 89, 112, 151
Pun, 17, 22, 26, 35–37, 53, 67, 111, 115, 119, 127–28, 153

Le Quart Livre, 2–3, 21, 59, 114

Rabelais, François, 2–3, 6, 12, 17–19, 21–22, 33, 38, 40, 53, 59, 63, 88, 90, 94, 101–7, 112, 114, 119, 122, 130, 146, 149, 164
Racaut, Luc, 23–24
Rape, 3–4, 153
Readers, 22–24, 27, 38, 59, 69–70, 73–75, 77, 80–81, 84, 88, 94–95, 101–2, 104, 108, 111, 113, 117, 129, 137, 146, 148
Reformation, 1, 12, 16, 26, 33, 57, 93, 120, 137, 140, 163–65
Les Regretz, complainctes, et lamentations, d'une damoiselle, laquelle s'estoit retirée à Genesve pour vivre en liberté, avec la convertion d'icelle estant à l'article de la mort, 73
Reid, Dylan, 121–23
Religious conversion. See Conversion
Remonstrance au peuple de France, 144–48
Remonstrance envoyee au roi, 3–4
Renner, Bernd, 112, 150
Reputation, 22, 120, 130, 132, 138, 149, 151, 153
Response au livre d'Artus Desiré, intitulé: Les grandes chroniques et Annales de Passe-partout, 73
Response aux calomnies contenues au Discours et Suyte du Discours sur les Miseres de ce temps, Faits par Messire Pierre Ronsard, jadis Poëte, et maintenant Prebstre, 149–56
Response aux injures et calomnies, de je ne sçay quells predicans et ministres de Genève, 11, 148, 156–62
Revulsion, 2, 123
Rhetoric / Rhetorical strategy, 51, 57–58, 69, 71, 80, 83–84, 86, 88, 91, 101, 111, 140, 149–50, 153–54, 164
De risu paschali, 111
Risus sardonicus. See Sardonic laughter
Robert, Simon, 25
Roche-Chandieu, Antoine de la, 11, 149–52, 156–57, 160–61
Ronsard, Pierre de, 8–9, 11–13, 129, 133–62, 164
Rouen, 11, 58, 66, 86, 120–24, 129
Roussel, Gérard, 38–39
Roy, Bruno, 130–32

The Sacred / Sacred ritual, 1, 15, 49, 58, 61–69, 71–72, 76–77, 82–85, 89, 94–96, 99, 104, 106, 110–11, 115–17, 140, 145, 162, 165
Saints, 28, 34–35, 55, 64, 78–79, 94, 96, 103, 106, 123, 126, 128
Sarcasm, 16, 20, 22, 28–29, 35, 45, 57, 66, 69, 73, 79, 85, 89, 101, 107–8, 111, 124, 140, 143, 145–46, 148, 154, 156
Sardinia / Sardinian laughter, 5–7
Satire, 1–13, 163–66; in Désiré, Artus, 59–91; in farce, 33–38; in Hangest, Jérôme de, 23–25; in Marcourt, Antoine, 16–21; in Marguerite de Navarre, 39–54; in morality plays, 125–32; in Rabelais, François, 2, 22, 53, 101, 107, 122, 149; in Ronsard, Pierre de, 137–62
Satires (Horace), 113
Satyres chrestiennes de la cuisine papale, 18, 71, 108, 111–15, 117–18
Saulnier, V.-L., 40, 47

De scandalis, 99, 114
Schadenfreude, 12, 137
Screech, M. A., 7–8
Scripture. *See* Bible
Sermons, 39, 81, 111–12, 115–16, 135, 160
Servants, 3–4, 24–25, 42, 44–49, 51, 54, 76, 111, 122
Shock, 2, 4, 21, 24–25, 71, 77, 84
Sick patient (character), 30, 32–48
Slaughter, 8, 21, 44, 85, 119, 135
Smiling/ Smirking, 5, 13, 38, 111
Social class / Social order, 24–25, 66, 122, 127, 146, 153
Sociétés joyeuses, Conards de Rouen, 11, 49, 120–32. *See also* Basoche
Sorbonne, 8–10, 16–17, 22, 36–39, 42–43, 46–48, 50, 57, 60, 62–64, 83, 85, 101, 114, 155
Sottie des béguins, 30–32
Sottie du monde, 30–32
Sottie pour le cry de la Basoche, 130
Stage direction, 2, 45
Status quo, 41, 44, 50, 54, 116, 130
St. Bartholomew's Day Massacre, 15, 134, 162
Stock characters, 31, 41, 47, 108, 116, 127, 131
Street performers, 77, 89, 95, 108–9, 144, 162
Stuart, Mary, 133
Style, 23, 30, 66, 80, 101, 102–3, 105, 108, 114, 138–39, 151, 156
Superstition, 28, 93, 99, 102–4, 121
Symbolism, 4, 8–9, 19, 26, 50–51, 53, 76, 94, 109, 129, 133
Szabari, Antónia, 2, 85

Teeth imagery, 5, 28–29, 53, 73, 105, 142, 164, 166
Tendentious humor, 4–5, 19, 25, 28, 38, 52–53, 137, 140, 152

Theatricality, 2, 19, 96, 109–10, 116, 144, 153
Theologians, 8, 10–11, 22, 36–38, 42, 47–48, 57, 60, 62, 65–67, 69, 72, 88, 95, 159
Tone, 12–13, 16, 18, 25, 28, 32, 52, 57, 59, 72, 81, 88–89, 108, 137, 139, 142, 149–50, 156, 163
Tory, Geoffroy, 101
Traité du ris, 6
Translation, 19, 38, 49, 61–64, 81, 93, 100, 107, 146, 151
Transubstantiation, 20, 84, 111, 118
Trickster, 17–19, 36–38, 60, 72, 102
Les Triomphes de l'Abbaye des Conards, 122
Trop Prou Peu et Moins, 30, 40, 52–54

Vernacular language / literature, 11, 24, 59, 62–63, 101, 146
Vingle, Pierre de, 33
Violence, 2, 5, 8, 13, 15, 36, 49–50, 53, 55–57, 59, 65, 68–70, 75–76, 84–86, 121, 125–29, 131, 134
Viret, Pierre, 10, 70–73, 92–119, 141, 143, 162, 164
Virgil, 79, 107
Virility, 19, 142–43, 148, 152, 153, 163
Vitriol, 13, 15, 57, 59, 61–63, 76, 81, 98, 148, 151, 164
Voltaire, 106, 165

Wars of Religion, 2–3, 8, 10–11, 23, 81, 86, 91–92, 112, 121, 123, 129, 131, 133, 136
Women, 3–4, 19, 24–28, 37–38, 41–42, 46–47, 58–59, 60–63, 64–68, 76, 95–96, 106–7, 111, 115, 134, 147–48, 158
Wordplay, 22, 36, 48, 68, 73, 107, 114, 119, 128

Zealots, 3, 15, 19, 22, 118, 155, 165

www.ingramcontent.com/pod-product-compliance
Lightning Source LLC
Chambersburg PA
CBHW032040300426
44117CB00009B/1133